Dialectic of Defeat

Dialectic of Defeat

Contours of Western Marxism

Russell Jacoby

Cambridge University Press

Cambridge
London New York New Rochelle
Melbourne Sydney

PUBLISHED BY THE PRESS SYNDICATE OF THE UNIVERSITY OF CAMBRIDGE
The Pitt Building, Trumpington Street, Cambridge, United Kingdom

CAMBRIDGE UNIVERSITY PRESS
The Edinburgh Building, Cambridge CB2 2RU, UK
40 West 20th Street, New York NY 10011–4211, USA
477 Williamstown Road, Port Melbourne, VIC 3207, Australia
Ruiz de Alarcón 13, 28014 Madrid, Spain
Dock House, The Waterfront, Cape Town 8001, South Africa

http://www.cambridge.org

First published 1981
First paperback edition 2002

A catalogue record for this book is available from the British Library

Library of Congress Cataloguing in Publication data
Jacoby, Russell.
Dialectic of defeat.
Includes index.
1. Communism – History. 2. Communism and philosophy.
3. Marx, Karl, 1818–1883. I. Title.
HX36.J22 335.4′09 81-3904 AACR2

ISBN 0 521 23915 X hardback
ISBN 0 521 52017 7 paperback

For Naomi

Contents

Preface		ix
Introduction		1
Chapter 1	Conformist Marxism	11
Chapter 2	The Marxism of Hegel and Engels	37
Chapter 3	From philosophy to politics: the inception of Western Marxism I	59
Chapter 4	From politics to philosophy: the inception of Western Marxism II	83
Chapter 5	The subterranean years	105
Chapter 6	Class unconsciousness	117
Journal abbreviations used in notes		127
Notes		129
Index		191

Preface

A rough egalitarianism belongs to the twentieth century; it has chopped down political hopes and beliefs of every stripe. From Liberalism to Marxism, none has survived intact. Talk of the Gulag is hardly answered by talk of Auschwitz; nor can analysis of one replace analysis of the other. The wreckage extends in every direction. The vastness of the junkyard encourages, almost compels, retreat and resignation.

Yet, as Herbert Marcuse once remarked, there was no God that failed, only men and women. The debacle allows no escape. With care and caution we must sift through the theoretical rubble. Marx and Weber and Freud remain our contemporaries not because little of import has been said since they wrote but because the society they dissected, and sometimes denounced, still wheezes along. The temptation to flee into the future and begin conceptually afresh is marked by fright, and it yields staler results than less ambitious efforts to think through the past.

This book was written in the spirit of rescue and retrieval. To be sure, recently there has been no dearth of histories of Marxism. This one, however, parts from the usual textual study or narrative monograph; it is both more and less modest. It is more modest in that I do not seek to elucidate the entire oeuvre of Marx; it is less in that I am not content with a flat historical reconstruction. I do not view this study as a Sunday tour through the museum of Marxism, stopping here and there to gaze upon extinct specimens. There are no simple lessons here nor instructions on how to save the world. Yet I hope to offer something more than a brisk survey of artifacts and fossils. Without passion and commitment, history is not only without a soul, it is without a mind.

In some quarters of the academy it has become the convention to expand acknowledgments into a complete directory of friends, family, professional acquaintances, foundations, departments, governments, libraries, seminars, and sometimes restaurants and cafés. To the fair-minded this evidences the generous spirit of intellectual life. To the jaundiced this suggests not only preparation for future favors but intimidation of any dissatisfied reader or reviewer. I break with this convention less out of courage than necessity. For reading the whole or parts of this manuscript, and for moral aid and intellectual sustenance, I thank Naomi Glauberman, Paul Breines, Paul Piccone, Christopher Lasch, Peter Reill, Mark Poster, Eliott Eisenberg, Carl Boggs, Georg Iggers, Martin Shapiro, and Joel Kovel.

Earlier versions of some material from these chapters have appeared in "The Inception of Western Marxism: Karl Korsch and the Politics of Philosophy," *Canadian Journal of Political and Social Theory/Revue canadienne de théorie politique et sociale* III/3 (Fall, 1979), pp. 5–33; "Political Economy and Class Unconsciousness," *Theory and Society*, V (1978), pp. 11–18; and "The Politics of Philosophy from Lukács to the Frankfurt School," *Telos*, 10 (1971), pp. 119–146.

Los Angeles
December 1980

Russell Jacoby

Introduction

The literature on Marxism threatens to drown both the theory and its students. To the cynical it confirms the obsolescence of Marxism: It has fled the streets and factories for the halls and offices of the university. The struggle to publish replaces the class struggle. Academics jet to conferences to hawk competing brands of Marxism. A consumer's guide is required to stay abreast of the offerings and the recalls: structural Marxism, semiotic Marxism, feminist Marxism, hermeneutical Marxism, phenomenological Marxism, critical Marxism, and so on.

This is not surprising. Marxism is not immunized against its object. After a century of contact the critique of the commodity succumbs to the commodity. Marx quipped that the criminal augments the market by producing the professor of criminology, who produces the commodity, the textbook on criminal law.[1] Today the revolutionary joins the criminal. The briefly popular slogan "The revolution will not be televised" was optimistic. The revolution will be televised. Nonetheless, to recognize that Marxism has been made a commodity is no reason to write it off. It proves that Marxism does not escape the social conditions that it has always denounced as determinant.

Nor does "commodification" exhaust the vulnerability of Marxism to its own historical situation. Everywhere Marxism has assumed characteristics of its specific environments. A single, homogeneous Marxism belongs to the past. Marxism takes on the color, and sometimes the content, of its conditions. Marxism devolves into Marxisms. This diversity is not benign. The world map of Marxism includes academics and political parties, entire states and cemeteries. There are

Marxist revolutionaries and poets; there are also Marxist careerists, premiers, and executioners.[2] A common vocabulary, reality, and loyalty cease to exist. Boundaries between traditions and experiences rigidify.

Vital differences among the Marxisms encourage a theoretical resignation. Forms of Marxism are treated as distinct specimens or cases. Each Marxism is unique, with its own history, texts, leaders, accomplishments, and crimes. Yet it is too soon to settle for case studies and surrender general approaches. Moreover, allegiance to specific forms of Marxism can be sustained only by attention to the general context from which they emerged. In less abstract terms, this context was defined by its dominant variety, Soviet Marxism. Other Marxisms defined themselves, or were defined, by their distance from Soviet Marxism.

Today no study can avert its eyes from the dark shadows that fall upon Marxism. If civilization can be judged by its prisons, refugees, and victims, Marxism cannot claim exemption. The darkness is due not simply to its opponents but to its proponents. To deny this is to falsify in advance any critical inquiry into Marxism. The swagger of some Marxisms suggests – to borrow a phrase – that Stalinism has a great future. A contemporary study cannot afford to be neutral lest it collaborate in the misdeeds; it requires a critical evaluation of the fate of its subject.

"Fate" is a loaded word; it includes its own judgment. Those who finish on top write the histories and hand out the medals. That the victors sponsor the museums and textbooks to honor themselves is no longer a novel insight; it has guided much "revisionist" history that has reclaimed the silenced and defeated. Yet the full implications of this insight rarely have been pursued. For the defeated are victimized not only by the victors but by themselves. The losers also draw the lessons; and their lessons smack of an ethos that the victors cherish, the ethos of success.

Success: Both capitalists and Marxists speak its language. Bank presidents and revolutionaries bestow their highest honors on achievers. The exploiters and the exploited extol their winners. Lenin was an inconnu until he succeeded. Martov, the defeated Menshivik leader, remains one. It seems just that the long-suffering and defeated celebrate their few successes. They should honor Lenin instead of Martov, or the Russian Revolution instead of the (defeated) Munich Soviet Republic. The smell of success sweetens the sourness of daily setbacks and insults.

Yet between honor and fetish are both a half-step and a chasm. Few boldly maintain the identity of success and truth; few resist its spell. Success confirms the truth of the theory; defeat is its own verdict. Failure bespeaks an erroneous theorizing. On the bottom line of the account book of Marxism, Leninism shows a net profit. For investor and revolutionary, successful performance is the best report.

Little has eviscerated Marxism more than its acceptance of the judgment of history as truth itself. The success of the Russian Revolution, and later the Chinese Revolution, dazzled generations of Marxists (and non-Marxists).[3] Conversely, the failure of other Marxisms, notably a distinct European Marxism, confirmed their inadequacy. Lenin, Stalin, Mao, and others attracted attention because of their successes. Attention could not be cleaved from imitation, however. Hence the model and theories of the Russian Revolution were not only exported but also enthusiastically imported by countless Marxists. That the subverters respected the judgment of reality is only proper; that they worshipped it crippled Marxism by substituting mimicry for thought.

To answer an immediate objection, no improvement transpires by flipping the conceptual coin. To progress from a fetish of victors to a fetish of defeated is progress in fetishism. If victory is not proof of truth, neither is defeat. Historical studies, as well as a political left, exhume the most oppressed and victimized as if they stood closer to truth. In the distribution of defeat, the most defeated are the most blessed. After his fourth exile and seventh flight in twenty years, Victor Serge in his great memoirs reminds us that the European left was not fated for defeat. "And we have known how to win, we must never forget that... No kind of predestination impels us to become the offal of concentration camps."[4]

Success and defeat are facts to be recognized, nothing more; they are mute, requiring interpretation and analysis. The "success" of the Russian Revolution does not prohibit evaluation. Marxism is not exhausted by the attainment and maintenance of state power. Engels, in a celebrated passage, commented that "the worst thing that can befall a leader of an extreme party is to be compelled to take over a government in an epoch when the movement is not yet ripe for the domination of the class which he represents."[5] This passage should not be used as glib judgment of the Russian Revolution; rather it recalls that success is not its own argument: Its limits, consequences, costs, and relevance elsewhere are open to scrutiny.

Defeat is also a fact; it registers the constellation of forces, not the quality of insight, theory, and even practices. These must be elicited from the dense web of events; they are not simply contiguous with the defeat itself. Moreover, success and defeat are not insular realities; they partake of each other. The success of Soviet Marxism contributed to, and often directed, the defeat of other Marxisms. To ascribe endless setbacks to Western Marxism and endless victories to Soviet Marxism, as if the Soviets did not suppress the opposition, confuses arson with faulty wiring. This is of course true for the opposition within Soviet Marxism. That Trotsky was defeated, and finally assassinated, is not a comment on his theories and writings but on power. Homage to success is homage to violence.

Capitalism fabricated the myth of individual success; the Marxists marketed their own brand. Formula and inspiration were built in. The instructions were simple: imitation. Hence every Leninist group in the world publishes a newspaper in accord with the instructions of Lenin's *What Is to Be Done?* There is no denying that Lenin and the Bolsheviks came to power; one can question whether the same tactics can be replicated successfully in Western Europe and North America. Under the harsh rays of success, vivid differences in social conditions and history wash out. For several years in the 1960s and 1970s Maoism, a theory of peasant revolution and national liberation, flourished in Europe and North America. In the urban wildernesses of New York and Paris, Maoists championed poor peasants and land reform.

This book challenges the ethos of success that has drained off the critical impulse of Marxism; it seeks to salvage a Western Marxism that rarely knew victory. The history of Western Marxism does not resound with official proclamations and marching bands; it is the history of the murder of Rosa Luxemburg, the imprisonment of Antonio Gramsci, the exile of Karl Korsch, the flight of the Frankfurt School, and the fate of countless Marxists who bucked the current and paid the price. Again, defeat does not anoint the defeated; it only implies that the other side was stronger. Defeat may enclose future victories. Conversely, the effort to replicate distant victories – in time and space – may only perpetuate a past of defeats.

Is this the dialectic of defeat? Do the defeats of unorthodox Marxism harbor openings for the future? Do the successes of orthodox Marxism only mask its dismal record in the advanced capitalist countries? The achievements of the Russian Revolution need not be denigrated. Yet their evaluation cannot renounce history and society. The issue here is less the record of Soviet Marxism in the Soviet Union than its record in Western Europe and North America. As Fernando Claudin has convincingly argued, the balance sheet is not encouraging.[6] Moreover, neither victory nor defeat can be measured with a single transhistorical yardstick; they must be refracted through the specific historical possibilities. The defeats of all Marxists before nazism, for instance, were not monotonously identical. The possibilities open to the Western Marxists, by then isolated individuals, sharply differed from the options of the German Communist party, a major political formation.

If the reality of defeat undermined the spell of success, the spell could be renewed by a powerful amulet: science. The following chapters examine a Marxist challenge to the consecration of Marxism by science. That Marxism is a science is regularly, almost obsessively, restated in orthodox texts. Here Marxism is infatuated with the bourgeois society it despises. If Marxists wanted to expropriate the expropriators, they also fell in love with their instruments: science and technology. In these pages the question is less science itself than its uncritical adoption.

Marxists were convinced that they were the appointed and rightful heirs to the science of bourgeois society – a science that guaranteed success. The greatest insults in the standard Marxist dictionary were "prescientific," "nonscientific," "mystical," "utopian," and "romantic." Vulnerability to these charges intimidated the Marxist critics of science. The suppressed critiques took their revenge. Marxism succumbed to science; it shriveled up into blueprints and state engineering. The most provocative interpretations of science migrated to those outside of the mainstream and to those outside of Marxism.

For the same reason, searching analyses of mass culture, leisure, and urban life found little nourishment in mainstream Marxism. Mesmerized by the glitter of science and progress, Marxists dreamed of new proletarian owners and revolutionary commissars but not a fundamental restructuring. The will to revamp a class society did not flag, but the substitution of the proletariat for the bourgeoisie exhausted the theory and its hopes. The trappings of bourgeois society were left inviolate. Authentic conservatives, extinct nowadays, who were unsympathetic to the tempo of industrial life often advanced more penetrating insights into the "commodification" of daily life than did the Marxists.

To challenge Marxism as science does not encourage the occult or mysterious. The single alternative of science or the irrational is posed by the inflexible scientific mind. Rather the challenge is directed against a repressive concept of science, perhaps more accurately dubbed "scientism." The strict natural sciences, elevated to the sole model of knowledge, censor critical thought. Anything that cannot be squeezed into scientific categories is proscribed or neglected.

Marxism not only yielded distinct schools and national traditions, but its covalent bonds weakened. The coherence of the original theory has often been overstated; nevertheless, during a century, Marx's "critique of political economy" fractured into philosophy, politics, and economics. To each belonged a distinct history, a body of literature, and specialists. The cause of this was not only the intellectual division of labor, which rendered philosophers and economists incomprehensible to each other, but these developments of Marxist theory testified to a profound transformation of the social reality.

"The critique of political economy" expressed not only a reality but a hope that the idioms of philosophical consciousness and economic activity overlapped. As the twentieth century tossed up problems unanticipated by classical Marxism, the hope receded. The defeats of the European revolutions, socialism in one country and fascism in several, made the original economic vocabulary inadequate, although not necessarily inaccurate. For some decades Marxist economics languished as Marxists turned to other disciplines – philosophy, aesthetics, psychology, sociology – to supplement and reevaluate the original texts.

The focus in these pages on philosophy and politics, and not economics and politics, is not arbitrary; it is loyal to the projectory of Western Marxism.[7] As often noted, the major figures of Western Marxism have been philosophers – from Lukács to Sartre – not economists. The predominance of philosophical works signified not a retreat but an advance to a reexamination of Marxism. Here I differ with Perry Anderson's deft *Considerations on Western Marxism.*[8] I do not view Western Marxism as an unfortunate detour from "classical" Marxism; nor do I look forward to its extinction. The myth of a heroic Marxism, harmonizing philosophy, economics, science, and praxis, overwhelms the feeble efforts to rethink Marxism.

Yet I do not mean to ratify, but to recognize, the distance between philosophy and politics; and I endeavor to establish some of the links. Philosophical Marxism incorporated an implicit, sometimes explicit, politics. In my account this is not simply an interesting postscript to the main story. Although not always visible, philosophical propositions pervaded political choices and tactics. The political antagonism between Western and Soviet Marxism was ultimately sustained, and regularly refired, by philosophical antagonisms.

These philosophical antagonisms had already coalesced in the nineteenth century. The reception of Hegel in Western Europe and Russia anticipated and infused later political differences. Nature, science, subjectivity, consciousness, and dialectics, interpreted in divergent modes, became conceptual templates for contending political practices. I argue that an index, if not a cause, for the separation of Western and Soviet Marxism was the reception of Engels as well as Hegel. Although it is frequently maintained that the critique of Engels commenced with Lukács, it originated at the turn of the century with earlier Western Marxists.

I should emphasize that I do want to simply indict Russian and Soviet Marxism for upholding a regressive scientific Marxism as if this were due to moral insensitivity or philosophical crudity. Philosophical differences cannot be ripped out of social and political contexts. The economic and political situation of the first Russian Marxists encouraged a Marxism that spoke to different imperatives than in Western Europe. The cult of science and objectivity resounded dissimilarly in Russia and Western Europe.

The examination of the reception of Hegel and Engels cannot be set off cleanly from an evaluation of texts. Recently in historical and literary studies the scrutiny of texts has become an obsession. Especially under the impact of French poststructural thought, a fetish of the text has been launched replete with a new and shifting vocabulary: discourse, parole, semiotics, grammatology, and so on. In the name of the text, the context has again lapsed. To structural and poststructural thinkers, the mess of history – denounced as historicism – pollutes the purity of the method. By remaining glued to the text the hope is to escape being unglued by the world.

Yet the shadows that cling to Marxism cannot be dispelled solely by desk lamps. After a certain point a study of *Capital* can explain Stalinism as much as a study of the Bible can explain the Inquisition. A moratorium on textual studies is hardly necessary; a recognition of its limits and dangers may be. Although I make some brief forays into what Hegel, Marx, and Engels "actually said," I am more concerned with their reception. Moreover, a sufficient, and growing, literature exists that dissects the texts and logic of Hegel and Marx.

This study is antiencyclopedic; it does not seek to discuss all figures, movements, and eddies of Western Marxism commensurate with their importance. Where the existing literature is adequate, I have not hesitated to abridge my own discussion. This is most noticeable with Gramsci, whose presence in these pages does not correspond to his significance: Since reliable studies of Gramsci constantly augment, a full discussion would be tiresome. He is mentioned as a confirmation of the pattern of Western Marxism, and he enters these pages where he becomes a problem: in the exchange with Bordiga and the opposition to Soviet Marxism. The treatment of Merleau-Ponty, Sartre, and French Marxism in general is brief for the same reason. Although I have not essayed a comprehensive narrative, I have tried to situate all the major figures and groups. I have been guided by two concerns: to examine those often slighted – the Dutch Marxists, Paul Levi, the German Communist Worker's party (KAPD) – and to select events and concepts that sharpen the outlines of Western Marxism. The approach, finally, is guided by the material and argument.

A number of remaining decisions and difficulties informing this study should be mentioned. Vocabulary is not the least of them. If Marxism passes into Marxisms, exact designations lag behind. National and geographical classifications can be misleading: Soviet Marxism, Chinese Marxism, Yugoslavian Marxism, and so on. Forms of Marxism are clearly transnational. Soviet Marxism or orthodox Leninism appeared, exported and imported, everywhere. They became, and are used in this study as the official versions, the orthodoxy – and the benchmarks for evaluating all heresies. Western and European Marxism are used interchangeably; they are also not rigorously geographical terms but refer to a body of thought and practice. Western Marxism appeared in several European countries; it is indigenous to advanced capitalism but is hardly the dominant form. For instance, Western Marxism in France is far overshadowed by the French Communist party, which with some strains continues to represent the orthodoxy.

Finally, any discussion of Western Marxism is incomplete without a consideration of its efforts to incorporate psychoanalytic thought. I surveyed some of these efforts in *Social Amnesia: A Critique of Conformist Psychology from Adler to Laing* and do not repeat my discussion here.[9] My aim in that work, however, differed, almost opposed, my aim here. In *Social Amnesia* I critically examined a post-Freudian psychology that succumbed to an overwhelming subjectivism. In a situation where the social noose is invisible and the gasps of the individual are recorded as cries of liberation, I recalled and defended an objective (or nonsubjective) theory of subjectivity.

Marxism hardly needs that lesson; objectivity is its watchword and opium. Yet the compulsive objectivity of orthodox Marxism is more compulsive than objective; it flees the subjective as if it were the threat it may be. Hence in these pages I recount the history of a Western Marxism that has not obliterated the individual or the subject. My concern, however, represents not a change of mind but a change of topics. To prize the formal logic of argument over the illogic of reality sacrifices thought to mechanics.

1

Conformist Marxism

I

"So much the worse for the facts." With these words of Fichte, Lukács closed the first draft of "What Is Orthodox Marxism?" To the skeptical, perhaps to the sympathetic, the words are outrageous. Marxism is not contradicted by the facts. The facts are duplicit, or, at best, mute. To quantify, classify, or categorize facts is to capitulate to them. "Truly orthodox dialectical Marxists paid little attention to the so-called 'facts.' "[1]

The obverse is plainer and more convincing: The facts confirm Marxism. The large events, as well as the small, prove the truth of the theory. The Russian and Chinese revolutions, imperialism, and the crises of capitalism all demonstrate the continuous validity of Marxism. Marxism is compelling precisely because it is accurate and, finally, because it is successful: It works. The strength of the working class, as well as the victory of several revolutions, leaves little doubt. Success is the proof.

Success: This is the rub. How does one evaluate success? The Seventeenth Congress of the Soviet Communist party (1934) announced that the party had "triumphed" everywhere. Stalin declared that socialism was now "the sole commanding force." The official account dubbed this meeting the "The Congress of Victors."[2] Several decades later, in 1956, Khruschev indicated how the victors fared: "Of the 139 members and candidates of the party's Central Committee who were elected at the Seventeenth Congress, 98 persons, i.e. 70 percent, were arrested and shot . . . The same fate met . . . the majority of the delegates to the

Seventeenth Party Congress. Of 1,966 delegates . . . 1,108 were arrested on charges of revolutionary crimes, i.e. decidedly more than a majority."[3]

The banal truth is that today's success is tomorrow's failure. Everybody wants a winner. Nobody likes a loser. That nothing succeeds like success is true not only for bourgeois society but for its critique, Marxism. Marxists also want to win or, at least, to side with the winners.

Orthodox Marxism has chased after success, and this hunt has paralyzed its critical nerve, past and present. Before World War I, the German Social Democrats exercised hegemony by virtue of their strength and electoral victories. After their moral and political collapse in World War I, the Russian Revolution and the Bolsheviks assumed this role. With the discrediting of the Russian Revolution, the Chinese Revolution and Maoism stepped in. Because each worked, each promised to deliver the magic formula for success. The final argument flung by the Leninists at the non-Leninists was that Lenin succeeded. The non-Leninists were not only wrong, they failed.

The lure of success and the sweet smell of victory fuel orthodox Marxism. Marxism–Leninism exudes the no-nonsense of how to succeed. This is the source of its perpetual attraction as a doctrine; unlike anarchism, syndicalism, or council communism, it has proved itself, offering victorious revolutions for emulation. Everything pales before the fact of victory. The adherents of orthodox Marxism extol and promote the victorious revolutions and parties as the route to success, until their shortcomings or failures become too blatant; then another is adopted.

The ex post facto element damns this Marxism to apologetics. Marxism degenerates into public relations for revolutionary movements; it turns critical only at last resort. It may suffice for philosophy to attain wisdom at dusk, but Marxism must commence its flight earlier. To condemn the failures after the verdict is too late.

The issues are complex. Future events are beyond grasp. History provides no refunds, guarantees, or insurance policies. The misappraisal of the successful revolution or the revolution-in-the-making, the premature celebration, the mistake, or the retraction forms the marrow of the human experience in history. Therefore the charge that a mistake has been made, or has been belatedly corrected, is itself compromised; it assumes a position outside of history, where there are no choices, failures, mistakes, or successes. The charge implies that it is better not to choose and retreats to the tired wisdom that history is bunk and vanity; or it hides behind academic knowledge too cautious to think and judge.

If this is true, it is also insufficient. This rejoinder slips into the *c'est la vie* attitude, which excuses indifferently all theories and commitments. It is no sin to be wrong, but it is no virtue to be wrong consistently. This is the question that orthodox Marxism provokes. History is assembled from a series of discrete mechanisms; if one breaks down, another is always available. This approach is immunized against criticism by a continual shifting of its object: Last year, Maoism; this year, the prison movement; next year, the working class.

A minor example is Charles Bettelheim, a respected French Marxist, who resigned from the Franco-China Friendship Association (May 1977), marking his break with post-Maoist China.[4] For many years he enthusiastically praised the Cultural Revolution and Maoism. Now he believes that the campaign against the "Gang of Four" commenced a "great leap backward."

The ease with which the advances of Mao's Cultural Revolution are being undone suggests to Bettelheim that the seeds for the reversal were planted earlier. Something must have been amiss with the Cultural Revolution itself that allowed it to be set aside so rapidly. Indeed, Bettelheim tells us "when we look back and analyze what has happened since 1965–66, we can say that this change in the relation of forces was already apparent in the first months of 1967." He goes on to identify some features of this change: introduction of coercion, displacement of mass participation, rise of sectarianism, and so on.[5]

This may be fine and good, but why do we learn this only now? The answer is obvious: Although Bettelheim says that the changes were "already apparent" in 1967, they were not apparent to him (and many others) for another ten years. The reasons that he now adduces for the "great leap backward" were presented as successfully overcome in his *Cultural Revolution and Industrial Organization in China* (1973). He wrote then that "through discussions and struggles involving millions of workers and vast sections of the population, a new road was opened up in the struggle for socialism . . . It constitutes a decisive and permanent achievement, as decisive and permanent as any scientific or social experience which discovers new processes or new objective laws."[6]

Nor was this the first time that Bettelheim identified permanent scientific achievements that did not turn out to be permanent, scientific, or achievements. He analyzed imperfectly the Russian Revolution and the transition from capitalism to socialism. In the mid-1960s Bettelheim defended Stalin's ideas on the law of value in a socialist society against "Che" Guevara.[7] The rejoinder by "Che" decried Bettelheim's mechanical and undialectical approach.[8] Several years later (1969) Bettelheim debated the same issue with Paul Sweezy.[9]

In 1974 Bettelheim admitted that his writings in the period 1962–1967 on the transition from capitalism to socialism were "not satisfactory." The problem was that until 1956 he had taken the Soviet Union as a "model" for revolution. The problem persisted for another ten years, however. Only the "lessons" of the Chinese Cultural Revolution "induced" him to "modify very seriously the terms of my analysis."[10] Hence Bettelheim began a major reevaluation of the Russian Revolution, in *Class Struggles in the USSR* (1974). Two additional problems emerge here. His serious modification of the evaluation of Russia is not very serious.[11] Bettelheim repeats the (past?) quasi-official Chinese position on the Russian Revolution. And now that the Cultural Revolution has proved deficient, he may have to reevaluate it. Consequently, his reevaluation of the Russian Revolution may have to be reevaluated, and so on.[12]

Is this gloating? To stand utterly outside the fray is hardly virtuous: It purchases purity by cashing in critical intelligence and commitment. To enter into the fray inevitably yields mistakes, including major ones. "There are no innocents in politics."[13] Yet neither is everyone equally guilty. Distinctions can, and must, be made. Political intellectuals who are perpetually on the hunt for successful revolutions betray their ethos: success.

The issue is not the failings of an individual but a style and procedure that eviscerates Marxism. Success is peddled until it fails, and then it is peddled again in a new form. At any single instant, the success appears more than convincing; the facts are on its side, whereas the critics command only theories and harping objections. The Russian, Chinese, and Cuban revolutions silence critics by their very existence and success. Debray's 1967 *Revolution in the Revolution* enthusiastically prescribed the Cuban model of revolution for all of South America. Ten years later the situation was sobering, the successes nonexistent. Gérard Chailland titles his recent analysis of Debray's theory "Guerilla Inflation: The *Foco* Theory as a Theory for Failure."[14] Debray himself hardly disagrees with this judgment; he now calls his pamphlet "a book of the moment."[15]

Some of this can, and has been, characterized as "Third Worldism," the pursuit and promotion of Third World revolutions by North American and Western European intellectuals. Yet the style has worked as effectively and perniciously within the industrial nations. The black movement, urban guerillas, the prison movement, women, youth, national minorities, and the working class itself have all been objects of instant mythologizing.

Not the least of the ills of orthodox Marxism is the wake it leaves of demoralization and cynicism. Hopes perpetually raised and dashed take their toll. If its more public figures can switch objects without losing a beat, others have graver difficulties. Who can transfer their loyalties without doubt from the Soviet Union to China to North Korea to Albania? or from the working class to the student movement to the black movement to the Third World back to the working class? The committed are leached out. The old anticommunist "God that failed" becomes the weary "gods that failed."

For many Marxists, an old routine has been refurbished to account for perpetual mistakes: self-criticism. Louis Althusser developed this into a fine art and an effective marketing strategy. As an art it neatly absolves past mistakes, makes way for new ones, and implies that the critics are spiteful and malicious for harping on the past. Who wants to criticize those who criticize themselves? As a commercial strategy it is marketed by the engineers of the planned obsolescence of thought; each theoretical innovation is fabricated from defective parts, designed for breakdown and replacement. The intellectual turns into a perpetual book buyer, compelled to buy the latest work to replace the preceding one.

Althusser not only invented "theoretical practice" but pioneered in its malpractice. First he argued that Marx definitely broke with Hegel. Several years later he confessed: "I must admit that I have given a much too abrupt idea of this thesis."[16] Then, he admitted that in his notion of Marx's "epistemological break," "I . . . made two mistakes"; it was neither epistemological nor a break.[17] He also erred in *Reading Capital,* calling philosophy "a theory of theoretical practice." This mistake was not simply "terminological ambiguity but one of an error in the conception itself."[18] He also mistakenly concluded that "philosophy is a *science*" and has an "object" and "history." Later he discovered that "philosophy is not [a] science" and has "no object" and "no history."[19] He also remembered in passing that he forgot about class struggle in *For Marx* and *Reading Capital.* "This is certainly the biggest mistake I made."[20]

The list, if honest, is hardly enviable; nor is it exhaustive.[21] Moreover, what Reich said of Freud – even where he was wrong, he was right – can be said in the inverse of Althusser – even where he is right, he is wrong.

Althusser represents a Marxism that is forever wrong, or right too late. To explain his multiple miscalculations, he reaches for an alibi beyond reproach: history. The irony is missed: Althusser and his followers have dedicated themselves to slaying the dangerous dragon of historicism. Historicism threatens the autonomy, rigor, objectivity, and, finally, the success of Marxism. For Althusser, historicism corrupts with Hegelian effluents the science of Marxism.[22]

Yet Althusser justifies all his mistakes by claiming that they were committed at a particular time and place, as if there could be some doubt about this. In Althusser's jargon the "conjuncture" ("the exact balance of forces . . . at any given moment"[23]) is the universal excuse for errors. The fetish of indicating the exact time when they wrote, rewrote, and corrected their manuscripts characterizes all the Althusserians. This furnishes the gloss of precision while anticipating a revision of the theory when the "conjuncture" changes. Nicos Poulantzas closes his *Fascism and Dictatorship* melodramatically: "Given the aim of this book, I prefer to give this conclusion a date. *Paris, July, 1970.*"[24]

"To understand these essays," Althusser tells us in the Introduction to *For Marx,* "and to pass judgement on them, it is essential to realize that they were conceived, written and published . . . in a particular ideological and theoretical conjuncture."[25] Or he suggests that the "exceptional situation" in which his essay on Lacan was written explains why it has to "either be corrected, or expanded."[26] The evil is not in the appeal to history; rather history becomes the insurance policy for the perpetual theoretical malpractice suits. The theory or theorist is never wrong and never reconceived; the guilt resides in the historical process – the conjuncture. In this way orthodox Marxism immunizes itself. If it is always wrong or too late, the fault lies elsewhere.

Althusser's response to one of his critics, John Lewis, indicates his achievement. He chastises Lewis for ignoring the historical situation in which *For Marx* was written and then awards himself a badge for courage and perspicuity. "Mr. Lewis never . . . talks about this political history . . . In *For Marx*, – that is, in 1965, . . . I was already writing about Stalin."[27] Some 30 years after the Moscow trials, or 10 short years after Khruschev denounced Stalin, Althusser was "already" criticizing Stalin. Althusser dreams he heads the theoretical parade while tidying up years after the procession has passed him by.

If success needs rescrutiny, so does failure. Neither success nor failure can be accepted as a blank fact. Success or its absence is only one factor in the evaluation of a politics. We do not condemn the collaborators with nazism because they picked the losing side; nor do we condemn the Spanish Loyalists and Republicans because they lost. The history of the opposition to orthodox Marxism – council communism, "left" communism, dissident currents, and so on – is without doubt a history of failure. Yet it is none the less valuable. Failure proves nothing, except who lost.

This is often forgotten. No one likes losers. The history of revolution is usually presented as a string of victories, blemished by some setbacks and defeats. Rarely does one find honesty comparable to that of Marx. After the revolutions of 1848 he wrote, "With the exception of a few short chapters, every important part of the annals of the revolution from 1848 to 1849 carries the heading: Defeat of the revolution!"[28] Summarizing the intervening period some fifteen years later he wrote, "If, then, there had been no solidarity of action between the British and the continental working classes, there was, at all events, a solidarity of defeat."[29]

Outside Marxism the same issues of success and failure have surfaced, although not in the same form. In historical and sociological studies controversy has flourished for years about the autonomy and resistance of various social formations: American blacks, working class, Jews, women, and so on. Evaluations differ on their degree of independence and resistance within the oppressive environments of slavery, concentration camps, and bourgeois society. Interpretations tend to fall into two types. One stresses autonomy and relative success at resistance; the other stresses the converse, the power and ability of the establishment to repress or incorporate an opposition.

The issues are emotionally and, finally, politically charged; this is the point. A politics governs and fuels this debate; a left tends to elevate the advances and autonomy of the underlying class or group, and the right extols the power (or genius) of the establishment. To be sure, the politics is often implicit, but for this reason it is so much the more potent. It is never questioned and thus congeals into a dogma: The left always and everywhere finds advances of the subaltern groups.

As a dogma it might be better than most, and it does seem to rest on a self-evident proposition: Victims in history resist. They are also subjects of history. Yet it also draws upon the myth of success, an upbeat vision of past and future conflicts. An examination of the strength of the establishment is dismissed as reactionary. Analysis of social relations that induced identification and not independence and resistance is precluded. Is it the task of a left to always find victories and successes of the suppressed? This degrades the critique of capitalism to cheering the home team, and it ill serves its subject by minimizing the density and complexity of the oppressive social relations. That the oppressed were terrorized by terror conveys no insult; that they sold out to eat and live suggests no dishonor. The urge to people the desert of history is public relations for the moguls who have wasted it.

The configuration of these debates testifies to the same pressures at work inside Marxism: the inclination to present the struggle as upward and successful. Certainly in the recent historical and sociological studies the provocations have never been lacking. To argue that there was little resistance to slavery, as Stanley Elkins did,[30] or to Nazi extermination, as Bruno Bettelheim and Hannah Arendt did,[31] or to bourgeois power, as working-class studies did,[32] was to insult; and the insult was compounded when it was further argued there was not only little resistance but complicity and cooperation.

These works of Elkins, Bettelheim, and Arendt marked one swing of the pendulum. In more recent years historical studies have moved in the opposite direction and have stressed the forms of resistance by slaves,[33] Jews,[34] the working classes,[35] and women.[36] If more just, this perspective begins to shade into a mythic vision of resistance and progress. At this point it raises more questions than it answers. The image of success and victories vies with the actual defeats and setbacks. If, for instance, the working classes were progressing in their culture, struggles, and class consciousness, their defeat or relative passivity would become not more but less understandable. If the structure and toll of domination are omitted, history is traded for cosmetics. "A 'history from above' – of the intricate machinery of class domination – is thus no less essential than a 'history from below': indeed, without it the latter in the end becomes one-sided (if the better side)."[37]

For those who imagine that dialectics consists of matching mathematical opposites, no problem exists. On one hand there is domination, on the other, resistance. Marcuse's *One Dimensional Man* was regularly derided as undialectical. Marcuse forgot that society was two-dimensional; domination always incites resistance. This is the Official Marxist Interpretation of Everything, or the power of positive thinking for Marxists. Any suggestion of the victory of the state or bourgeois culture is countered by stressing the victory of the working classes and their culture. Each negative statement is answered by a positive. The total is zero.

This mathematical interpretation of history issues into a picture of forces of liberation battling the forces of domination. If this is adequate for actual warfare, it fails as a model for the existence and persistence of capitalism. Capitalism does not simply rely on perpetual military subjugation. For this reason any blank juxtaposition of "history from above" and "history from below" threatens to conclude in two-volume works, with few transitions. The crucial question is the relationship between these two histories.

The official proletarian culture of the III International and, most recently, China portrayed only smiling, working, and powerful peasants. Frowns, sickness, betrayals, and defeats were eschewed. Andrei Zhdanov, proponent of Socialist Realism, explained why optimism and heroism were the guiding slogans: "Our [Soviet] literature is impregnated with enthusiasm and the spirit of heroic deeds . . . It is optimistic in essence because it is the literature of the rising class of the proletariat."[38] This is the open and hidden logic of orthodox Marxism and recent historical studies. The need to stress the victories of the oppressed is deep seated and humanistic, but it maltreats its subject when the objective defeats and surrenders, political and psychological, are whitewashed and remain unrecognized and uncomprehended.

Let there be no misunderstanding: The vision of unresisting victims by the social worker or the philanthropist is no better. This is a static view of history or the administrative dream of the world. The application of the "dialectical" scheme that decays into a behavioral psychology must also be avoided: Stimulus provokes a response, or repression yields rebellion. Both visions corrode into myths.

II

Distancing oneself from the political plane reveals the theoretical outline of orthodox Marxism, which is marked by a commitment to science. An esteem for science is hardly unique to Marxism; it infuses modern society. Science guarantees success. Marxism inherited this proposition from bourgeois society and hammered it into a deadly weapon. For Marxists, it became the revolver for shooting dissidents and opponents. The primal and final charge that orthodox Marxism invokes is that its opponents have violated the canons of science; they are prescientific, nonscientific, literary, romantic, utopian, historicist, humanist, aesthetic.

Marx labeled his own work scientific, contrasting it to utopian and other brands of socialism. "There is no royal road to science," he cautioned his French readers of *Capital.*[39] Yet Marx employed the term "science" sparingly, wary of excess usage. More important, for Marx, science meant *Wissenschaft*, a term that resounds with Hegelian tones. That the English and French "science" is more limited than the German *Wissenschaft* is a point regularly made in cultural and intellectual studies.[40] Because it involves the entire question of Hegel's impact on Marxism, however, it merits more attention than a footnote.

If Marx deemed his own work scientific, he distrusted a religion of science.[41] On more than one occasion he disassociated himself from the term "scientific socialism." Marx charged Proudhon with fetishizing science. "No school of thought has thrown around the word 'science' more haphazardly than that of Proudhon."[42] For Proudhon, science "reduces itself to a slender proportion of a scientific formula; he is the man in search of formulas."[43] Years later, responding to Bakunin's accusation that "scientific socialism" (*wissenschaftlicher Sozialismus*) was elitist, Marx clarified: "'Scientific socialism' was only used in opposition to utopian socialism, which wants to attach the people to new delusions, instead of limiting its science to the knowledge of the social movement made by the people itself."[44]

That "science" here meant "knowledge of the social movement made by the people itself" (*Erkenntnis der vom Volk selbst gemachten sozialen Bewegung*)[45] suggests the divergence between the Hegelian *Wissenschaft* and the French and English "science." This can be overstated, but the terms illuminate, and ultimately sustain, two conflicting Marxist approaches to history and society. The distinction between *Wissenschaft* and "science" gains currency only outside of the natural and exact sciences; this already structures the problem. The issue was how to transfer the methods of the natural sciences to the social, political, and philosophical terrain. The palpable advances of the natural sciences rendered this a compelling project. In duplicating the methods of the natural sciences, the hope was to duplicate its achievements.

This project inspired myriad thinkers, from Auguste Comte to Emile Durkheim, Karl Popper, and contemporary social scientists, and it forms the nub and hub of positivist (non-Hegelian) science. The history of these efforts is neither simple nor monotonous, and it is cluttered with reservations and qualifications.[46] Each thinker selected and prized only some of the features of the natural sciences: quantification, natural laws, objectivity, clarity, and so on. Comte is illustrative; he originally considered sociology a "special kind of physics." By name and substance Comte patterned social physics on the natural sciences. He regarded "all phenomena as subjected to invariable natural *laws*. Our business is . . . to pursue an accurate discovery of these laws with a view to reducing them to the smallest possible number . . . The best illustration of this is in the case of the doctrine of gravitation."[47]

In one fashion or another positivist "science" imitated and adopted the procedures of the natural sciences. For example, the program of the Vienna Circle sought to replicate the progress of the natural sciences. The "scientific world conception," the program explained, was "empiricist and positivist" and applied "logical analysis." These features called forth others; a scientific world conception necessitated the "search for a neutral system of formulae, for a symbolism freed from the slag of historical languages . . . Neatness and clarity are striven for, and dark distances and unfathomable depths rejected."[48]

"The slag of historical languages" is the heap that separates the positivist science from the Hegelian *Wissenschaft*. In the Hegelian tradition, the slag of history is as valuable as the nuggets. History is not footnoted or discarded, rather it infuses the theory. This is where Hegelian and positivist science separate. The natural world, and its sciences, knows history only externally; history does not determine structure or method. The difference between the study of the moon and the French Revolution is history. Inquiries of human behavior inspired by the study of the moon or the atom suppress or belittle the historical dimension.

"History" does not mean here a chronicle of events but the story of humanity as actor and victim. As Hegel's greatest student wrote, "Men make their own history," adding the crucial qualification, "but they do not make it just as they please."[49] Positivist science tends to eliminate history as so much slag or intellectual baggage. To be sure, the natural world and the natural sciences are hardly impervious to history. The problems and approaches are themselves a product of history; but, finally, the structure of the moon or the atom is not historical. "Human history," wrote Marx citing Vico, "differs from natural history in that we have made the former, but not the latter."[50]

The Hegelian *Wissenschaft* is not wider or larger than the positivist science; rather it is impregnated with history. The natural reality and natural sciences do not know the fundamental historical categories: consciousness and self-consciousness, subjectivity and objectivity, appearance and essence. In direct opposition to Hegelian logic, Otto Neurath (with Hans Hahn and Rudolf Carnap) wrote for the Vienna Circle: "In science there are no 'depths'; there is surface everywhere." Or, "a scientific description can contain only the *structure* . . . of objects, not their 'essence' . . . Subjectively experienced qualities – redness, pleasure – are as such only experiences, not knowledge."[51]

Yet Hegelian thought must not be confused with mysticism or irrationality; it does not promote the cult of depths and essences. Positive and empirical sciences are not false, but limited.[52] "To such questions as, when Caeser was born, or how many feet there were in a stadium, etc. a neat answer should be given, just as it is surely true that the square of the hypotenuse equals the squares of the other two sides of a right-angled triangle. But the nature of such so-called truths is different from the nature of philosophical truths."[53] The logic of the empirical sciences and common sense is not so much true or untrue as correct or incorrect; it does not attain truth. The judgment "the rose 'is red' or 'is not red' " can only be "correct" within the "limited circle of perception."[54]

To Hegel, the ideal of the positive sciences – mathematics – is vulnerable to the same criticism. As a single mode of cognition it is "external and indifferent," as well as limited. "Our knowledge would be in a very awkward predicament if such objects as freedom, law, morality, or even God himself, because they cannot be measured and calculated, or expressed in a mathematical formula, were to be reckoned beyond the reach of exact knowledge."[55]

As object and method, Hegel's *Wissenschaft* is saturated with history; this finally constitutes Hegel's protest against the positive and empirical sciences. They are historically blind and treat truth as formal and static. "Truth is not a minted coin which can be given and pocketed ready-made."[56] History is a means and an end. "The harmoniousness of childhood is a gift from the hand of nature; the second harmony must spring from the labour and culture of the spirit"[57] – from the historical process.

These teachings of Hegel were neither well received nor well preserved. The story of the impact of Hegelian thought takes volumes. It is germane here in regard to a single issue: The critique of positivist science that does not collapse into irrationality or existentialism is unthinkable without Hegelian thought. This is why the reception of Hegel by Marxists is fundamental. As the following chapter seeks to demonstrate, this reception preceded and defined the texture of Marxism.

Hegel remains an outsider to the major philosophical traditions. For instance, Anglo-American courses in the history of philosophy typically end with Kant and recommence in the twentieth century with Ludwig Wittgenstein, Bertrand Russell, and the Vienna Circle. The nineteenth century, with the troubling Hegel – as well as Marx, Kierkegaard, Nietzsche, and Schopenhauer – is regularly omitted or palmed off to the literature departments or to teachers not-yet-hired or about-to-be-fired. Karl Popper's evaluation, if not representative, at least suggests the deep and general mistrust. In *The Open Society*, a book that he tells us is grounded in a "rational attitude" of "openness of criticism,"[58] Popper introduces as "excellent" the following judgment of Hegel:

"Hegel . . . was a flat-headed, insipid, nauseating, illiterate charlatan, who reached the pinnacle of audacity in scribbling together and dishing up the crassest mystifying nonsense. This nonsense has been noisily proclaimed as immortal wisdom by mercenary followers and readily accepted as such by all fools."[59]

If Hegel fared better in the Marxist traditions, it was perhaps because he attracted little interest. He was easily situated, interpreted, and forgotten with the aid of some phrases by Marx or especially some texts by Engels. Hegel was honored as the originator of idealistic dialectics, which with juggling could be rendered materialistic and scientific. They were ultimately codified by Stalin into a set of laws.[60] What Lenin scribbled down during the enforced leisure of World War I when he began to study Hegel remained an isolated statement. "It is impossible completely to understand *Capital* . . . without having thoroughly studied and understood the *whole* of Hegel's *Logic*. Consequently, . . . none of the Marxists have understood Marx!!"[61]

Yet Hegel's role, or lack of a role, should not be exaggerated. Neither the presence or absence nor the accurate or inaccurate interpretation of a single thinker can be held accountable for the vagaries of political and social movements. In this sense the relation of Hegel to Marxism (or Darwin to social Darwinism) is not cause and effect. The founders succumb to the imperatives of their followers. That Hegel has been consistently misread or unread suggests something important about the fabric of orthodox Marxism: Hegel proved a threat to the dominant idea of science. Consequently, orthodox Marxism has sought either to reduce Hegel to a positivist notion of science or to purge him from Marxism.

This has remained a current project of orthodox Marxism. In recent years Althusser assumed this task; he is a short course on "what is orthodox Marxism." His work has been marked by two closely related elements, a phobia of Hegel and a passion for science. "We have the right . . . and the duty, politically, to use and defend – by fighting for the *word* – the philosophical category of 'science' . . . To use and defend the word 'science' . . . is a necessity, in order to resist the bourgeois subjective idealists and the petty-bourgeois Marxists."[62] The main weapon of the petty-bourgeois hordes is history, or "historicism" in Althusser's lexicon. History and historicism compromise the rigor of science. Marxism is no more historical than language, "which as Stalin showed escapes it [history]."[63]

Next to history, the main danger to science is Hegel; Althusser has met this danger through exorcism. He argued that the "young Marx *was never strictly speaking a Hegelian*" except in 1844, when he broke with Hegel.[64] Althusser learned that this was never, strictly speaking, true, except when he said it in 1965. Later he discovered Hegel everywhere and recast his thesis to save it: Marx was engaged in a lifelong flight from Hegel, and he attained safety only in death. With Althusser, anything short of rigor mortis lacks rigor. The living Marx was tainted with Hegel. "The famous *Preface* of 1859 is still profoundly Hegelian evolutionist."[65] Althusser's geiger counter picks up Hegelian radiation even in *Capital;* its one percent of Hegelian radioactivity is "flagrant and extremely harmful."[66] Only Marx's notes on Wagner, written the year before his death, are "*totally and definitely exempt* from *any* trace of Hegelian influence."[67]

That generations of Marxists have been seduced by a popular idea of science cannot simply be traced to intellectual confusion; it is rooted, rather, in the ambivalent relationship between Marxism and bourgeois society. If Marx was capitalism's greatest critic, he was also its greatest admirer. Marx's own position can be presented theoretically with some precision, but more – or less – theoretically it has presented individual Marxists of specific societies with endless difficulties. Capitalism was denounced for its exploitation, its brutality, pollution, hypocrisy – the list goes on. Yet it was welcomed, even celebrated, because it represented a giant step out of a prebourgeois order. Socialism could only be established on the foundation and wealth that capitalism produced. Capitalism was not only indispensable, it was desirable.

The message for individual Marxists was more complex, especially for those located in societies where the work of capitalism was incomplete. This included all Marxists, with the possible exception of the English. In all other countries capitalism remained a progressive force, and the working class was to abet capitalism until the material foundations for socialism had been created. The lesson was difficult and unpalatable. In January 1849 Marx advised the German Democrats and workers, "We are certainly the last people to desire the rule of the bourgeoisie." Yet "it is better to suffer in modern bourgeois society, which by its industry creates the material means for the foundation of a new society that will liberate you all, than to revert to a bygone form of society which . . . thrusts the entire nation back into medieval barbarism."[68]

This says it exactly, perhaps too exactly. For this provoked responses from an "ultra-left" impatient with its evolutionary logic. Although these objections are generally ignored or slighted in the official histories,[69] they touch a raw nerve of Marxism. In the aftermath of 1848, when these objections were raised, Marx advocated incremental social transformation. Protests emerged from various quarters and finally split the Communist League, to which Marx and Engels belonged.[70] Andreas Gottschalk asked Marx sarcastically: "Why should we make a revolution? Why should we, men of the proletariat, spill our blood? Should we really escape the hell of the Middle Ages by precipitating ourselves into the purgatory of decrepit capitalist rule . . . ? You are not serious about the liberation of the oppressed."[71]

The charge was not fair; yet it located a tension in Marxism that regularly degenerated into a simple affirmation: Where capitalism was incomplete, Marxists were required to finish its work. The evil of retrograde social development was met by blessing capitalist development, which would finally issue into a new social order. This evolutionary logic was more than logic; it brought in its train attitudes and beliefs that corroded the theoretical and psychological impulse to subvert capitalism.

The evaluation of colonialism by Marx displayed these same features. Brutal robbery and exploitation marked colonialism. Insofar as the material foundations of capitalism were established, however, colonialism progressed willy-nilly toward socialism. This, in brief, constituted Marx's appraisal of the English colonization of India. "The devasting effects of English industry, when contemplated with regard to India . . . are palpable and confounding." But England has a "double mission" in India, destroying the old society "and the laying of the material foundations of Western society in Asia." "Modern industry . . . will dissolve the hereditary divisions of labour, upon which rest the Indian castes, those decisive impediments to Indian progress and Indian power."[72]

From *The Communist Manifesto* to *Capital,* the same dialectical vision informed Marx's analysis of modern industry. Marx never doubted that the drive for profits constantly impelled the bourgeoisie to revolutionize the instruments of production. "Modern industry never views or treats the existing form of production process as the definitive one. Its technical basis is therefore revolutionary, whereas all earlier modes of production were essentially conservative." Yet the social relations in which the "technical basis of production" was enmeshed constituted the devasting "negative side."[73]

If the terms are clear enough, the substance is not. That it has taken countless scholars to determine exactly what Marx was saying only suggests the difficulty of Marxists faced with political options and choices. The history of Marxism is the history of the loss of the dialectical critique of bourgeois society. The irresistible temptation was to cast the dialectical movements of society into a one-way and upward path. Progress in capitalism was read as progress toward socialism. The texts of Marx could always be interpreted in this light. Marxists were confident that their "science" was grounded in the actual movements of society; this distinguished Marxism from other (and utopian) socialisms, which fled into the past or into rural enclaves. For the Marxists, however, the critique of capitalism was corroded by the endorsement of its achievements.

Every chapter in the history of Marxism has been rent by this dialectic, or inconsistency: The denunciation of capitalism vied with its affirmation. The beginnings of Russian Marxism conformed to this pattern. Appealing to economic or cultural realities, the Populists argued that Russia would or should escape the disaster and evil of capitalist development. The Marxists retorted that capitalism was, and should be, developing in Russia; this laid the foundation for a proletariat and, finally, a socialist, revolution. For these reasons capitalism could be evaluated as progressive. Lenin's *Development of Capitalism in Russia* (1900) pursued this in detail.

Inasmuch as the Russian Marxists strained to demonstrate the factual and positive impact of capitalism, they were tempted to minimize its destructiveness. If "more" capitalism was preferable to "less," was the critique of capitalism itself vitiated? Lenin directly addressed this question: "Recognition of the progressiveness of this role [of capitalism] is quite compatible . . . with the full recognition of the negative and dark sides of capitalism."[74]

Yet for many Russian Marxists this recognition proved difficult to maintain in practice; they extolled capitalism so enthusiastically that they forgot about socialism, or tired of it. They no longer grasped how or where socialism differed from capitalism; this set the stage for a return to religion. The "legal Marxists" were especially prey to these options. Serge Bulgakov exulted, as a Marxist, that "every new factory, every new industrial enterprise carries us forward . . ."; and he ended as a priest decrying the "mechanical necessity" of Marxism.[75] Struve, a legal Marxist, closed his major study with the words "Let us confess our cultural backwardness and let us go and learn from capitalism" and ended as a liberal.[76]

The same ambiguity corroded the Marxist opposition to colonialism. The II International condemned colonialism as a violent appendage of capitalism. To some Marxists, however, it served a necessary and positive function, in propelling the colonized along the path of industrialization. As one exponent of a "positive" colonial policy phrased it: "The primitive peoples will reach civilization only by bearing this cross [of capitalism]. It is therefore our duty not to hinder the development of capitalism, an indispensable chain in the history of humanity; we can even favor its appearance."[77]

The evaluation of technology by Marxists succumbed to the same pressures; a dialectical critique was sloughed off. Marxists did not doubt that technology constituted the greatest achievement of capitalism, distinguishing it from all previous societies. The suffering or misfortune resulting from technology was caused by the social context, not the apparatus itself. Such logic stuffed technology into familiar categories of means and ends; technology was at best and worst a neutral endeavor. The evil resided only in the ends to which it was used.

This approach infused orthodox Marxism; it could not be accused of distorting Marx. Marx had always been a sharp critic of utopian, feudal, and romantic socialism; each was oblivious or antagonistic toward the technological advances of capitalist industrialization. Little seemed more certain than that Marxists accepted and even accelerated these advances. Nevertheless, a yawning gap between the general principles and the particulars vitiated a critical appropriation of a technological world. Technology everywhere was welcomed as facilitating socialism and, for that reason, was exempted from critical inspection.

Marx was of course completely cognizant of the destructiveness of the labor process. On occasion, however, he had suggested that the divisions of labor within the factory were "planned and regulated," whereas those in the larger society were unregulated and anarchistic.[78] The notion was attractive and popular because it inferred that the factory and technology were the progressive elements of capitalism. Irrationality was confined to the marketplace and found its boundary at the factory gate. Furthermore, the notion accorded with common sense, which could confirm the confusion and lawlessness of the market but was mute before the apparent rationality and efficiency of production itself. Yet such a perspective capitulated to the mystique of technology; it reduced revolution to sacking the bosses while protecting as sacrosanct the technological base.[79]

Lenin's evaluation of technology, and of Taylorism in particular, participated in this logic. The weakness of capitalist technology and Taylorism lay in their confinement to the factory. "Capital organises and rationalises labour within the factory . . . In social production as a whole, however, chaos continues to reign and grow."[80] Lenin recognized that the Taylor system, "like all capitalist progress, is a combination of the refined brutality of bourgeois exploitation and a number of the greatest scientific achievements." The lesson was clear: "The Soviet Republic must at all costs adopt all that is valuable in the achievements of science and technology in this field. The possibility of building socialism depends exactly upon our success in combining the Soviet power and the Soviet organisation of administration with the up-to-date achievements of capitalism. We must organise in Russia the study and teaching of the Taylor system and systematically try it out and adapt it to our own ends."[81] Stalin later defined Leninism as a combination of "Russian revolutionary sweep with American efficiency."[82]

The uncritical enthusiasm for technology was not grounded simply in the textual complexities of Marx; nor was the plan to adopt and accelerate capitalist industrialization based simply on a misreading of Marx. Such an argument ascribes too much importance to the texts. Rather the social–economic imperatives of backwardness suppressed the dialectical critique of technology. This resounds throughout Lenin's writings. The work of capitalism was palpably incomplete; and if this was obvious to the Russians, then Marxists in Italy, France, and Germany were just as convinced.[83]

If today large regions within the industrially advanced countries are "underdeveloped," this was evidently more striking a century ago. Of course, what constituted "under" developed or "over" developed is the essence of the matter.[84] Marx studied England because he was convinced that other West European countries would replicate its history. "The country that is more developed industrially only shows to the less developed, the image of its own future." Germany, in comparison, suffered "not only from the development of capitalist production, but also from the incompleteness of that development."[85]

The "incompleteness" of economic development, as fact or conviction, encouraged the acceptance of evolutionary theories. For the first generation of Marxists after Marx, capitalism proved its ability to not only limp along but to develop and expand. The last part of the century witnessed both the perfecting of new industrial technology – cheap steel, electric power – and the transformation of consumption – sewing machines, cheap clocks, bicycles, electric lighting.[86] That these were not equally distributed is not to the point: They never had been. They suggested, however, that capitalism had hardly ceased to progress. The evolutionary progress of capitalism called forth and ratified the evolutionary and scientific doctrines of Marxists.

The critique of bourgeois society – Marxism – progressively lost its bite; the distance between Marxism and bourgeois society narrowed. Marxists and their opponents shared the belief in science, progress, and success. Revolution was not simply adjourned; rather the Marxists embraced the scientific and industrial rationality as their own. They saw themselves accelerating the advances of capitalism.

The phenomenon of Marxists extolling and finally succumbing to capitalism did not go completely unnoticed. If the participants were blind, those on the outside or margins of Marxism were not. It is hardly fortuitous that *the* historian and sociologist of capitalist rationality, Max Weber, recognized the spirit of capitalism in the lair of the Marxists. He visited a Party Congress of the German Social Democrats (SPD) in 1906 and concluded: "These gentlemen no longer frighten anyone."[87] The following year he debated conservative sociologists on the threat of SPD electoral victory in several German cities. "I see no danger for bourgeois society in surrendering our cities . . . to the SPD," said Weber. He noted that "no revolutionary enthusiasm" was expressed at the recent SPD Congress, and he anticipated that a victorious SPD would follow a "mercantile policy," encouraging the growth of capital.[88]

The profound complicity of orthodox Marxism in bourgeois industrialization is exposed by an absence. In the Marxist tradition a searching critique of the "secondary" characteristics of capitalism is lacking. Secondary refers to those features that stand once removed from the primary economic organization of wages, working conditions, imperialism, and the market. It refers to a series of relations, such as urbanism, mass media, psychological life, and leisure. These are not necessarily second in importance, but are second in that they cannot exist apart from the basic political–economic organization of society.

In recent decades these areas have increasingly drawn the attention of Marxists, but earlier Marxists ignored them. The few analyses offered have been pedestrian and predictable. The secondary features have been disposed of by concepts taken from the basic dictionary of Marxism: superstructure, relations of production, accumulation, and so on. If none of these concepts have been wrong, none have grasped the specificity of the phenomenon.

The usual explanation for the banality of Marxism refers to the ills of "vulgar" Marxism. Vulgar Marxism is vulgar in its economic reductionism; everything lacks substance and reality beyond an economic base. This does not suffice as an explanation for the lameness of Marxism. Not only vulgar Marxism but its vulgar critique needs to be surmounted.

The vulgar critique of vulgar Marxism glosses over the complicity between the Marxists and the secondary features of capitalism. This was the reason for blindness. They did not perceive these features as fundamentally changing; hence there was no reason for scrutiny. The Marxists would inherit the cities and the mass newspapers; only the signs and headlines would be changed. Rockefeller Plaza would become Leninplatz. The basic rapport with industrial life paralyzed the critique.

This can be stated in the obverse more emphatically: The most compelling and illuminating analyses of the secondary processes derive from a conservative, sometimes reactionary, tradition. This runs from Nietzsche and Spengler to contemporary – and surely lesser – critics, such as Jacques Ellul and Ivan Illich. This is hardly a coherent tradition, and it is radically flawed in more than one respect. Yet the analyses that are proferred are unmatched – and unassimilated – by Marxists.

For example, Spengler's analysis of the daily press from 1919 found no counterpart in the literature of the Marxists:

> English–American politics have created *through the press* a force-field of world-wide intellectual and financial tensions in which every individual unconsciously takes up the place alotted to him, so that he must think, will, and act as a ruling personality somewhere or other in the distance thinks fit... Man does not speak to man; the press, and its associate, the electrical news-service, keep the waking-consciousness of whole peoples and continents under a deafening drum-fire of theses, catchwords, standpoints, scenes, feelings, day by day and year by year... The scattered sheets of the Age of Enlightenment transformed themselves into the "Press" – a term of most significant anonymity... To-day we live so cowed under the bombardment of this intellectual artillery that hardly anyone can attain to the inward detachment that is required for a clear view of the monstrous drama... The liberal bourgeois mind is *proud* of the abolition of censorship, the last restraint, while the dictator of the press – Northcliffe! – keeps the slave-gang of his readers under the whip of his leading articles, telegrams and pictures. *Democracy has by its newspapers completely expelled the book from the mental life of the people* ... The people read the *one* paper, "its" paper, which forces itself through the front doors by millions daily, spellbinds the intellect from morning to night, drives the book into oblivion by its more engaging layout, and if one or another specimen of a book does emerge into visibility, forestalls and eliminates its possible effects by "reviewing" it... What the Press wills, is true. Its commanders evoke, transform, interchange truths. Three weeks of press work, and the truth is acknowledged by everybody... The reader neither knows, nor is allowed to know, the purpose for which he is used... A more appalling caricature of freedom of thought cannot be imagined. Formerly a man did not dare to think freely. Now he dares, but cannot.[89]

This assault on capitalism can also be found in Nietzsche's analysis of morality and bad conscience or, more recently, in Illich's discussion of the medicalization of society.[90] These conservative critics penetrate and grasp phenomena that the Marxists revere and pass over. The sources of their insight are at hand; unlike the Marxists, they find capitalist rationality and progress grating. This allows and encourages insights barred to the Marxists, who are less hostile to the beat of capitalism. The Marxists hear the squeaks and groans where the mechanism needs oil and new bearings; to these critics the hum itself is offensive.

To many of the conservatives, Marxism itself appeared as simply another industrialization scheme. Conventional liberalism and wisdom feared Marxism as a threat to capitalist industrialization. These critics feared the opposite: Marxism accelerating industrialization. Spengler considered Marxism a version of the English industrial revolution: It concentrated on business, profits, and classes. Marx was an "exclusively English thinker," adopting the terms, ethics, and categories of the industrial revolution. "He took his principles from the very thing he was fighting." Marx intended to *extend* capitalism to the working class, turning each worker into a merchant who would sell his labor at the highest prices. In the light of the history of Marxism and trade unions, Spengler's judgment cannot be rejected as simply perverse: "Marxism is the capitalism of the working class."[91]

It is not coincidental that the few Marxists who swam against the tide of capitalist rationality did not sever all links to conservatism, romanticism, or utopianism; they remained attached to a noncapitalist logic. They include William Morris, of the nineteenth century, and Ernst Bloch, André Breton, and the Frankfurt School, of the twentieth century. Their intellectual sources enabled them to see through the mirror of the economy; they were alerted not simply to the falling rate of profit but to the falling rate of intelligence and beauty.[92] These figures are linked by their resistance to socialism as a souped-up version of capitalism.

The unorthodox Marxists retrieved the substance of Marx: Socialism promised more than a rise in wages or an expansion of cities. A rise in wages, Marx wrote in *Capital*, "only means in fact that the length and weight of the golden chain the wage-labourer has already forged for himself allows it to be loosened somewhat."[93] Neither the elevation nor the equalization of wages was the goal of Marx's socialism; Marx, early and late, denounced "barracks communism [*Kasernenkommunismus*]."[94] Liberation is more than electing the bosses, thereby trading subjugation for self-subjugation. "Criticism has plucked the imaginary flowers on the chain not in order that man shall continue to bear that chain without fantasy or consolation but so that he shall throw off the chain and pluck the living flower."[95]

The idioms diverge, but the basic thinking of the unorthodox Marxists does not. Morris cautioned again and again not to confuse "the machinery of socialism" with socialism; to substitute "a business-like administration in the interests of the public" for a laissez faire and coercive regime would be a great gain, but not the goal.[96] Socialism is not utilitarianism; it is leisure. "The leisure which Socialism above all things aims at obtaining for the worker is also the very thing that breeds desire – desire for beauty, for knowledge, for more abundant life, in short."[97]

Bloch salvaged the utopian and romantic note in Marxism.[98] The "naked economic orientation" paralyzed orthodox Marxism.[99] If the economy had been analytically subverted by the Marxists, the "soul" and "belief" to replace it were lacking.[100] For Bloch, the path from utopia to science – the title of Engels's popular pamphlet – skipped too much; it eliminated the driving force of the utopian vision. What Bloch called the "warm current" of Marxism must be retrieved, lest it be suffocated by the "cold current" of technocratic Marxism. Breton, like Bloch, refused to sever links to supraeconomic logic and terrains; he refused the either/or of orthodoxy: either industrialization or imagination. "In the realm of facts, as we see it, no ambiguity is possible: all of us seek to shift power from the hands of the bourgeoisie to those of the proletariat. Meanwhile, it is nonetheless necessary that the experiments of inner life continue."[101]

In the cant of orthodox Marxism all of these figures are charged with the same infraction: violating the code of science. The code adumbrated various subsections, itemizing romantic, pessimistic, subjective, and utopian violations. For one guardian, *History and Class Consciousness* was "the first major eruption of the romantic anti-scientific tradition of bourgeois thought into Marxist theory."[102] The charge against the Frankfurt School runs: "In the place of revolutionary science, enters bourgeois cultural pessimism."[103] T. W. Adorno and Max Horkheimer were accused of "spiritualism" and Marcuse of "petty-bourgeois anarchism," a crime that is extended "to all those who have taken him seriously."[104] Wilhelm Reich and his followers did not escape the police raid. "Your starting point is consumption, ours is production; therefore you are not Marxists."[105] The surrealists were indicted for blocking capitalist development. "It is necessary to affirm plainly that the movement that one could call *technological* [*machiniste*] is destined to develop in the world in an irresistable fashion . . . Communism should be one of the principal factors of its development."[106]

Against the dirty words – romanticism, subjectivism, aestheticism, utopianism – the clean ones are invoked – science, objectivity, rigor, structure. Here the final, almost psychological, contours of orthodox Marxism come into view. Adorno's characterization of positivism as "the puritanism of knowledge" holds true for orthodox Marxism.[107] The goal is rigorous self-control and self-discipline. The asceticism of orthodox Marxism despises unregulated insight as if it were the threat it actually is. The sexual code is internalized as conceptual commandments: Suggestions of utopia and romanticism are tabooed as too suggestive. Scientific Marxism dreams not of a life without anxiety but of master plans and interoffice memos. Structural Marxism not only examines but is in love with structures: It fears the unstructured.

Asceticism is the conceptual center of gravity of orthodox Marxism. Concepts are multiplied to stamp out dissolute thought and thinkers. The object is to become an object; hence the hatred for the subjective. That the dissenters have been regularly derided as infantile implies the psychosexual core: Authority is threatened.[108] One critic is offended that nowhere in *History and Class Consciousness* is Marxism recognized as a "real and responsible science."[109] The gun of science is cocked whenever thought thinks too much. Another critic growls that unless we "move on from the discovery of the horrors of capitalism to an attempt to understand it scientifically" we will be plagued by "another 40 years of paralyzed virtuosity" of the Frankfurt School.[110] The threat of paralyzed virtuosity is met by preventive arrests and five-year plans. "The first concern," wrote Horkheimer about orthodox Marxists, "when they think about freedom is the new penal system, not its abolition."[111]

Along with Benjamin Franklin, orthodox Marxism is infused with the spirit of puritanism. The mental apparatus with permanent-press concepts tames the chaos of desire. Orthodox Marxism confirms what Mary Douglas called the "purity rule": An increase "to disembody or etherealize the forms of expression" corresponds to a tightening net of social domination.[112] The dirty words of Marxism – and humanism itself – recall the corporal and carnal reality that gives the lie to pristine theories of metastructures. As a cohort of Althusser put it: "I shall not be satisfied until I either situated it ["the word man"] . . . in the necessity of the theoretical system . . . or *eliminated* it as a foreign body."[113]

The conformity of orthodox Marxism serves the cold passion for science and authority. Althusser tells us that ideology belongs to the future as well as to the past. He means: Keep your uniforms. The logic of "so much the worse for the facts" challenged the regulations that have domesticated Marxism. Nevertheless, the choices are not between facts and fantasy, conceptual rigor and free association, science and poetry, or optimism and pessimism. These are the bad choices that perpetuated Marxism as caricature. The pieces do not fit neatly together, but neither does society. This suggests at least one guide for a critical Marxism: Do not lose the pieces.

2

The Marxism of Hegel and Engels

Unorthodox Marxism is unthinkable without Hegel. The irreplaceable starting and returning points for surpassing conformist Marxism are found in Hegel. From Gramsci to Merleau-Ponty, Marxists escaped the constraints of orthodoxy by tapping Hegelian waters. Critical Marxism obtained coherence and significance in countries where Hegelian thought remained alive: Italy and Germany.[1] Conversely, where a Hegelian tradition never rooted, dissipated, or arrived late – in the United States, England, France – orthodox Marxism not only dominated but suffocated alternatives.

Yet this assertion is too crude and requires qualifications. Apart from the difficulty of identifying national traditions of Marxism, the relationship between Hegel and a critical Marxism explodes a simple cause and effect. Diverse schools of Marxism have appealed to Hegel. In the nineteenth century Russian Hegelianism was second to none. In the twentieth century Soviet as well as European Marxism rest on Hegelian bases. Yet a pattern emerges that is more than a pattern: It illuminates the logic and essence of Marxism. The Hegel that has informed (and sometimes decorated) Marxism has been divided into *two* types. Two Hegelian traditions crystalized, and each infused two major Marxisms of the twentieth century, Soviet and European.

The failure to discern the two Hegelian traditions obscures the history of Marxism. Partly because of the division of intellectual labor, the distinction between the two Hegels has rarely been studied. Russian specialists regularly concluded that Soviet Marxism is Hegelian in form and inspiration. Conversely, specialists of European history argued that Western Marxism remains fundamentally Hegelian.[2]

These judgments are accurate, but imprecise and unilluminating. Soviet and European Marxism relied on antagonistic Hegelian traditions. This is more than an interesting (or uninteresting) fact. The interpretation of Hegel is an index to the history of Marxism; and it is a source. Marx arrived at his own theory by way of Hegel. The interpretation of Marx by subsequent Marxists was decisively colored by their reception of Hegel.

The issue is not arcane or scholastic; the goal is not to discover when, where, and who read each text of Hegel. Nor is the issue which tradition read Hegel more accurately; rather the task is to broadly characterize the Hegelian literature. Two traditions can be identified: the "historical" and the "scientific" Hegel. Each prized different texts and opposite formulations from the oeuvre of Hegel. The historical Hegelians gravitated toward the Hegel of history, subjectivity, and consciousness; their preferred text was *The Phenomenology of Mind*. Hegel was the philosopher of the subject attaining consciousness through history. The scientific Hegelians valued Hegel as the comprehensive and scientific philosopher; they elevated the total system, the laws of development, and the formality of the dialectic. They preferred the *Science of Logic*.

The Hegelians tended to divide, as did the Marxists, over the interpretation of nature. Hegel himself developed a philosophy of nature that sought to confirm dialectical movements in pure chemical and physical nature. Its details are not important here, but this philosophy of nature demonstrated to the scientific followers the rigorous and universal method of Hegel. The "laws" of dialectics, valid not only in history but in nature itself, proved the comprehensiveness of the system. Conversely, the philosophy of nature fared poorly with the historical Hegelians. They judged it at best irrelevant, at worst erroneous.

These conflicting evaluations of Hegel's philosophy of nature permeated the Marxist controversy on the dialectic of nature. Soviet Marxists generally defended the dialectic of nature; the laws of dialectics were not confined to history but were equally valid in nature. In the vocabulary of Soviet Marxism, as certified by Stalin, "dialectical materialism" was the "world outlook" of Marxism that encompassed nature. "Historical materialism" was a specific "application of the principles of dialectical materialism to the phenomena of the life of society."[3] To the Western theorists, by drowning Marxism in a universal system, the Soviets killed its essence. The search for general dialectical laws eclipsed the heart of Marxism: the revolutionary process grounded in the subject attaining the consciousness. These processes were unknown to nature.

Engels's contribution shows convincingly that the issue did not simply divide along national lines. The historical Hegelians predominated in Italy and Germany, and later in France. The scientific Hegelians held the edge in Russia. Yet Engels belonged emphatically in a scientific Hegelian camp. For this reason orthodox Marxism leaned heavily on Engels while a Western Marxism critically reexamined Engels and his relationship to Marx.

I

Russia yielded a rich variety of Hegelians. By 1840, when Hegel had been established in Russia, Ivan Kireevsky, who had attended his lectures in Germany, commented acidly that in Russia "even the 10 year olds" speak the language of Hegel.[4] The study of Hegel led to widely divergent conclusions, spanning Vissarion G. Belinksky's (brief) reconciliation with reality and Michael Bakunin's subversion of reality. "To me," wrote Belinksky, "it [Hegel's philosophy] was a liberation . . . I understood that there is no such thing as savage material force . . . There is no arbitrary power. Nothing happens by accident."[5] Several years later Bakunin wrote, "Contradictions have never been so sharply presented as now . . . The spirit of revolution is not subdued . . . it is burrowing – if I may avail myself of this expression of Hegel's – like a mole under the earth."[6]

Initially, Hegelian philosophy lacked emphatic connection to a specific cultural or political tendency. With each passing decade, however, Hegel was sucked into the century-long conflict between the Westernizers and Slavophiles. Russian Marxism itself emerged out of and against Russian populism; and the dispute between the Marxists and Populists composed one chapter in the longer conflict between the Westernizers and Slavophiles. Essentially, the issue turned on the nature of Russian development. The Westernizers, or Europeanizers, argued, to cite

Nicolas Berdyaev, that "the future of Russia lay in its taking the Western path." Conversely, the Slavophiles believed that Russia offered a "special type of culture," a distinct Russian civilization.[7]

Hegel might seem extraneous to this controversy. Nonetheless, implicitly, and finally explicitly, a conceptual issue coalesced that encompassed and defined Russian Hegelianism. The Westernizers, and later the Marxists, were drawn to *universal* categories of reason and development; these categories did not allow a special or unique role for Russia. They suggested, rather, a single developmental path, shared by Russia and Western Europe.

The Slavophiles and later the Populists, on the other hand, cultivated the categories of individuality and subjectivity. These categories freed Russia from the fate of imitating a single and universal Western model; they permitted a particular and unique Russian development, unknown in Western Europe.[8] These conflicting imperatives controlled the reading of Hegel; adherents and opponents defined themselves according to the value they bestowed on universal scientific categories.

While sometimes passing through a Hegelian phase, the Slavophiles and the Populists ultimately found Hegel uncongenial.[9] Slavophiles who were attracted to Hegel, such as Kireevsky, finally rejected him.[10] "Hegelian rationalism was the enemy of all transcendence."[11] They judged Hegel the panlogician, the rationalist, and the Westernizer who sacrificed the individual and specific Russian virtues – the hope for the Slavophiles and Populists. Hegel, stated one Slavophile, stands in "opposition to the religious, civil and intellectual life of our people."[12] The impression that Hegel endangered the individual, and unique Russian realities, provoked his rejection from Belinsky to Mikhailovsky.[13]

Conversely, the Westernizers, and emphatically the Marxists, discovered an ally in Hegel. He was considered a universal thinker, whose philosophy was applicable to Europe and Russia.[14] Toward the end of the century this was *the* issue among Russian social thinkers: the nature of Russian development – its distinct or universal features – and the validity of Marxism to Russia. Philosophical categories were scrutinized for their receptivity to unique Russian development or to universal and ineluctable Western evolution. For the Marxists, Hegel, already refracted through the Western–Slavophile dialogue, assumed the role of the theorist of objective and universal development.

The two major figures in this conflict were Nicholas Mikhailovsky and Georgi Plekhanov. Mikhailovsky, a Populist and a critic of Marxism, defended individual ethical and moral choices; in this respect he also resisted fatalism and determinism in social theory. It is not fortuitous that he dubbed his contribution "subjective" sociology and that the Populists generally formed a "subjective" school of sociology. Mikhailovsky denounced a purely objective theory.[15] As he argued in his "What Is Progress?": "The exclusive use of the objective method in sociology . . . would be tantamount to measuring weight with a yardstick . . . supreme control must be vested in the subjective method."[16] Hegel, consequently, was judged the foe of the individual and an exponent of an oppressive objectivity. "There is no system of philosophy which treats the individual with such withering contempt and cold cruelty as the system of Hegel."[17]

The substance of Plekhanov's reply to Mikhailovsky was adopted and repeated by the first Russian Marxists. Unlike Mikhailovsky, Plekhanov celebrated Hegel, commemorating him in the German Social Democrats' *Die Neue Zeit*.[18] His full answer to Mikhailovsky, *The Development of the Monist View of History*, "reared," according to Lenin, "a whole generation of Russian Marxists."[19] Plekhanov accented the objective, deterministic, and universal qualities of Hegel and Marx. With Hegel, "the accident of human arbitrariness and human prudence give place to *conformity to law*, i.e. consequently to necessity."[20] Or, as he asserted in his polemic, "The 'subjective method' in sociology is the greatest nonsense."[21]

The Marxists gained the upper hand in their feuds with the Populists. They were able to pin on Mikhailovsky the charges of confusion, idealism, and vacillation while claiming to be scientific and objective. Subjective wants and desires for the future of Russia did not count; it was objectively developing toward capitalism, argued many of the first Russian Marxists, including Lenin. Inasmuch as this was already a chapter in the longer exchange between the Westernizers and Slavophiles, the Marxists were more than ready to stress objective, scientific, and universal categories.[22] For the Russian Marxists, the term "subjective" was irrevocably tainted by its association with the Populist argument for a non-Western and non-Marxist future for Russia.[23] Soviet Marxism inherited, and augmented, the distrust of subjectivity.

The Soviet version of Marxism as a scientific and unified theory encompassing society *and* nature was prefigured in the response to Mikhailovsky. For Mikhailovsky, in accord with his concern for subjectivity and the individual, separated society from nature.[24] He complained that the positivists devalued the individual by deploying methods appropriate for biology and chemistry. The rejoinder by Russian Marxists defended the continuum of nature and society; they considered this the test of the rigor and objectivity of a science. A reading of Hegel, science, and subjectivity took shape that was the inverse of the European tradition.

II

The reception of Hegel that imprinted European Marxism sharply diverged from the Russian. By the last quarter of the century the Hegelian traditions had dissipated, especially in Germany.[25] Marx averred in 1873 that he was a "pupil of that mighty thinker," because Hegel was currently treated as a "dead dog."[26] Nearly everywhere Hegel had been supplanted by positivism, social Darwinism, or neo-Kantianism.[27]

Within a weakening Hegelianism, Italy could boast the most visible and forceful representatives.[28] Karl Rosenkranz, one of Hegel's German disciples, noted with "astonishment" in 1868 that although Hegel is considered "obsolete" in Germany, he "comes to life again in the Italian language."[29] The study of Hegel flourished in Naples, where Antonio Labriola, the "first" Italian Marxist, received his education. Years later, in 1894, Labriola asked Engels for a copy of the rare *The Holy Family*, Marx and Engels's polemic against the young Hegelians of the 1840s. After reading it, Labriola wrote to Engels, it recalled "the Hegelians of Naples among whom I lived in my earliest youth, and it seems to me that I understood and appreciated that book more than others . . . I, also, lived in my young days, as it were, in such a training hall and I am not sorry for it."[30]

Labriola's teacher, Bertrando Spaventa, perhaps the most original of the Neapolitan Hegelians,[31] offered a politically acute reading of Hegel.[32] As Spaventa explained in his first important writing, *Studii sopra la filosofia di Hegel* (Studies on the Philosophy of Hegel) (1850), while Hegel's philosophy was dead in France and Germany, it was spreading in Naples despite opposition from police and clerics. For

Spaventa, Hegel's philosophy opened a route toward national independence and revolution.[33] In words that recalled a text by Marx he did not know, Spaventa argued that Hegel's philosophy was the intellectual arm of the national revolution. If material force sufficed to fight the foreign invaders of Italy (the Austrians), it did not suffice to surmount the cultural and religious domination of the pope, cardinals, and priests. "If the musket is necessary to destroy the former, it will not suffice to annihilate the latter."[34]

The Hegel of Spaventa was the Hegel of consciousness and the dialectic of subjectivity.[35] The strength and the weakness of Spaventa, and an entire Italian Hegelian tradition, resided in concentration on subjectivity. Yet the charge of subjectivism leveled against Spaventa forgets that he cut his subjectivism from the same cloth as did Marx. "Man makes himself what he is," wrote Spaventa. "His world, his knowledge, and his happiness – all which he is as a man – is his own work. In general, this is the significance of the great concept of *work* and history, which are fundamentally the same."[36] Like many of the Western Hegelians, Spaventa was drawn to *The Phenomenology of Mind* as "the real light of the whole system."[37] The categories of consciousness, subjectivity, and history moved to the fore. "Knowledge is generally inexplicable – impossible – if the spirit – subjectivity – is simply a spectator. Knowledge is essentially *self-knowledge.*"[38]

National traditions alone cannot unravel the history of Hegelianism and Marxism. The rupture between the historical and scientific Hegels did not simply correlate with national traditions; it also took place *within* an Italian framework. If Spaventa and his circle proved more important and enduring, initially an "orthodox" school of Hegelians represented by the Italian Augusto Vera enjoyed a far wider reputation.[39] Vera, an enthusiastic Hegelian, was responsible in Italy, France, and England for innumerable commentaries on and translations of Hegel, including one published in the United States by the St. Louis Hegelians.[40] His productivity and singlemindedness earned him broad recognition. Rosenkranz considered him the "most rigorous systematizer" of Hegel.[41]

For Vera, the *system* was the beginning and the end of Hegel, the absolutely vital element. That *The Phenomenology* preceded the system was a "subjective and accidental fact." The "system" was primary.[42] Vera wrote in his (French) translation to *The Phenomenology:* "The system . . . is everything."[43] Not *The Phenomenology*, he argued elsewhere, but the *Logic* was the "key to the whole system."[44]

Literal loyalty to Hegel's texts defined Vera's orthodoxy;[45] he did not mince words. With Hegel "the circle of philosophy" closed. To comment "mechanically" on Hegel's "deductions" was all that remained for philosophers.[46] Spaventa thought this criminal: "In true philosophers there is always something more than themselves . . . this is the germ of a new life. To mechanically repeat a philosopher amounts to suffocating this germ."[47] That Spaventa and Vera sharply differed on the validity of Hegel's philosophy of nature is hardly surprising. For Spaventa, it was replete with faults, mistakes, and "erroneous affirmations." These objections were resolutely rejected by Vera, who defended "the systematic unity of Nature."[48] Even Rosenkranz, who lauded Vera as the sole philosopher to examine Hegel's philosophy of nature, was stirred to question his defense of Hegel's views on astronomy and Newton.[49]

The Neapolitan Hegelians prepared the grounds for an Italian Marxism, which runs from Spaventa to his student Labriola, and from Labriola's student Benedetto Croce to Gramsci. These Italians concentrated on the categories of history, subjectivity, and consciousness, and they regarded with suspicion a positivist inclination to interpret Marxism as a universal and scientific system. Labriola criticized Plekhanov on exactly this point: "This arrogant way of speaking of science will make *scientific* socialism laughable before the whole world. The guilt resides in the fact that many people look upon Marxism as a new kind of universal wisdom [*Allweisheit*]."[50]

The difficulty of characterizing Labriola's thought in a brief compass[51] derives partly from its very nature. Because of his antipathy toward positivism and systems, Labriola was deliberately unsystematic and fragmentary; he preferred the informality of letters and teaching to professional monographs. One of his major works consisted of letters (to Sorel). He explained: "It has never been in my mind to write a standard book . . . I choose the form of letter because interruptions, breaks in the continuity of thought, and occasional jumps . . . do not seem out of place and incongruous there."[52] Or more emphatically: "For twenty years I have detested systematic philosophy. This attitude . . . made me more apt to accept Marxism."[53]

The weakness, nearly the absence, of an Italian Marxism in the 1880s forced Labriola to discover and rethink Marx for himself. To do this he mined his own Hegelian past and resources. In this sense Labriola came to Marxism as Marx did: through German idealism. As he told Engels in 1894, he arrived at socialism by way of his "rigorous Hegelian education."[54] He did not learn about Marxism "from the mouth of a great teacher."[55] Marx's books were his only means, and even these were difficult to find. Only a single copy of Marx's *Critique of Political Economy* could be located in Rome.[56] His letters to Engels often complained of the dearth of Marx's texts in Italy.

The timbre of Labriola's Marxism resounded in his vocabulary; his terms testified to his efforts to distance himself from positivism and vulgar Marxism. Leery of the term "science," he preferred "critical communism." "That is its true name, and there is none more exact for this doctrine."[57] He wrote to Engels of his misgivings about the terms "science" and *Wissenschaft*; for Engels, *Wissenschaft* implied a "more profound, more organic, more complex" meaning than the "science of the positivists," which supplanted it in Italy. For the same reason Labriola preferred "genetic method" to the term "dialectical materialism." Dialectics in Italy had degenerated into rhetoric and sophistry. "No one knows any longer the Hegelian tradition."[58] In a similar vein he protested the "conventionalism" and the "stereotyped phrases" that inflicted the socialist press.[59]

Labriola continuously resisted positivist and Darwinian Marxism. He criticized the "mania" of Marxists who "bring within the scope of socialism all the rest of science"[60] and who "chase" after that "*universal philosophy*, into which socialism might be fitted as the central point of everything."[61] Although he did not reject Darwin or evolution, he repudiated the amalgam of Marx and Darwin. "What a fine sight! Materialism–Positivism–Dialectics, a holy trinity!"[62] If Marx and Engels respected Darwin, according to Labriola, they did not consider him "the discoverer of the laws of entire humanity."[63] "Our doctrine must not be confounded with Darwinism, and it need not invoke anew the conception of a mythical, mystical, or metaphorical form of fatalism." "History," Labriola summarized succinctly, "is the work of man . . . There are, then, no reasons for carrying back that work of man which is history to the simple struggle for existence."[64]

Labriola's objections to semantic concessions to positivism were not misplaced. In *The Materialist Conception of History* he discussed popular conceptions of causation in history, such as chance or determinism. He stated that these "superficial" approaches will dissolve as soon as "scientific" criticism appears – at least this is what his English readers think he wrote.[65] Labriola did not use the term "scientific" here: He wrote that these superficial modes will vanish with the appearance of "la critica della conoscenza," the "critique of consciousness."[66]

Labriola's choice of words denotes the presence of the historical Hegel. His very first work, in fact, defended Hegel against Kant.[67] To the end he remained committed to a Hegelian core of Marxism, the idea of humanity producing itself through its own praxis.[68] Among the theorists in the II International, Labriola stood out as the sharpest critic of vulgar and positivist Marxism;[69] the acuity of his judgment was honed on a Hegelian stone. He denounced the "vulgar expounders of Marxism" who in reducing it to a simple doctrine of economic change "robbed" it of its "imminent philosophy."[70] He stated in one of his best passages:

> Critical communism does not manufacture revolutions, it does not prepare insurrections, it does not furnish armies for revolts. It mingles itself with the proletarian movement, but it sees and supports that movement in the full intelligence of the connection which it has, which it can have, and which it must have, with all the relations of social life as a whole. In a word, it is not a seminary in which superior officers of the proletarian revolution are trained, but it is neither more nor less than the consciousness of this revolution and especially the consciousness of its difficulties.[71]

By virtue of his late arrival to Marxism and his disdain for systematic writings, Labriola's major works were few and fell within a brief period: *In Memory of the Communist Manifesto* (1895), *On Historical Materialism* (1896), and *Socialism and Philosophy* (1897). (He died in 1904.) Yet directly and indirectly Labriola inspired a Marxist literature that drew on the historical Hegel. Works on Marx soon appeared by Benedetto Croce, his pupil, and Giovanni Gentile. Although not a direct student, Gentile came under the sway of Labriola's teacher, Spaventa. In 1900 he edited the first of several volumes of Spaventa's writings.

In a series of essays begun in 1896 (and collected in 1900), Croce dissected the positivist reading of Marx. He launched into Achille Loria, who had been attacked previously by Engels. The determinist and evolutionary cast of Loria's theory "deprived" Marxism of "moral and voluntary elements," rendering it "quietistic." Loria failed to understand that Marx did not interpret history as an "automatic" process.[72] Paul Lafargue, Marx's son-in-law, also found no favor with Croce. He charged that Lafargue reduced Marxism to a "facile formula," opening it to ridicule.[73]

Much to Labriola's chagrin, however, Croce quickly distanced himself from his teacher's socialism. He chipped away at the conceptual status of Marxism, denying it was a "philosophy of history." He preferred to call it a "summary of new data," a "realistic conception of history," or a "canon of interpretation." By this Croce sought to privilege ethics and morality by sharply separating them from Marxism. As a method of history Marxism should not be confused with ethics and philosophy. Moreover, Croce attacked Marx's theory of surplus value, a "term without meaning in pure economics."[74] He told Gentile that he considered his own book a "bier" for Marxism.[75]

Croce's contributions severely tested his teacher's friendship; and Labriola dispatched a barrage of critical letters. He was incensed that Croce was drawn into the wider circles of Marxist revisionism, which was becoming public and menacing. For Labriola to check revisionism required increasing commitment and clarity. Furthermore, Labriola himself was distressed to be implicated insofar as he had been associated with both Croce and Sorel, another spokesman for revisionism. That Eduard Bernstein could even inquire whether he agreed with Croce shocked him.[76]

The intensity, or at least fragility, of positions adopted can be illustrated by Labriola's *Socialism and Philosophy*. This appeared, encouraged by Croce, in 1897 (in Italian) as a series of friendly letters to Sorel. By the time the French translation had been prepared, the story had changed; both Sorel and Croce had discredited themselves as revisionists in Labriola's opinion. Bernstein himself was referring to Croce as an ally.[77] While Sorel was innocently suggesting to Labriola that Croce write the Introduction to the French translation, Labriola penned a new Preface and Postscript. His letters to Sorel appeared in French in 1899 with a Preface attacking Sorel and a Postscript attacking Croce.[78]

Labriola charged Croce with the gravest sin in his code: scholasticism. The distinctions that Croce drew inside Marxism gratified only abstract logicians. "There is a profound difference," he wrote to Croce, "in considering science and philosophy as a *task*, a mission, a *Lebens- and Weltanschauung*, and considering it simply as an intellectual pastime."[79] Labriola heaped scorn on Croce's reply that he was uninterested in politics. Politics is 95 percent of Marxism. "If Marx was only a professor (i.e. the other 5 percent) I would be as interested in him as much as I am interested in the logic of Wundt."[80]

Gentile, like Croce, was primarily interested in the five percent of Marx. Although his later career is blackened by his association with fascism,[81] his book on Marx was more provocative and original than Croce's.[82] Even Lenin noticed and recommended it. "The book of an Hegelian idealist Giovanni Gentile, *La filosofia di Marx*, Pisa, 1899, deserves attention. The author points out some important aspects of Marx's materialistic dialectics which usually escape the attention of the Kantians, positivists, etc."[83]

While Gentile was working on his book on Marx he was also preparing a volume of Spaventa's writings. He was introduced to Spaventa's thought by his neo-idealist teacher, Donato JaJa.[84] In reply to some hostile reviews when the volume appeared in 1900 he maintained: "There is a tradition that we must take up again and develop if we wish to gain the right road; and that tradition is in the works of Spaventa."[85] For Gentile, Spaventa developed a concept "implied in *The Phenomenology*." "Knowledge is not simply knowledge, but knowledge is acting, working... This concept which Bertrando Spaventa lucidly presented is in our opinion the golden key to the new epistemology after Kant... It was also one of the most profound ideas of the most celebrated disciple of the philosopher from Stuttgart [Hegel], who in this respect was certainly unknown to Spaventa: Karl Marx."[86]

Gentile challenged Croce's argument that philosophy was a secondary and extraneous addition to Marxism. Perhaps for this reason Gentile won Labriola's approval.[87] According to Gentile, Marx was a "philosopher before he was a revolutionary."[88] As a whole his book on Marx represented a fusion of Feuerbach and Hegel; the subjective dialectic predominated.[89] Marx's criticism of Feuerbach, he believed, served to distinguish a critical Marxism from a crude materialism.

Gentile, in fact, was the first to translate into Italian Marx's "Theses on Feuerbach." The first and famous thesis presented the issue succinctly: "The chief defect of all hitherto materialism – including Feuerbach's – is that the object, actuality, sensuousness, is conceived only in the form of the *object* or *perception,* but not as sensuous human activity, praxis, not subjectively."[90]

Gentile's "philosophy of praxis" returned to a Marxism that transcended flat materialism. The stock teaching that Marx substituted materialism for idealism slighted the concept of praxis. Idealism furnished this concept, knowledge as subjective activity. Without it, materialism inclined toward "passivity." To Marx, reality was a "subjective product of man – that is product of sensuous activity, not of thought, as Hegel and other idealists believed."[91]

III

Although broad intellectual and political relationships often mislead, the fate of Hegel and Marx in France confirms a connection between a historical Hegel and a Western Marxism. In brief, a Western Marxism emerged only after a historical Hegel had struck a chord in French cultural life; and compared to Germany and Italy, Hegel arrived "late." Loyal translations and forceful commentaries date only from the 1930s and 1940s. Jean Hyppolite's translation of *The Phenomenology* appeared in 1939 and 1941 and his commentary, in 1946. Alexandre Kojève offered lectures on Hegel in the mid-1930s, which he published in 1947. These efforts prepared the way for the most significant, or the most public, theorists of French Western Marxism: Maurice Merleau-Ponty and Jean-Paul Sartre.[92]

This is also an exaggeration that ignores the much earlier commentaries and translations of Hegel.[93] Translations of Hegel's major works date from the 1860s; and nineteenth-century France witnessed a number of efforts to introduce Hegel. These ran the gamut from the "eclecticism" of Victor Cousin to the orthodoxy of Augusto Vera. Each was seriously handicapped, however. A deficient knowledge of Hegel (and of German) characterized Cousin's lectures and writings.[94] Rosenkranz, who gave Vera high marks, judged Cousin harshly. If Cousin had grasped Hegel "more deeply and accurately," Rosenkranz stated, Hegel would have enjoyed more success in France.[95]

Vera represented the opposite weakness: extreme loyalty to Hegel with little originality. As mentioned previously, Vera, later an opponent of Spaventa, resided for years in France and completed some of the first French translations and extended commentaries on Hegel. He proclaimed that his life was dedicated to the triumph of Hegelian philosophy.[96] Later Frenchmen found few triumphs. The translations made from German to French by this Italian were considered "uncertain" and his commentaries "mediocre."[97] More sympathetically, Vera has been judged unable to shake "the indifference of the public, nor modify its prejudices."[98]

After the demise of the weak nineteenth-century French Hegelians, other currents and individuals can be charted that finally coalesced into a French Western Marxism. Lucien Herr and Charles Andler studied Hegel at the turn of the century. Subsequently, but prior to Kojève and Hyppolite, Jean Wahl, André Breton, Henri Lefebvre, and Alexandre Koyré presented Hegelian thought to a French public.

Many of these formed a series of interlocking relationships. Wahl inspired Hyppolite as well as Sartre.[99] In 1930 Koyré himself addressed the question of why a "Hegelian school had not been able to form in France."[100] He also wrote on the Hegelian tradition in Russia and hoped to nurture a French Hegel renaissance.[101] When Koyré was compelled to interrupt his course on Hegel, he asked Kojève to succeed him.[102] In the 1930s Lefebvre (with Norbert Guterman) translated Lenin's Hegel notebooks, Hegel's writings, and texts of the early Marx. They anticipated, as well as participated in, the post–World War II flowering of French Marxism.[103] Nor should the serious interest of the surrealists, especially Breton, in Hegel be slighted. "You cite Hegel," Breton complained, "and in revolutionary circles you immediately see brows darken."[104] In the early 1930s the surrealists published selections from Lenin's Hegel notebooks; and a former surrealist (Raymond Queneau) edited Kojève's lectures on Hegel.[105] These individuals all turned to the historical Hegel while denigrating or ignoring Hegel's philosophy of nature.[106]

At the turn of the century Lucien Herr, Charles Andler, and Georges Sorel represented weak versions of Labriola, Croce, and Gentile.[107] These Frenchmen also retrieved the Hegelian dimension of Marxism. Yet they had little to draw upon;[108] by the 1890s what existed of French Hegelianism had evaporated. The French were communicating with their Italian counterparts, however. Sorel and Labriola exchanged letters that were to constitute one of Labriola's books. Their friendship soon ended, because Labriola decided that Sorel, perpetually shifting positions, was a "psychiatric case."[109] Croce, on the other hand, considered Sorel a kindred spirit[110] and remained his regular correspondent.[111]

The few Marxist texts of this French circle displayed the same contours as the Italian contributions. They turned to the historical Hegel and, while recalling the subjective and philosophical spirit of Marxism, denounced its vulgar and positivist deformations. Herr, whose influence on French socialism extended beyond his modest writings,[112] wrote one of the few pieces on Hegel of this period, an entry in *La Grande Encyclopédie.*[113] His major project, a three-volume study of Hegel, conceived in the late 1880s, remained uncompleted at his death in 1926. A draft of a Preface for the second volume projected following the development of the Hegelian school until "nothing more exists which merits its name."[114] An unpublished pamphlet from 1906, *La Révolution sociale,* echoed themes of a Western Marxism. Referring to Croce, Herr criticized labeling Marxism materialistic and scientific. "It is utterly exact that Marxism is *scientific* socialism, but it is necessary to define this scientific character . . . Marxism is knowledge of the law of the proletariat *prise du dedans.* It is the consciousness of the proletariat."[115]

If only because of his continuous revisions, Sorel is difficult to summarize. Like Gentile, he advanced a subjective critique of orthodox Marxism, and, like Gentile's, it threatened to become exclusively subjective. He challenged Marxist determinism and pretense to science.[116] Marxists have erred in establishing a "scientific party."[117] For Sorel, science and determinism overlapped. "The fatalist prejudice," he wrote in "Necessity and Fatalism in Marxism," "derives in large part from the false idea of science formed by the socialists."[118]

Sorel's critique of orthodox Marxism, however, was rooted as much in Bergson as in Hegel.[119] Through his correspondence with Croce, however, he warmed to Hegel. By 1907 he affirmed that it was necessary to show the French public, which believed Hegel was "dead and buried," that his theories were "alive and active."[120] Several years later he agreed with Croce that Hegel had opened a new era.[121]

IV

In the 12 years that Engels survived Marx (1883–1895), he assumed and completed an astounding number of tasks and projects. Contemporaries often commented upon his energy. Not only did he edit Volumes 2 and 3 of *Capital*, provide endless advice, and enter in theoretical debates about exchange value and profit rates, but he penned *The Origin of the Family*, *Feuerbach and the End of Classical German Philosophy*, and prefaces to Marx's *Civil War in France* and *Class Struggles in France, 1848–1850*. In the last five years of his life, Yvonne Kapp writes, "Engels has some 135 works of greater or less importance to his credit. These ranged from volume 3 of *Capital*, which to all intents and purposes, he may be said to have written from Marx's very rough first draft – and revisions of the English translation of volume 1 . . . to lengthy interviews, weighty articles . . . new prefaces . . . innumerable translations, many of which he supervised . . . an output that he himself at the age of 74 thought 'work enough for two men of 40.' "[122]

By virtue of his collaboration with Marx, his prodigious output, and the lucidity and simplicity of his own texts, Engels enjoyed respect and authority.[123] He was only challenged sub rosa. Some of Engels's final letters protested the unauthorized editing of his new Preface to Marx's *Class Struggles in France*. "I appear as a peaceful worshipper of legality at any price," he complained.[124] That Bernstein, an anointed successor to Engels, waited until Engels died to publicly challenge Marxism does not seem accidental.[125] The texts of Engels became essential reading; and because of their brevity and clarity, they displaced the longer and more complex writings of Marx.[126]

Yet Engels illustrates and indexes two divergent traditions of Marxism, which in turn rest on contrasting interpretations of Hegel. It is not necessary to belittle Engels or saddle him with all the ills of later Marxism[127] to recognize that as a popularizer of Marxism he followed his own inclinations. Although Engels railed against dogmatic Marxism, especially in private letters, he publicly presented Marxism as a unified objective system encompassing Nature and History.[128] In brief, Engels stood firmly with a scientific Hegelian tradition. Attracted to the natural sciences, he sought to demonstrate the universal validity of dialectics:

> What therefore is the negation of the negation? An extremely general – and for that reason extremely comprehensive and important – law of Nature, history and thought; a law which, as we have seen, holds good in the animal and plant kingdoms, in geology, in mathematics, in history and in philosophy . . . When I say that all these processes are the negation of the negation, I bring them all together under this one law of motion . . . Dialectics is nothing more than the science of the general laws of motion and development of Nature, human society and thought.[129]

A reliance on Engels marked orthodox, especially Soviet, Marxism; Engels legitimated Marxism as an objective and systematic science. The basic texts of Lenin, Stalin, and Mao drew almost exclusively upon Engels.[130] Conversely, Western Marxists challenged Engels; they charged he misconceived the relation of dialectics and nature. The search for universal scientific laws swallowed the specific subjective moment of Marxism.

To jump ahead, one heresy of Georg Lukács's *History and Class Consciousness* lay exactly here. Lukács accused Engels of missing the essence of the dialectic method, "*namely the dialectical relation between subject and object in the historical process.*" In a footnote, Lukács elaborated:

> It is of the first importance to realize that the method is limited here to the realms of history and society. The misunderstandings that arise from Engels' account of dialectics can in the main be put down to the fact that Engels – following Hegel's mistaken lead – extended the method to apply also to nature. However, the crucial determinants of dialectics – the interaction of subject and object . . . the historical changes . . . etc. – are absent from our knowledge of nature.[131]

Defenders of orthodox Marxism rebuked Lukács with dispatch; they tolerated no breach between Engels and Marx. The parameters of this debate were continuously reestablished. Engels, a scientific Hegel, and a dialectics of nature composed an orthodoxy that was committed to a universal and scientific Marxism. The unorthodox challenged Engels and rescued the historical Hegel. Lukács himself might not have been fully aware, and recent accounts of Marxism have ignored, that the critique of Engels did not commence in 1923 with *History and Class Consciousness*.[132] Rather the Italian and French Hegelians of the 1890s had already discussed and evaluated Engels's contribution. Moreover, this earlier critique may have been transmitted to Lukács by Ervin Szabó, a Hungarian Marxist, and Sorel, who were both important in Lukács's development.[133]

It may have been Gentile who first questioned at length Engels's distortion of Marx. Similar thoughts were echoed by Croce, Sorel, and Andler. By 1906 Croce had remarked upon the extended Italian discussions on Engels.[134] In 1912 a substantial result of these discussions emerged: Rodolfo Mondolfo's *Il materialismo storico in Federico Engels* (The Historical Materialism of Friedrich Engels), which was a detailed analysis of Engels, contrasting his "dialectical materialism" with Marx's "philosophy of praxis."[135]

Gentile challenged Engels's understanding and appropriation of Hegel. He cited Engels's pamphlet on scientific and utopian socialism, in which Hegel is criticized for failing to understand the objectivity of the world.[136] In retort, Gentile charged that Engels demonstrated that he understood nothing of Hegel's "subjectivity"; nor did he understand that it was necessary to grasp *The Phenomenology* before the *Logic*.[137] Writing to JaJa about this very issue, Gentile affirmed that although Engels might be a "valiant economist," it was regrettable that he was celebrated as a "great philosopher."[138] Engels's *Anti-Dühring*, he argued elsewhere, never reached the "genuine sources" of Marx and never "profoundly penetrated the philosophical part of the theory of his friend and teacher."[139]

Croce commented more prudently that treating Marx's and Engels's writings as identical was a mistake; the "mental shape" of Engels did not resemble that of Marx.[140] Labriola, it should be noted, did not accept these critiques of Engels, perhaps because Engels had been a personal friend. "I am such a cretin," he wrote to Croce sarcastically, "that I do not see the difference [between Marx and Engels]."[141]

Sorel belittled Engels freely in his letters and public writings. He wrote to Croce that it was "certain" Engels deviated from Marx and that Engels did not command an extensive philosophical background. "He did not have very clear ideas, notably on Hegelianism. He has contributed a great deal in leading historical materialism down the path of evolutionism and making it an absolute dogma."[142] Sorel, a former engineer, stated that Engels's ideas on science were "vague." Referring to Engels's pamphlet on scientific socialism, he concluded: "Thus not much importance should be attached to the terms he uses.

The expression 'scientific socialism' flattered current ideas on the omnipotence of science, and it flourished."[143] From this vantage point Sorel denounced Lafargue, also criticized by Croce, as a disciple of Engels, not Marx. "I believe that these ideas [of Lafargue's] are not at all Marxist, but it must be recognized that they are based on the principles posed by Engels."[144]

Sorel referred often in his letters to Charles Andler, a friend and the later biographer of Lucien Herr. Like Herr, Andler was conversant with German culture and philosophy. In 1897 he criticized in passing the term "scientific socialism."[145] In 1901 he published a lengthy commentary on *The Communist Manifesto*. He ferreted out its French sources, and he argued that some incoherence of the text derived from divergences between Marx and Engels.[146]

In the mid-1890s Andler offered a course on the "decomposition of Marxism" and planned a book on the same subject.[147] The book never appeared, and Sorel took the term for his own in *The Decomposition of Marxism* (1908).[148] A piece of the course on Engels appeared later (1912–1913), subtitled "Fragments of a Study on the Decomposition of Marxism."[149] Andler admitted that although it might be strange to argue that Engels "vigorously contributed to the decomposition of Marxism, since he has long been regarded as the most authoritative interpreter, his destructive influence on the doctrine is a fact." For Andler, Engels was "the first disciple of Marx who presented Marxism not only as a subversive economic doctrine but as a complete system of philosophy."[150] Moreover, an "industrial spirit" permeated Engels. Whereas Marx used terms such as "class itself" as a revolutionary force, Engels substituted productive forces. "No one has manifested more ingenious dilettentism in all kinds of sciences than this founder of scientific socialism."[151]

Apart from some isolated contributions, such as those by the Czech Thomas Masaryk[152] or the Pole Stanislaw Brzozowski or the Hungarian Ervin Szabó,[153] the most extensive critiques of Engels emanated from the Italians. Their criticism was primarily grounded in Feuerbach or in a reconsideration of the relationship among Hegel, Feuerbach, and Marx. This reconsideration formed the basis for the work of Gentile and Mondolfo, as well as for Arturo Labriola (no relation to Antonio). As noted earlier, Gentile translated Marx's "Theses on Feuerbach" into Italian, and the accuracy of this translation informed the debate. Arturo Labriola, at that time a syndicalist and an acquaintance of Sorel, wrote the Preface to the French translation of one of Sorel's books. His critique of Engels in *Marx nell'economia e come teorico del socialismo* (Marx on Economics and as Theorist of Socialism) (1908) was emphatically Feuerbachian. He cited the first thesis on Feuerbach and stated: "Here is the nucleus and the point of departure for all of Marxism." For Arturo Labriola, *Capital* itself was a gloss on Feuerbach.[154]

It is not surprising that the "Theses on Feuerbach" was the touchstone for these critics of Engels. Inasmuch as the theses were directed against passive materialism, or a materialism without a subject, it was a perfect foil to use against Engels – even though Engels himself had published them. Arturo Labriola drew the most violent conclusions about Engels. He judged that Engels possessed "an intelligence of modest proportions . . ." "I seriously doubt whether he had understood the radical profundity of the thought of his friend and teacher." He even conjectured whether Engels was "familiar" with all the work of Marx: He charged that Engels reduced Marx to a natural science, and he pondered the "enigma" of why Marx tolerated "the adulteration of Engels."[155]

Mondolfo's discussion of Engels was more measured and sympathetic. Unlike Croce, Gentile, and Arturo Labriola, Mondolfo remained a lifelong socialist.[156] Without doubt he was one of the ablest theorists of the period.[157] His starting point was also Feuerbach. His first writings on Marx, "Feuerbach and Marx" (1909), examined their philosophical relationship. "To understand Marx well it is necessary to first directly grasp Feuerbach."[158] Marx avoided the bad choices of fatalism and voluntarism through a "critical–practical conception." "From a critical consciousness of the social reality to historical praxis: this sequence signals the supersession of the antithesis of voluntarism and fatalism." Mondolfo took *Umwälzende Praxis* (revolutionary praxis) from the theses as the vital concept fusing subjective and objective moments. Capitalism is not constituted solely of objective tendencies.[159]

Mondolfo did simply denigrate Engels in comparison with Marx. In response to a review,[160] he clarified that he separated the two thinkers "to better demonstrate their essential identity."[161] This was an overstatement; his study highlighted the deficiencies of Engels. To Engels's "dialectical materialism" Mondolfo contrasted Marx's "philosophy of praxis." According to Mondolfo, the initial problem for Marx was knowledge; for Engels it was being. Consequently, Marx, departing from the critique of consciousness, moved toward a philosophy of praxis while Engels, rooted in a natural philosophy, concluded with materialism. Much of the dogmatism and obscurity of Engels resulted from lacking the concept of revolutionary praxis.[162]

Anticipating Lukács's critique, Mondolfo analyzed Engels's "mistake" as repeating Hegel's. He drew upon Croce's *What Is Living and What Is Dead of the Philosophy of Hegel* (1906), which devoted one chapter to the "error" in the concept of Hegel's philosophy of nature. For Croce, a philosophy of nature was a "contradiction in terms." "It implies philosophical thought of those arbitrary concepts which philosophy does not know and upon which it consequently has no hold."[163] Engels, unable to escape this error, affirmed the natural and scientific reality of dialectics. To Mondolfo, Engels reversed Hegel while preserving the essential mistake: "The Hegelian absorption of science by philosophy is transformed in Engels into the absorption of philosophy by science."[164]

"When Hegel was lying on his deathbed," teased Heinrich Heine, "he said: 'Only one man has understood me,' but shortly afterwards he added fretfully: 'And even he did not understand me.' "[165] The history of Marxism does little to deflate the joke. Yet Hegel, misunderstood or understood, dogged and sometimes led Marxists. Theorists of Marxism did not arrive at Marxism cleansed of history and culture; or, to borrow a phrase from Mao Tse-Tung, Marxists do not fall from the sky. They attained Marxism already tempered by their cultural past; this past included Hegelian thought and, more broadly, ideas of science, history, and the individual. The materialist doctrine that belittled the impact of ideas always demonstrated the opposite.

The Hegel that lurked behind Marxism split into two traditions, scientific and historical. The distinct Hegelian traditions did not yield by themselves Soviet and Western Marxism; they preformed and informed the ensuing Marxism. Soviet Marxism was regularly sustained by a scientific Hegel, and European Marxism was regularly sustained by a historical Hegel. Each demarcated a common terrain and language: universal laws of nature and society, and historical processes of consciousness and action.

In the revolutionary surges after World War I, the philosophical border between the historical and scientific Hegelians translated into a political fissure between Western and Soviet Marxism. The major theorists of Western Marxism - Lukács, Gramsci, and Korsch - were drenched in German idealism and the historical Hegel. Later Western Marxists - Marcuse, Sartre, and Merleau-Ponty - returned to Hegel to escape the constraints of orthodox Marxism. Of course, philosophical issues were not always urgent; yet they were always more than an afterthought. They did not dictate politics, but sketched the possibilities and the hopes.

3

From philosophy to politics: the inception of Western Marxism I

The term "Western Marxism" (and "European Marxism") entered Marxist dictionaries in the early 1920s.[1] The Soviet edition listed it as derogatory. By implying that a specific Marxism belonged to Western Europe, the universality of bolshevism and the III (Communist) International (Comintern) was threatened. To the participants, this threat was not instantly evident. Moreover, the political and philosophical layers of Western Marxism unpeeled sequentially; at least this is how it appeared to Korsch when he looked back. First a specific Western Marxist politics took shape, and later its philosophy was elaborated.

"As it moved westwards," Korsch explained in 1930, "this Marxist Leninist philosophy [of the Russians] encountered the work of Lukács, myself and other 'Western' Communists which formed an *antagonistic philosophical tendency within the Communist International itself.*" He added: "This philosophical discussion was only a weak echo of the political and tactical disputes that the two sides had conducted so fiercely some years before." Of these political disputes, Korsch mentioned two: Rosa Luxemburg's criticism of the Russian Revolution and the conflict between the Bolsheviks and the "radical left tendency" led by the Dutchmen Anton Pannekoek and Hermann Gorter.[2]

A "weak echo": World War I, the collapse of the II International, the radicalization of the working class, the Russian Revolution, brief Western European revolutions, the founding of the III International and the new Communist parties resonated for decades. The magnitude and profundity of these upheavals damned philosophical discussions to irrelevancy. By 1923, however, when Korsch and Lukács published their major philosophical works, the revolutionary surges had subsided. Politics lost an immediacy, or, at least, the options contracted. This was not only hindsight. Lenin, Trotsky, and others remarked on the slowing of the historical tempo.[3] The task was to dig in and prepare.

If the political collisions are forgotten, the weak echo might be mistaken for the thunder itself. The philosophical feuds cannot be understood abstracted from the preceding political conflicts; nor are they identical to these conflicts. Politics permeated philosophy but did not replace it. Latent political choices infused the theoretical debates.

The density of philosophy and politics in this period was not unique in the history of Marxism. However, no formula for the relationship of philosophy and politics exists; this relationship is complex and historically specific. Philosophy participated in a constellation of tactics and organizations; it cannot be reduced to them or, for that reason, dismissed. Lenin himself fell victim to the entanglement of philosophy and politics. His major philosophical work, *Materialism and Empirio-Criticism,* sharply attacked the followers of Ernst Mach and Richard Avenarius. Yet a political embarrassment marked his philosophical offensive. Many followers of Mach were political allies of Lenin, as was A. Bogdanov, for a period. Conversely, the philosopher that Lenin prized most, Plekhanov, was a political opponent. For these reasons Lenin sought to separate the philosophical and political issues.[4]

For a few years after World War I the political arena seemed wide open. By the end of 1923, the last post–World War I offensive – the German October – was history; and even by 1921 the defeat of the European revolutions was a fact. Yet the brevity of the period does not deprive it of importance. In these years the political contours of a Western Marxism surfaced; the situation rarely reoccurred. The consolidation of the Russian Revolution and the rise of fascism, if they did not spell imprisonment and death, compelled unorthodox Marxists to silently table their heresies or retreat from the political barricades. The history of Western Marxism between the mid-1920s and the 1950s is largely a history of these two choices.

A word of caution: To shift in parts of this and the next chapter from delineating two traditions of Hegel to the politics of the Comintern and Communist parties is to enter a new world. No longer is the talk of Hegel's *Logic* or *Phenomenology* but the "21 Conditions," the March

Action, and even *Bettelheimerei.* The cast of characters and political parties is long. What N. O. Brown wrote to explain his use of the "strange language" of Freud – "But this strange world is the world we all of us actually live in"[5] – can perhaps be reformulated: This strange world is the world they, if no longer all of us, actually lived in. For this reason it cannot be avoided.

This chapter, however, seeks to pare away, as much as is feasible, extraneous details, names, and events. In this way the danger of drowning in a sea of political incidents may be prevented and the contours of a political Western Marxism thrown into relief. The story, in any case, was fragmentary, brief, and finally "unsuccessful."

Yet Rosa Luxemburg, Paul Levi, and Dutch and "left" Communists posed a series of political alternatives to the rapidly consolidating Soviet communism. They challenged the validity for Western Europe of the Russian experience and the Leninist model. As often, perhaps always, in the history of Marxism, the question of organization proved to be the terrain for political and theoretical jousting. This question incorporated a group of principles that set Marxist against Marxist. Lukács stated succinctly: "Organization is the form of mediation between theory and practice."[6]

A simple preference for democratic organizations did not dictate the Western Marxist repudiation of Leninism; rather to the Western Marxists the yawning political and social gap between Europe and Russia prohibited an identical praxis for each. Leninism bore the indelible marks of specific Russian conditions: a relatively small proletariat, a massive agrarian population, a feeble bourgeois culture. The last was decisive: The impact of bourgeois and national culture sharply distinguished Western European from Russian society. As Gorter wrote, in the Netherlands – the oldest capitalist country – bourgeois culture and values were drummed into the working class for centuries. The same could not be said of Russia.

Leninism was not blind to bourgeois culture; it responded by contracting to a tighter and more disciplined party. The infection of bourgeois culture was attributed to trade unions or an "aristocracy" of the working class. Since the infectious source was discrete, the organizational prescription could be sharply defined. To the Western Marxists, however, bourgeois culture was endemic and inescapable; an organizational solution did not suffice.

The Western Marxists responded by retrieving from Marxism the processes of class consciousness and proletarian subjectivity. Their accent on process resulted from their conviction that class consciousness was not a thing to be commanded or divulged but attained by the class itself. Herein dwelled the democratic ethos of Western Marxism. The network of bourgeois culture and passivity could not be undone by superior discipline or directives; these remained locked within its terms regardless of the purity and dedication of the party and its members. Rather bourgeois hegemony could be contested only by engaging the whole of the proletariat, its hearts and minds. When class consciousness and proletarian subjectivity fused, the landscape of capitalism would light up.

In this period the coherence of Western Marxism and "left" communism was little evident. That many "left" Communists considered themselves loyal Leninists, and that it took Lenin to disabuse them of the illusion, suggests the confusion. Nor were the theoretical sources identical. Korsch, Lukács, Gramsci, the Frankfurt School, and, later, French Marxism were rooted in German idealism and the historical Hegel. This is not true of the Dutch Marxists, who looked more to Dietzgen than to Hegel. Exceptions do not prove the rule. Yet the Dutch Marxists are not exceptions in that the same categories surfaced in all corners of Western Marxism.

I

Korsch mentioned Rosa Luxemburg's critique of the Russian Revolution as one political backdrop to the philosophical disputes. Despite, or because of, all the secondary literature, Luxemburg resists classification. If the interpretation of Engels indexed the philosophical separation between Western and Soviet Marxism, Luxemburg indexed the political split. For years in the III International, "Luxemburgism" spelled heresy. The fate of her collected works suggests the difficulty of slipping her into conventional categories. Their publication, sponsored by the Communist party, ceased in the late 1920s. Only after some 40 years of delay did the project recommence.[7]

Perspectives on Luxemburg and Lenin, or Luxemburg and the Bolsheviks, are themselves subject to a historical dynamic.[8] In recent years her differences with Lenin have been belittled; with no hesitation she is given the official stamp of orthodox Marxist.[9] Originally this effort hit serious snags, and one of the most serious was her successor in the German Communist party (KPD), Paul Levi.

Levi mediated the impact of Luxemburg on European Marxism. He not only led the most important Communist party outside the Soviet, but Levi published Luxemburg's critique of the Russian Revolution as proof of her profound antipathy to bolshevism. Although neither her pupil nor her equal, he remained a loyal follower. Beginning as her lawyer in 1913, he belonged to both her personal and political inner circle. Shortly after her assassination (January 1919), Levi succeeded her as leader of the German Communist party. Within two years he moved from the leadership to opposition, to expulsion (1921). Some 10 years after the murder of Rosa Luxemburg, Paul Levi committed suicide.[10]

In any discussion of Levi, Luxemburg, and subsequent splits in the party, the fundamental importance of German communism to the Russian Revolution and the III International should not be forgotten. The German party was not another, or even major, party; it was *the* party, and initially nearly overshadowed the Russian party. Before World War I, the German Social Democrats (SPD) were the leading party. After the war, it was desperately hoped that the German revolution would bail out the Russian Revolution. Early conferences of the Comintern were conducted in German,[11] and its Moscow headquarters was considered stopgap until the wider European revolutions rendered possible its relocation to Berlin.[12] Nor was this all fantasy. The KPD wielded considerable clout. For instance, in 1924 the KPD received 3.7 million votes in Reichstag elections; in 1927 it was publishing 36 *daily* newspapers.[13] Considering the dire straights of the Russian Revolution and the wealth, experience, and apparent expertise of the German working-class movement, all of its developments were carefully monitored, guided, and finally controlled.

Levi's presence at the Congress of Livorno (January 1921) provoked his first public opposition to the Soviets.[14] At this Party Congress, the Italian Communist party (PCI) was founded by splitting the Italian Socialist party (PSI). This was neither surprising nor unanticipated. It was in accord with Comintern policy to expel or withdraw from the reformists of the old Socialist parties. In Italy the political parties and groups debated for months which conditions of entry into the Comintern were acceptable. The Comintern and its representatives encouraged a hard line, a clean break with a wide number of reformists. They achieved their aim, but with only one-third of the votes from the Congress, they departed to form the PCI. Because less than half the membership of the PSI renewed in either party, some historians considered the split at Livorno a fatal mistake for the Italian left. "Although a schism of the Party seemed warranted by the facts, the particular schism that occurred at Livorno was disastrous. Thanks to that Congress – and to Mussolini – the Italian Left was eliminated from political life for the next twenty-two years."[15]

Levi returned from Livorno upset by what he had witnessed;[16] he was repelled by the crudity of the Comintern representatives who promoted the split.[17] He presented a criticism of the Comintern tactics to his own Central Committee.[18] To those who argued that it was better to be "few in numbers but firm in principle" Levi replied that "principles without followers constitute a party no more than followers without principles."[19] In Levi's eyes the Comintern employed tactics unsuitable for Western European parties.

Levi objected to the "mechanical split" of the Italian party, preferring the "organic bringing-up" of the masses. "To create parties within the Communist International not through organic growth with the masses but through deliberate splits" was risky and unproductive. "If the Communist International functions in Western Europe in terms of admission and expulsion like a recoiling cannon . . . then we will experience in Western Europe the worst possible setback."[20]

In Levi's opinion the Russians erased the distinction between Western Europe and Russia; they blindly applied the same organizational principles to each. "It seems to me that the comrades did not clearly realize that splits in a mass party with a different intellectual structure [*ein andere geistige Struktur*] than, for example, that of the illegal Russian party – which performed brilliantly in its own way – *cannot be carried on the basis of resolutions, but only on the basis of political experience.*" The language and approach recalled Luxemburg's distrust of politics commanded by inflexible resolutions. Levi appealed directly to her legacy. "I do not want to conceal anything: the old difference between Rosa Luxemburg and Lenin emerges here again."[21]

Levi's criticism of the Comintern's conduct at Livorno was unacceptable to the new orthodoxy; nor did it help that he raised the sensitive issue of relocating to the West the Comintern headquarters.[22]

He was outvoted in his own Central Committee. With other supporters he resigned from the Central Committee and consequently watched from the sidelines the increasing subordination of KPD to the Comintern.[23] He did not have long to wait. Within weeks of his resignation the Comintern decisively intervened in the KPD in what came to be known as the March Action (1921). This has been called the "first insurrection in Europe attempted at the instigation and under the leadership of a team specially sent from Moscow."[24] As a revolution, it was a debacle; the KPD membership dwindled from 450,000 to 180,000 as one consequence. It also marked a "turning point" in the relation of the KPD to Moscow.[25] From this time on, the integrity and autonomy of the KPD dramatically declined.

To Levi, the ill-conceived and ill-executed March Action proved that the KPD and the Comintern were out of touch with the proletarian masses. As Levi explained in a letter to Lenin, the March Action wrecked the painstaking work of the past two years. Not only the effort to numerically enlarge the Communist party but the effort to root it "culturally [*seelisch*]" in the proletarian masses was profoundly set back. The "trust" of the proletarian class that the former leadership had sweated to gain was sabotaged.[26]

Levi's full indictment of the March Action earned him expulsion from the party.[27] In *Unser Weg: Wider der Putschismus* (Our Path: Against Putschism) (1921) he charged that the party and the Comintern representatives organized a putsch, not a Marxist revolution. Theoretically his critique moved within the parameters of Western Marxism: The Soviet party by virtue of its past as an illegal party in an agrarian country was incapable of understanding the revolutionary traditions of the West European proletariat. The Russians bypassed the "cultural structure" to incite the proletariat directly by a battery of resolutions and leaflets. He commented later:

> It's the same old nonsense that Moscow always wants to believe, namely that a Soviet-type revolution would have occurred by now if there weren't a Seratti in Italy or a Levi in Germany standing in the way. The Muscovites completely overlook the fact that conditions in Western Europe are utterly different from those in Russia. There you had an agrarian revolution – revolution with some 95 per cent of the population in favor... In Germany the peasants are counterrevolutionary. In Western Europe the proletariat is tightly organized; in Russia the masses

> were not organized. These are some of the differences that Moscow one day will have to try to grasp.[28]

Unser Weg denounced the March Action as the "greatest Bakuninist Putsch in history." The party misevaluated the "subjective factor." Rather than establishing a viable relationship to the working class, the party substituted itself for the class. "Any action that expresses solely the political needs of the Communist Party, and not the subjective needs of the proletarian masses, is in itself defective."[29] Moreover, the political imperatives that triggered the March Action were not exclusively German. As Levi wrote to Lenin, shortly before the March Action, a Comintern representative informed the German Central Committee that Russia found itself in an extremely grave situation, and he counseled that "it is absolutely necessary that Russia be relieved by movement in the West; for that reason the German party must immediately commence action . . . to overthrow the regime."[30]

The Comintern, Levi concluded, was "isolated" from Western Europe, "its most important proving grounds." The lines of communication are poor and unreliable, the Comintern representatives second-rate. Alluding to Béla Kun's role in the March Action, Levi caustically observed that naturally Russia could not afford to send its best emissaries. "Western Europe and Germany became a training ground for all kinds of petty bureaucrats."[31]

The following year Levi published Rosa Luxemburg's critique of the Russian Revolution. In his Introduction he quoted Luxemburg's earlier critique of Lenin, which concluded: "Finally, we must frankly admit to ourselves that errors made by a truly revolutionary labor movement are historically infinitely more fruitful and more valuable than the infallibility of the best of all possible 'central committees.' "[32] Levi did not challenge the revolutionary commitment of Lenin and Trotsky, but he wondered about the future once they passed from the scene. The "old" guard formed a small section of the party. This situation gave rise to Lenin's "deepest error." He "isolated" and "enclosed" the party like a pure specimen in a laboratory, which could be maintained or improved through "purification." He assumed a "partition could be erected between the party and the broad masses . . ." On this question a "deep antagonism" existed between Luxemburg and the Bolsheviks.[33]

Levi represented Luxemburg in the first period of bolshevization of the world communist movement. His loyalty to her ideas quickly ended his career in the party and propelled him, willy-nilly, on a route parallel to Western Marxism. He concluded that without the spirit and sentiment of revolution the proletarian organization was vacant and ineffectual. "It is not only the size and numbers of things; it is a spirit [*Geist*] which blows over everything which alone can raise the proletarian revolution" to its greatness.[34] Lenin and the Bolsheviks failed to weigh the cultural atmosphere of Western Europe, which damned the insular party to irrelevancy. Lenin's ideas on organization were not "absolutely false" but bore the imprint of the specific stages of the Russian Revolution: absolutism, feudalism, illegality. "Certainly in the western lands there is a subjugation of the proletariat by the bourgeoisie. But the bourgeoisie practices its domination in the form of 'democracy'... These were the conditions in which Rosa Luxemburg lived and worked."[35]

The challenge to revolution by command or example pulsated throughout Rosa Luxemburg's work. The proletariat as the actor/subject of revolution defined her central loyalty; she distrusted the substitution of party, leadership, or the bureaucracy for the proletariat. Citing Marx and Engels that the emancipation of the working class must be its own work, she expanded: "But that does not mean that some committee of intellectuals, what deceptively calls itself the leader of the working class, 'orders' or 'decides,' when and how the working class will begin on its goal of emancipation; but that, the broad masses of the proletariat *itself* must recognize the need, the condition and the means for emancipation, and through its *own* will... enter into open struggle."[36] To underline her belief in the proletariat as the actor and subject, she reversed a sentence of Marx's. In the famous passage in *The 18th Brumaire* Marx stated that men make their own history, but they do not make it just as they please. In Luxemburg's formulation: "Men do not make history just as they please, *but they make their own history.*"[37]

Yet the gap between Rosa Luxemburg and Luxemburgism might be as wide as those between Marx and Marxism, and even Lenin and Leninism. On a series of issues – nationalism, imperialism, and organization – Luxemburg delineated a unique position, distant from the major contemporary Marxists – Bernstein, Kautsky, and Lenin.[38] The difficulty of grasping the specific contours of her oeuvre is no reason to assimilate it into the prevailing orthodoxy. By dismissing some of her texts, especially her analysis of the Russian Revolution, as products of mis- or limited information and by reinterpreting several others, her heresies are explained away. Lately the effort to certify her orthodoxy has increased.[39]

Her evaluation of the Russian Revolution cannot be easily dismissed, however; nor can it be severed from her 1904 critique of Lenin. She was one of the few who possessed the linguistic and political knowledge to critically appraise Lenin's organizational proposals, and she did so when Kautsky had barely heard of Lenin.[40] If Marxism cannot be satisfied with attaining insight ex post facto, it must not be forgotten that Rosa Luxemburg advanced prescient criticism not only of the Russian Revolution in 1918 but of Bernstein in 1899, Lenin in 1904, and Kautsky in 1910. Against a generally dismal record of Marxists, Luxemburg's historical accuracy was superb.

In the wake of the Russian Revolution of 1905, Luxemburg did draw closer to Lenin; however, substantial differences remained.[41] The 1905 Russian Revolution partially provoked the issue of the mass strike among German Socialists, and it led to Luxemburg's alienation from Kautsky. To delimit its use, Kautsky argued that although effective in Russia, the mass strike was inapplicable in Germany.[42] Luxemburg contested Kautsky's reasoning of "the complete antagonism of Germany and Russia." The mass strike did not express peculiar Russian conditions but rather a general class struggle.[43] Moreover, when Plekhanov charged Lenin with Blanquism, she partly retracted her own criticisms. "There might be traces of it [Blanquism] in the organization plan that Lenin presented in 1902," she wrote in 1906, "but that lies in the past... The errors were corrected through life itself, and there is no danger they could be repeated."[44] Twelve years later she charged Lenin (and Trotsky) with Jacobinism.

Luxemburg did not worship spontaneity uncritically,[45] nor did she fully escape significant ambivalences. She did retain an unswerving commitment to the proletariat as the subject of history, however, and she conceived this not simply as a philosophical statement but as a political statement. Here she differed with Bernstein, Kautsky, and Lenin. Each crippled the processes of subjective development of the proletariat.

She indicted Bernstein and the revisionists for suppressing the "*subjective* factor of the socialist transformation."[46] They conflated means and ends, or they misinterpreted trade unions as a goal, and not as a means of awareness and consciousness. For Luxemburg, the process of the proletariat attaining class consciousness constituted the heart and soul of revolution. One reformist presented the choice of aiming a real pistol at the ruling class or the "pistol" of parliamentary majorities. Luxemburg believed that this missed the essence of Marxism, "the power of the class conscious proletariat."[47]

Luxemburg also broached a psychological dimension to this subjectivity. Although this was not decisive to her analysis, it marked a typical Western Marxist motif. The subject of history – the proletariat – was not simply a theoretical dream but flesh and blood, thought and feelings. Proletarian passivity could not be cleaved from psychological passivity. That Luxemburg raised the issue in her 1904 critique of Lenin suggested the very different impact and consequences of industrialization on the Western and Russian proletariats. Luxemburg reviewed *One Step Forward, Two Steps Backward* (1904), which with *What Is to Be Done?* represented Lenin at his most inflexible. Lenin celebrated the factory as a model for revolutionary organizations, and he derided criticism of it as aristocratic and intellectual:

> For the factory which seems only a bogey to some, represents that highest form of capitalist co-operation which has united and disciplined the proletariat, taught it to organise and placed it at the head of all other sections of the toiling and exploited population. And Marxism, the ideology of the proletariat trained by capitalism, has been and is teaching unstable intellectuals to distinguish between the factory as a means of exploitation . . . and the factory as a means of organisation (discipline based on collective work . . .). The discipline and organisation which come so hard to the bourgeois intellectual are very easily acquired by the proletariat just because of this factory "schooling."[48]

To Luxemburg, the model was critically flawed, an obstacle to revolution. To the extent that the Marxist organization imitated factory discipline and organization, it betrayed revolution. The Marxist or Social Democratic organization did not adopt and generalize past bourgeois formations, but it reconstructed them from the inside. The revolutionary organization required "a complete revision of the concept of organization, a whole new content for the concept of centralism, and a whole new conception of the reciprocal relation of the organization and struggle." "Independent direct action of the masses" belonged to the nucleus of the revolutionary organization. Consequently, it cannot be "based on blind obedience, nor on the mechanical subordination of the party militants to a central power."[49]

Luxemburg believed that the discipline and obedience instilled by factory life did not encourage but crippled revolutionary action: It is to be undone, not prescribed. She stated, "Socialism in life demands a complete spiritual transformation in the masses degraded by centuries of bourgeois class rule."[50] She distanced herself from Lenin's glorification of

> the educational influence of the factory on the proletariat, which makes it immediately ripe for "organisation and discipline." The "discipline" which Lenin has in mind is implanted in the proletariat not only by factory but also by the barracks, by modern bureaucratism – in short, by the whole mechanism of the centralized bourgeois state. It is nothing but an incorrect use of the word when at one time one designates as "discipline" two so opposed concepts as the absence of thought and will in a mass of flesh with many arms and legs moving mechanically, and the voluntary coordination of conscious political acts by a social stratum. There is nothing common to the corpselike obedience of a dominated class and the organized rebellion of class struggling for its liberation. It is not by linking up with the discipline implanted in him by the capitalist state . . . but by breaking, uprooting this slavish spirit of discipline that the proletariat can be educated for the new discipline, for the voluntary self-discipline of Social Democracy.[51]

Luxemburg's *Russian Revolution* does not require extensive discussion. Yet its West European perspective is often minimized; she did not condemn the Bolshevik practices in themselves but in regard to their impact on Western Europe. Their success encouraged slavish imitation: This was the danger. She feared that the European working class would succumb to imitating the Bolsheviks. Therefore she wanted to delay founding the III International until active West European parties could check the influence of the Bolsheviks. She also resisted adopting the name "Communist party" as foreign to German revolutionary traditions.[52]

Nor was Luxemburg in doubt about the decisive contextual fact of the Russian Revolution: the absence or failure of the West European revolutions. This failure exacted a double toll: It increased the attractiveness of the successful Bolsheviks and, at the same time, deformed their practices. Her analysis of the Russian Revolution moved within these parameters. External circumstances damaged revolutionary practices; consequently, the Russian Revolution was less a model to be emulated than it was an example of the difficulties of isolated socialism. Luxemburg set herself against the gravitational pull of success.

The brutal international situation dictated the brutality of the Russian Revolution; the "complete failure" of the international working class allowed few choices. "Under such fatal conditions even the most gigantic idealism and the most storm-tested revolutionary energy are incapable of realizing democracy and socialism but only distorted attempts at either." She had no doubts: The Bolsheviks must be supported enthusiastically. What they created "under the conditions of bitter compulsion and necessity," however, cannot be regarded by the international working class "as a shining example of socialist policy."

The abdication of the international proletariat, she reaffirmed at the close of her analysis, dominated the events of the Russian Revolution. "The starting and end term" of this abandonment was the "failure of the German proletariat." Under these conditions, socialism was necessarily distorted. "The danger begins only when they make a virtue of necessity and want to freeze into a complete theoretical system all the tactics forced upon them by the fateful circumstances and want to recommend them to the international proletariat as a model of socialist tactics."[53]

This guided her critique; she did not recommend choices that the Russian Revolution did not have. She criticized undemocratic policies not to reform the Bolsheviks but to break decisively with antidemocratic tactics of German socialism. The revolutionary action of the German proletariat cannot "be called forth in the spirit of the guardianship methods of the German Social Democracy . . . It can never again be conjured forth by a spotless authority, be it that of our own 'higher committees' or of the 'Russian' example." In words that recall Marx (and Labriola) she declared:

> Not by the creation of a revolutionary hurrah-spirit, but quite the contrary: only by an insight into all the fearful seriousness, all the complexity of the tasks involved, only as a result of political maturity and independence of spirit, only as a result of a capacity for critical judgement on

> the part of the masses . . . only thus can the genuine capacity for historical judgement be born in the German proletariat.[54]

II

The second political dispute that the philosophical conflict echoed was, according to Korsch, "the disagreement that culminated in the years 1920–1921 between the radical left tendency led by the Dutch Communists Pannekoek and Gorter and the Russian Bolshevik faction led by Lenin."[55] This was not a minor squabble but, in the first period of the Comintern, a divisive threat to Soviet Marxism; nor was it confined to the small Dutch party. German communism, in which Pannekoek and Gorter played roles, was equally menaced. Moreover, as Lenin himself discussed, the left tendency stretched across Europe.

That a small band of Dutch Marxists predominated in what became known as "left" communism may not be entirely fortuitous. Gorter observed that Holland was the oldest bourgeois country in Western Europe, older than England and France. By the very length of its rule, and its victories and power, the Dutch bourgeoisie profoundly dominated Dutch society. The bourgeois "spirit" (*Geist*) saturated the entire people. "There is no country more bourgeois than Holland," announced Gorter, "no country where the bourgeois spirit is more deeply rooted."[56]

This advance post of bourgeois society spawned advanced critics and theorists; at least the Dutch Marxists, or what became known as the "Dutch School," first coherently elaborated principles later adopted by "left" Communists. The singular impact of bourgeois culture and ideology on the working class constituted their point of departure. Their Marxism incorporated categories of *Geist,* mind, culture, and consciousness. Prior to the break with the Bolsheviks, Pannekoek argued that these categories were more than categories; they imbued social relations. Marxists could ignore them only by periling a revolutionary transformation.

For instance, Gorter's *Der historische Materialismus* (Historical Materialism) (1908) asserted that *Geist* pervaded the commodity society. The power of the bourgeoisie rested as much on its spiritual as its military or political arms. For the Socialists, spiritual propaganda was not extraneous but essential. "*Geist* must be revolutionized."[57] Although such statements might bely the materialism of Marxism, they must be evaluated in the light of their specific political contexts, the issues of the pre–World War I socialist movement.

Unlike Germany, in the Netherlands the prewar debates between the revisionists and the radicals among the Socialists led to a complete break.[58] In 1909 the Dutch Socialist party (SDAP) expelled the radicals, who then formed a competing and smaller party; many of its members later entered the Dutch Communist party. Before their expulsion, Pannekoek and Gorter (as well as Henriette Rolland-Holst) sharply criticized the SDAP for its "anti-socialist tendency," namely, its "search for direct success, the approaches to burger democracy, the abandonment of the class standpoint."[59] These Dutch had already distinguished themselves as uncompromising critics of revisionism, which added to their prestige as post–World War I critics of Soviet Marxism.

In 1906 Pannekoek moved to Germany to participate in the newly founded SPD Party School. The school, a stronghold of the antirevisionist left, included Luxemburg.[60] Pannekoek's proposal for his course, "Historical Materialism and Social Theory," included a section on the human or cultural sciences – *Geisteswissenschaft*. Kautsky, to whom the proposal had been sent, balked; Pannekoek retorted that a "clear understanding of the role and nature of spirit and the spiritual [*die Rolle und das Wesen des Geistes und des Geistigen*]" was imperative.[61]

With Luxemburg, Pannekoek was drawn into the debate on the mass strike that transpired in the German party, and, like Luxemburg, he criticized Kautsky. His analysis recalled Gorter's. The categories of subjectivity and *Geist* commanded. Over the next ten years the contours of his position changed little; Pannekoek articulated the same principles against Kautsky in 1912 and Comintern in 1920.

Pannekoek posed some elementary questions: Given its numerical and economic superiority, why had not the proletariat attained power? How did a smaller exploiting minority, the bourgeoisie, dominate a larger mass? The conventional answer of the political and military muscle of the bourgeoisie did not suffice. On a raw empirical level the working class possessed the greater power. Yet the cultural superiority of the bourgeoisie compensated for its material weakness. The bourgeois minority controlled the vehicles of culture and education: schools, churches, newspapers. By these means bourgeois values and perspectives infected the masses. "This intellectual dependence [*geistige Abhängigkeit*] on the bourgeoisie is one of the major causes of the weakness of the proletariat." The cultural atmosphere mediated and sustained the exercise of power. "Cultural power [*Geistige Macht*] is the most powerful force in the human world." Yet the technical reason for the reign of the bourgeoisie is not to be forgotten: It also wielded a superior organization, the state.

This analysis prompted two conclusions. The proletariat was faced with two tasks, attaining knowledge and an organization to challenge the state. Unlike the purely objective factors, such as the size of the proletariat, these allowed choice and decision. Knowledge was the "first and simplest form of class consciousness" and enabled the proletariat to free itself from "spiritual dependency" on the bourgeoisie.[62]

Organization could not be severed from class consciousness. This was the cutting edge to Pannekoek, anticipating Lukács. Class consciousness and organization were more than connected; they nearly merged. The proletariat could not militarily defeat the bourgeoisie, nor could it compete with state power. The fiber and strength of the proletarian organization lay, rather, in its solidarity, esprit, and discipline. The specific virtues of the proletarian organization, which negated individualism, were foreign to the bourgeoisie. The proletarian organization transcended a collection of individuals formally bound together. At its marrow were bonds, commitments, and relationships. For Pannekoek, these surpassed economic and political loyalties, shading into a cultural or spiritual dimension. "The essence of this organization is something spiritual [*Geistiges*]; it is the complete transformation of the proletarian character."

Referring to his proposal to curb use of the mass strike or mass action, Pannekoek charged Kautsky with "actionless waiting," "passive radicalism," and, more gravely, misconceiving the nature of organization. For Pannekoek, subjectivity, class consciousness, and organization welded together; they constituted the very essence, and hope, of the proletariat. The ethos of the proletarian organization not only rendered it resilient but signaled the commencement of socialism; it carved out territory beyond bourgeois individualism.[63]

In a continuation of the debate, Pannekoek responded to the counter-charge that the "spirit of organization" was ethereal, floating above society. To Pannekoek, it permeated and defined the proletariat. Kautsky failed to distinguish a proletarian organization from a whist club or any other group. If statutes and funds were required, they did not constitute a working-class organization. Kautsky attended only the "external form of organization." The internal processes, however, were critical; these sustained relations that challenged the domination of the bourgeoisie. Nor were they mystical or irrelevant; they included the transformation of the "character" of the proletariat. Both the strength of the proletariat and its emancipatory capacity rested on these processes. "The development of the proletariat organization in itself signifies the repudiation of all the functions of class rule; it represents the self-created order of the people."[64]

The source for some formulations of Pannekoek and the Dutch School was not so much Hegel as Joseph Dietzgen (1828–1888).[65] Especially after the turn of the century, Dietzgen, a tanner and an autodidact, attracted a group of enthusiastic adherents. The skeptical – including Marx – doubted his real achievements. From an independent and isolated standpoint he completed or complemented historical materialism. He drew on Feuerbach more than Hegel and wrote to Marx that "Feuerbach showed me the way."[66] In fact, Marx bemoaned to Engels that "precisely Hegel he [Dietzgen] did *not* study."[67] Dietzgen's impact was limited; Pannekoek noted in 1902 that he had not until then "exerted any perceptible influence on the socialist movement."[68] Nevertheless the Dutch School devoted much attention to Dietzgen. Pannekoek wrote incessantly on Dietzgen; Gorter translated him (into Dutch); Roland-Holst wrote a book on him.[69]

Dietzgen's first and most important work, *The Nature of Human Brainwork* (1869), extended dialectics to conceptual and abstract thought. What Dietzgen achieved is less important than what the Dutch found in him: a valuable mental and intellectual supplement to Marx.[70] The "weak" spot in Marx, according to Pannekoek, was that he never fully explained how mind (*Geist*) was entangled in the material process.[71] Marx affirmed and proved the general dependence of mind on the material conditions, but he did not set forth the specific links. Here Dietzgen entered.

Refracted through Pannekoek, Dietzgen illuminated subjectivity and consciousness. To follow Pannekoek: "There is no lack of economic development; the material world had long been ripe for socialism. What is lacking is men." Mankind is not a "marionette" of economic forces; these forces dominate by means of ideas and perceptions – through the mind. Reversing Marx (and following Luxemburg), Pannekoek stated that mankind does not make history as it pleases, but it makes history. "Spirit [*Geist*] must actively intervene. Economic development will yield social revolution only insofar as it produces in the spirit [*Geist*] of men revolutionary thought and revolutionary will... This is where Dietzgen's contribution lies. Marx gave us the science of social and human action. Dietzgen gave us the theory of the human spirit."[72]

III

With the rise of "left" communism in 1919, the Dutch Marxists received wider European attention. For orthodox Marxists, "left" communism passed into history only by way of denunciation in Lenin's *Left-Wing Communism, an Infantile Disorder*. In the Leninist vocabulary the quotation marks around "left" crystallized the definition: "Left" communism was left in name only. Nothing stood left of the official Communist parties. "Left" communism was more than a theoretical aberration, however. In 1919–1920 it was *the* threat to the Comintern.

"Left" communism surfaced throughout Europe; it did not constitute a coherent formation but a series of groupings, organizations, and journals. Pannekoek and Gorter were prominent in several. For instance, in the first year of the Comintern, Secondary Bureaus or Secretariats were established in Amsterdam, Berlin, and Vienna to coordinate European activities.[73] Two in particular challenged the Comintern by adopting "left" positions: Amsterdam and Vienna. The Amsterdam Bureau included Gorter, Roland-Holst, and Pannekoek, "its spiritual leader."[74] It openly criticized the Comintern and even held a conference. Moscow quickly closed it for its insubordination.[75] The Vienna Bureau fell under the sway of exiles from the defeated Hungarian Revolution, including Lukács, and met a similar fate.[76]

The organ of the Comintern Bureau in Vienna was *Kommunismus*, which printed many of the essays that later composed *History and Class Consciousness*. It also published Pannekoek. The same roles were assumed in Italy by Bordiga's *Il Soviet*, which published Lukács and Pannekoek,[77] and in England by Sylvia Pankhurst's *Worker's Dreadnought*. The *Worker's Dreadnought*, one of the best-informed and cosmopolitan newspapers of the period, ran Lukács, as well as fundamental texts of Gorter and Luxemburg; these included Gorter's "Open Letter" to Lenin (discussed later) and Luxemburg's critique of the Russian Revolution, which Levi had publicized.[78] These were theoretical icings, however, to larger political and social movements.

"Left" communism was a political expression of Western Marxism; they are inextricably linked but not identical. "Left" communism did not speak a philosophical language, although it contested the Bolsheviks politically. Briefly, "left" communism in Germany, Italy, and the Netherlands wrote off parliaments and trade unions as vehicles for revolution. Lenin prescribed their use, but to the "left" these institutions belonged to a reformist and bankrupt past of socialism. The Communists could not at will manipulate parliaments and trade unions, as if they were neutral instruments. By their very nature, parliaments and unions encouraged illusions in the working class about the revolutionary process.

Several other principles and sensibilities sustained these political positions. A gut hatred for authoritarianism and bureaucratization marked the "left" Communists; they prized autonomy and self-regulation of the proletariat. From this perspective they mounted a critique not only of the bourgeois institutions of the parliament but of the vanguard and Leninist party (with the important exception of Bordiga, who is discussed in Chapter 5). Consequently, they celebrated (again with the exception of Bordiga) workers' councils, factory councils, and soviets. Unlike parliamentary or trade union bureaucracies, these rested on the autonomy and independence of the proletariat. For the "left" Communists, the vanguard party shared a lethal weakness with bourgeois institutions: It substituted leadership for the self-movement of the proletariat. On its most theoretical level the "left" Communists justified their political positions by themes familiar to Western Marxism, the decisive role of class consciousness and subjectivity.

Pannekoek and Gorter were closely associated with one of the few "left" communist groups that seriously challenged Comintern leadership, the Communist Worker's party of Germany (KAPD). Pannekoek provided much of the theoretical inspiration for the program of the KAPD, and Gorter personally participated.[79] The circumstances from which the KAPD emerged are as follows.

The KPD, under Paul Levi's leadership, pursued a dual strategy: Clamp down on the "left" in the party to mollify, and finally unite with, the much larger and less radical Independent Social Democrats (USPD). Already at the Second Party Congress (October 1919) the party leadership clashed with the "left." A resolution attacked the "left" or "syndicalist" interpretation of the irrelevancy of parliamentary elections; it also sanctioned the use of trade unions and the "strictest centralization" in the party.[80] Each of these issues – parliaments, trade unions, authoritarian leadership – provoked the "left" wing. Not only did the resolution pass, but it called for the expulsion of the opposition.

This resolution, as well as dissatisfaction with the lack of activity of the KPD during the Kapp putsch,[81] formed the immediate backdrop to the most important split in the KPD in its initial years: the KAPD. At its foundation half the membership of the KPD belonged to it.[82] The KAPD's "call" for a new party (April 1920) denounced the KPD's reformism and corruption. It declared that the KAPD is "no party in the traditional sense. It is not a leadership party [*Führerpartei*]," and it pledged unity of the proletariat on the basis of councils.[83]

The theoretical perspective of Western Marxism and the political activity of "left" communism intersected briefly. Political and tactical issues of parliaments, trade unions, and bureaucratic leadership predominated. Yet these political positions, in turn, tapped theoretical principles of Western Marxism. Tacitly, as well as explicitly, revolution was dissected as a process of the subject (the proletariat) attaining class consciousness. The formulations threw into sharp relief the subjective dimension of the historical process, including its psychological contours.

The program of the KAPD (May 1920) stated that the economic and political situation in Germany was "over-ripe" for revolution. Insofar as the "objective conditions" existed, the restraining conditions were subjective.

> In other words: the ideology of the proletariat is still partly the prey of bourgeois or petty-bourgeois conceptual elements. The psychology of the German proletariat in its present composition carries only too clearly the marks of centuries of military enslavement, as well as marks of an insufficient self consciousness . . . The subjective movement plays in the German revolution a decisive role. The problem of the German Revolution is

> the problem *of the development in self-consciousness* [*Selbstbewusstseins-entwicklung*] *of the German proletariat.*[84]

In the same year as the KAPD program, Pannekoek published one of his most important pieces, "World Revolution and Communist Tactics." The text that *Kommunismus* published (it also appeared as a pamphlet) included an editorial note commenting that it was a "a very important contribution," although it "might stand in certain antagonism to the line of the Moscow Executive Committee."[85] This was an understatement. Pannekoek observed that in the "first flush of enthusiasm" for the Russian Revolution the "difficulties facing the revolution in Western Europe were underestimated."[86] The experience showed that the German Revolution will be a "slow, arduous process." For this reason tactics become more than tactics, translating into long-range choices grounded on general principles and observations.

Two propositions sustained the tactical choices: ideological and subjective pressures crippled the revolutionary process; and these pressures afflicted Western Europe more than Russia. In Western Europe the bourgeoisie dominated long and successfully.

> In November 1918, state power slipped from the nerveless grasp of the bourgeoisie in Germany and Austria . . . the masses were in control; and the bourgeoisie was nevertheless able to build this state power up again and once more subjugate the workers. This proves that the bourgeoisie possessed another hidden source of power which had remained intact and which permitted it to re-establish its hegemony when everything seemed shattered. This hidden power is the bourgeoisie's ideological hold over the proletariat. Because the proletarian masses were still completely governed by a bourgeois mentality, they restored the hegemony of the bourgeoisie with their own hands after it had collapsed.[87]

The hegemony of bourgeois ideology, or the control of education, culture, and schools, constituted the concrete force that suffocated the revolution; and this hegemony, rooted in the long history of a tenacious and supple bourgeoisie, distinguished Western Europe (and countries colonized by West Europeans – the United States, Australia) from the Soviet Union. The strength of the bourgeoisie, Pannekoek explained elsewhere, did not emanate exclusively from its money or arms, but also from

> the domination of bourgeois culture over the whole population, including the proletariat. During a century of the bourgeois period the bourgeois intellectual life [*Geistesleben*] penetrated the entire society, and produced a mental organization and discipline, which reached and dominated the masses through thousands of canals . . . Thus the resistances, which the proletariat in the old bourgeois countries must overcome *in itself*, are much greater than in the new countries of Eastern Europe which lack that bourgeois culture.[88]

Gorter's contribution from the same year took the form of an "open letter" to Lenin, responding to his pamphlet *Left-Wing Communism*. Gorter hammered away at the same issues as Pannekoek. He paid particular attention to the "powerful distinction between Russia and Western Europe" in regard to class formation; these differences questioned extrapolations of tactics and principles from the Russian to the West European situation. Europe lacked a large and impoverished peasantry; consequently, the proletariat was deprived of potential agrarian allies. The relative isolation of the proletariat compounded its task. Thrown back on its own sources and resources, it faced an entrenched bourgeoisie.

Unlike Eastern Europe, in the West the ideology of the bourgeoisie "overpowered the whole social and political life; it has sunk deeper in the minds and hearts of the worker." "How to uproot the traditional bourgeoisie thinking which paralyzes the proletariat" defined the tactical problem. The conventional dependence on leaders, parliaments, and trade unions would be worse than no help: It would ratify the forms of bourgeois domination.

Gorter closed his "letter" by repudiating Lenin's statement that the period of propaganda was past. Referring to the German, Austrian, and Hungarian situations, Gorter wrote, "The most serious economic crisis is there – and yet the revolution does not come. There must be another cause which brings about revolution, and when it is not active, the revolution fails or miscarries. This cause is the *spirit of the masses*."[89] The neglect of the spirit, the culture, the minds of the proletariat eviscerated the III International.

By 1921 the KAPD had suffered its first of many splits. After several years the history of the KAPD and "left" communism in Germany became the history of small groups. Orthodox Leninists relished this fate; it confirmed their criticisms of the irrelevancy of "left" communism. It is indubitably true that only for a historical moment did the factors jell in which German "left" Communists might have decisively intervened. Nor was "left" communism, and especially council communism, without serious flaws.[90] Yet their failure is a fact, nothing more. Fragmentation may not inhere in "left" communism; it may be a by-product of failure and defeat and, indeed, may have guaranteed them. What beclouds the historical record is the illusion that the victors – orthodox Leninism and the Comintern – won. They too failed – regularly, and perhaps with fewer justifications. The hypnotic spell of success conspires to perpetuate history as a permanent defeat.

4

From politics to philosophy: the inception of Western Marxism II

"From 1918 to the present day, every chapter of European history could be headed: *The defeat of the Revolution*."[1] So Pannekoek paraphrased Marx in 1927. By June 1924, when Lukács and Korsch were denounced as "left" Communists by the keepers of the Soviet orthodoxy, the major post–World War I upheavals were past but hardly forgotten. By their participation in these events, Lukács and Korsch each provided clues to the political significance of their philosophical writings. This explains the hostility that greeted *History and Class Consciousness* and *Marxism and Philosophy*, both published in 1923. Each book distilled past political experiences. Although neither book openly broached heretical political positions, neither could be insulated from a dense political atmosphere and past.

A philosophical denunciation of Lukács by the Russian philosopher Abram Deborin and his followers complemented the political denunciation. This philosophical confrontation etched the divergence between two Hegelian traditions. Lukács leaned heavily on Hegel. Deborin also drew on Hegel, and his "school" was identified, and eventually dismissed, as Hegelian. The Deborinites used the "scientific" Hegel to slay the "historical" Hegel of Lukács. Hegel collided with Hegel.

In an Afternote to the first edition of his book, Korsch expressed his theoretical solidarity with Lukács. Yet their theoretical closeness was partly an illusion. Their positions intersected, but each moved perpendicular to the other. Lukács shifted from a Hegelianized Marxism and "left" communism toward philosophical orthodoxy and political compromise. Korsch passed from a conventional philosophical and Marxist past to philosophical and political heresy. For an instant their paths crossed.

Neither Lukács's nor Korsch's philosophical works are discussed here in any detail; this has been done well elsewhere. This chapter, rather, seeks to illuminate the fog that shrouds the boundaries between philosophy and politics in Western Marxism.

I

The relation between the "early" pre-Marxist and the "later" Lukács continues to burn its way through books and studies.[2] Here it must suffice to recall Lukács's roots in philosophical idealism and literary criticism. Lukács himself situated his *Theory of the Novel* (1916) within the Hegelian revival and judged it Hegelian in spirit and letter.[3]

The continuities between the Lukács of this period and Lukács the Communist are hardly in doubt, and they are captured by the comment expressing an initial reluctance to accept Lukács into the Communist party: "A crazed Hegelian is still far from being a communist."[4] A 1907 essay (later included in *Soul and Form*) argued that Novalis and Schlegel did not represent art for arts sake but "pan-poetism," or "the ancient dream of a golden age. But their golden age is not a refuge in a past that has been lost forever, which occasionally haunts beautiful fairy tales; it is the goal whose attainment is the duty of life of everyman."[5] Eleven years later, Lukács, no longer everyman but Deputy Commissar of Public Education in the Hungarian Soviet Republic, declared that "beautiful and instructive fairy tales" be taught to the young.[6]

Shortly before joining the Communist party in 1918, Lukács enunciated the issues that were to dominate his thinking in the coming years: the relationship between political transformation and human emancipation. They were not identical. In "Bolshevism as Moral Problem" (1918) Lukács affirmed that the "objective relations" did not guarantee freedom. The class struggle might conclude with a victory of the proletariat. If "pure sociology" registered a social change, however, this change did not yet spell freedom. Freedom presupposed, but could not be confused with, a transformation of class relations. To ensure freedom, a subjective element must supplement the objective relations: the "will" to realize freedom. Without this "will," the proletariat as liberator was unthinkable.[7]

Subsequently, Lukács translated this ethical postulate into an organizational imperative: to incorporate emancipation into the very fiber of objective transformation. The revolutionary apparatus of political transformation remained locked within dead objective relations and did not automatically yield liberation. In his sharpest and baldest formulation Lukács, as a government official, proclaimed: "Politics is merely the means, culture is the goal."[8] If the term "culture" is loaded with ambiguity, the essential meaning is not. Culture encompassed human freedom. Political struggle and economic reorganization did not in themselves constitute the ends for human existence. Marxists participated in political conflict not for its own sake but to organize a society where politics receded before human emancipation.

Lukács's "The Old Culture and the New Culture" (1919) provocatively elaborated these ideas. Lukács defined capitalism by its reductionism, an insatiable market subordinating all to profit and money. Communists did not work to establish a better or more efficient economy but to disestablish its stellar structure. Freedom subverted the dictatorship of economic relations. Lukács's formulations recalled those of Marx: Emancipation was not freedom *of*, but freedom *from*, property.[9] "Liberation from capitalism," declared Lukács, "means liberation from the rule of the economy."

When the dominion of the economy is subverted, culture is revolutionized; it is no longer an instrument for something else, but an end in itself. The possibility for a "new culture" that would release the creative essence of humanity from the authority of the cash nexus was opened. The following passage pulsates with the utopian note of Lukács's analysis:

> The reason an economic reorganization is absolutely necessary is that because of the unique structure of human consciousness, immediate evils and miseries – even though they are on a much lower level than the ultimate questions of human existence – nevertheless (with few exceptions) block the ultimate questions from consciousness. These immediate evils and miseries are not, by themselves, capable of bringing to consciousness the final questions of existence. We can clarify this with a very simple example. Someone is racking his brain over a complex scientific problem; during his work he contracts an unrelenting toothache. Clearly, in most cases he would be unable to remain in the stream of his

> thought and work until the immediate pain is relieved. The annihilation of capitalism, the new socialist reconstruction of the economy means the healing of all toothaches for the whole of humanity.[10]

However utopian, idealist, or outrageous, this was authentic Marxism for Lukács. It did not rest on an arbitrary reading of Marx. In an essay from the same year, "The Changing Function of Historical Materialism" (1919) (later included in *History and Class Consciousness*), Lukács selected as Marx's basic proposition that consciousness does not determine existence, but social existence determines consciousness. Yet the very nature of the revolutionary transformation reverses this proposition. The economic structure is stood "on its head." Social consciousness no longer obeys, but issues the commands. This defines the uniqueness of revolution, a "leap" that abolishes the grip of reification.[11]

As Lukács recognized, in these analyses the category of consciousness ("first noted and elucidated in classical German philosophy"[12]) assumed a supreme role; Hegel and Marx intersected. Lukács unearthed the historical Hegel for Marxism. He criticized a scientific and positivist Marxism oblivious to the critical import of consciousness. Marx assumed "the greatest legacy of Hegelian philosophy," the idea of mind developing from "complete lack of consciousness to a clear, ever-growing self-consciousness." Alluding to vulgar Marxists, Lukács added that "only the superficiality and philosophical philistinism of his successors have obscured this crucial concept. Unable to comprehend Hegel's conception of history, they have turned historical development into a wholly automatic process, not only independent of, but even qualitatively different from consciousness."

To be sure, Marx modified Hegel. He did not simply substitute materialism for Hegel's idealism, however, as vulgar Marxists often taught. Rather Marx enriched and deepened Hegel by locating the development of consciousness in the living processes of society. Lukács appended a crucial qualification, emblematic of Western Marxism: "Marx was altogether too sober and profound a thinker to apply this method to the investigation of nature."[13]

The collapse of the Hungarian Soviet Republic after 133 days (August 1919) turned Lukács from an official of a revolutionary government into an exile in a factionalized Communist party. For the next several years his political contributions fell into two categories, addressing the specific issues of the Hungarian party and the wider ones of European communism. As Lukács noted later, a "cleavage" marked his contributions. In the Hungarian party, Lukács generally backed a moderate antibureaucratic, antisectarian, united front. Within the international arena, especially in Germany, Lukács associated with the "left" communists and supported the theory of the offensive.[14]

Although this divergence was real, Lukács's later presentation facilely hung his international leftism on the hook of "revolutionary messianism." The divergence was grounded in the antibureaucratic sensibility imbued in Western Marxism, however; insofar as this sensibility was not blind, it implied different tactics for Germany and Hungary. In Germany parliamentarism risked rebuilding the bureaucratic structures, and evils, of the Social Democratic past. In the authoritarian dictatorship of Hungary, antiparliamentarism lacked meaning; it could only be adopted as a slogan or bravado. On the tactical plane, an antibureaucratic impulse bound together the Western Marxists. Lukács, Gramsci, and Luxemburg are linked not by their appraisal of parliamentary strategies (or by the theory of the offensive); rather they converged in their repudiation of a bureacratization that threatened the independence or autonomy of the proletariat.

On this issue the echo of syndicalism and Ervin Szabó can be discerned. Lukács wrote that Szabó had brought him into contact with syndicalism and Sorel. To the unsympathetic, Lukács always remained Szabó's disciple.[15] Szabó, like Lucien Herr – for years a librarian – exercised an important impact on students, intellectuals, and a left opposition to the Hungarian social democracy.[16] The socialist student club he founded in 1902 included Lukács. In 1905 he published the first Hungarian edition of Marx and Engels. The French syndicalist Lagardelle wrote to him in the same year: "I agree entirely with you on the interpretation of Marxism."[17]

The left opposition that Szabó spearheaded in the Hungarian Socialist party presented a program in 1905 that attacked the reformism of electoral politics and dictatorial party leadership while defending inner-party democracy – all syndicalist principles. Contemporary with Sorel, Luxemburg, and Pannekoek, Szabó advanced a critique of the bureaucratization of the German Social Democrats (SPD). Ethical and subjective idealism inspired his critique. According to Szabó, Marxism suffered from universal vulgarization. The "iron laws of economic relations" subordinated the "subjective element."[18] The SPD was the prime sinner. His 1905 oppositional program stated that "we do not want embedded in our Hungarian party the praxis of the SPD, which has elevated *strict discipline* to a supremely dominating organizational and functional principle."[19] Nor did Engels escape Szabó's censure; as spiritual father of the SPD he was an arch opportunist.[20] Perhaps Lukács's critique of Engels originated in that of Szabó.

As an exile,[21] Lukács frequently contributed to *Kommunismus*, which regularly published "left" Communists.[22] As noted previously, like the Amsterdam Bureau and its journal, the Comintern Bureau in Vienna and *Kommunismus* were charged with "leftism" and finally dissolved. In discussing the journal, Lenin singled out Lukács's "The Question of Parliamentarianism" (1920) as especially guilty of leftism.[23]

The analysis that Lukács offered in this essay followed closely the earlier "Party and Class" (1919). Both the party and the parliament were judged bourgeois inventions and instruments. When the proletariat "fit its actions into the organizational framework of the party," it surrendered to "the forms of capitalist society." The party revealed that the proletariat was "too strong" to abstain from political action and too weak to impose its will on society. The party was the "external organizational expression of this inner crisis."[24] Lukács dissected parliamentary tactics with the same conceptual knife. Parliament, the bourgeoisie's "very own instrument," blocked the proletariat from refashioning the decisive extraparliamentary political reality. To the proletariat, electoral politics diverted and distracted; at best parliaments were only "defensive weapons" or preparations for real struggles.[25]

The inner logic of the analysis moved away from the bureaucratic party and parliamentary structures toward workers' councils as the authentic arena of proletarian activity. Yet the logic ran up against Lukács's own resistance. As formulated in the final essay of *History and Class Consciousness*, Lukács fused contraries, workers' councils, and the Leninist party. Loyal to his earliest analyses, he situated the workers' councils beyond bourgeois society, where they incorporated subjectivity and self-activity. Nevertheless, the political efficiency and theoretical justification for the Leninist party increasingly impressed Lukács; the party not only represented consciousness, it was consciousness. In the essays between 1920 and 1923, Lukács emphasized either the workers' council or the party, until finally in *History and Class Consciousness* he simply welded the two together. Although theoretically executed with sureness, the weld lacked strength.

To document Lukács's position on all the events of the communist movement would be pointless. Generally, the council motif eroded and the party gained the upper hand.[26] Yet Lukács found little difficulty in commending both centralized discipline and Luxemburgian spontaniety.[27] For instance, in the same year of his leftist "Question of Parliamentarianism" he published a "self-criticism" of his essay "Party and Class." He criticized himself and the Hungarian Communist party for misunderstanding the "indispensability" of the party in leading the revolution. Lukács noted that other parties of the revolutionary movement shared this failure and alluded to both the KAPD and the Amsterdam Bureau. He defined the error as "the belief that the party organization in essence was a child of bourgeois society, which in the proletarian class struggle could be replaced by a special proletarian organization (worker's councils, factory councils, industrial unions, etc.)."[28]

He never jettisoned his original critique of the bureaucratic party as alien to the working class, however. Here he came closest to the Dutch Marxists. Lukács rejected the proletarian organization as simply an instrument to gain state power; rather the revolutionary organization should incorporate freedom and autonomy. To Lukács, as to Pannekoek, this distinguished the proletarian organization from any other. Lukács's experience in the exiled Hungarian party ensured that the antibureaucratic note did not dissipate in his writings.

The Hungarian situation cannot be completely abstracted from the wider context, especially since Béla Kun, leader of the faction opposing Lukács, played a key role as a Comintern agent in the March Action. Perhaps because of his Moscow residency (Lukács was in Vienna), Kun obtained the goodwill of the Russian leaders. He attacked the Vienna group for its "Hegelian rubbish"[29] and raised the specter of its syndicalism and "Dutch Marxism";[30] he also proposed an aggressive policy for the Hungarian party. While the Vienna group cautiously cultivated reliable contacts with sympathizers in repressive Hungary, Kun advised the party leadership to return to Hungary regardless of the risk, to create a mass movement.[31] Because the probability of arrest was high, this plan appeared to the Vienna group to be political as well as personal suicide.

Lukács's "Politics of Illusion – Yet Again?" (1922) caustically attacked the politics that Kun championed. His polemic revealed the core of Lukács's organizational thinking within the territory he knew best, Hungary. In an analysis that smacked of Levi's indictment of the March Action,[32] Lukács charged that Kun had constructed a plan to please Moscow that ignored Hungarian realities. He designed his proclamations of an imminent revolutionary outbreak to secure his position in the international revolutionary movement. To Kun and his faction, the danger facing comrades in Hungary counted for little, but they were "certainly thinking seriously about those comrades who now enjoy the status of international celebrities and whose position would doubtless be strengthened if they could claim to represent, not a small illegal party, but a powerful mass party."[33]

"The soullessness of its bureaucracy" characterized Kun's organization. As it feigned revolutionary progress, corrosion set in. "Sham results" were required in order to impress Moscow and advance careers. The entire organization ineluctably turned corrupt. Comrades engaged in illegal work issued false reports that provided the expected good news. The central committee degenerated into an "empty bureacracy." Since no real work was accomplished, the party rested on pure authority and "blind and slavish submission." Lukács saw the future: "Such artificial and illegitimate cultivation of authority serves only to make the party bureaucracy even more hollow and soulless; it turns it into an *office*, with bosses and subalterns."[34]

The threat and reality of bureaucratic corruption did not induce Lukács to renounce the party; rather he emphasized all the more its nonbureaucratic human relations. In an essay from 1921, "Organization and Revolutionary Initiative," Lukács did not shy away from prescribing centralization and discipline. Yet Lukács's qualification touched the marrow of the revolutionary organization. "The centralization of a revolutionary party cannot possibly be achieved by bureaucratic and technical means . . . The fully developed consciousness of the party members . . . is . . . a prerequisite." In words that could be taken from Pannekoek and Gorter, Lukács affirmed: "Thus the question of organization reveals itself to be an intellectual [*geistig*] question." Organization is not a "technical question" but "*the supreme intellectual* [*geistig*] *question of the revolution.*"[35]

The double logic drove Lukács in a direction that few followed; on the one hand he militantly defended the centralization and discipline of the Leninist party; on the other he doggedly affirmed the nonbureaucratic and emancipatory nature of party life. A "left" communist impulse infused the Leninist party of Lukács. Party life was assembled out of patches of freedom: comradery, solidarity, trust, and so on. This was not a secondary consideration; these qualities set the proletarian party apart from other organizations. Without these bonds of freedom the party of revolution lost its raison d'être. *History and Class Consciousness*, especially "Towards a Methodology of the Problem of Organization," renounced neither authoritarian centralization nor nonauthoritarian freedom.

In that final chapter the arguments of the book coalesced. Lukács's wider analysis of capitalism bestowed a critical importance on the revolutionary organization that was less "technical" than "intellectual." Capitalism is not automatically metamorphosed into socialism, as vulgar Marxists often believed; capitalism leads to crises and wars, but no further. Between capitalism and socialism resides an empty space beyond determinism. At this juncture only the possibility exists that the hitherto "object of the economic process" – the proletariat – will become the subject. Since this conversion from object to subject is not automatic, it is a "free action." It depends solely on the proletariat attaining self-understanding and class consciousness. Lukács alluded to Gorter; this task is especially difficult in Western Europe because the proletariat can call upon no extraproletariat allies. Everything pivots on the insight of the proletariat.[36]

Within this framework Lukács situated the revolutionary organization, the conscious "leap" into freedom. The leap bore the traces of its capitalist past but also participated in future freedom. This was the intractable problem: the party as a vessel of freedom collided with the society of unfreedom. It straddled two worlds. The organization "consists necessarily of men who have been brought up in and ruined by capitalist society." The task was to "mitigate the catastrophic effects of this situation" while eschewing utopian hopes of a total transformation of its human material. "The inner life of the party is one unceasing struggle against this, its capitalist inheritence."[37]

Untouched by any depth psychology. Lukács reiterated that the incorporation of the "whole personality" is a "decisive weapon." "Party members enter with their whole personality into a living relationship with the whole of the life of the party." Active participation precluded that the party degenerated into "mechanical obedience." For Lukács, the party transcended a political tool. "Freedom – as the classical German philosophers realized – is something practical; it is an activity. And only by becoming a world of activity for everyone of its members can the Communist Party hope to overcome the passive role assumed by bourgeois man."[38]

History and Class Consciousness presented a defense of the Leninist party so extreme that it committed an offense. Inasmuch as no real party could measure up to its justification, the party stood condemned by its defense: This was the heresy of Lukács's orthodoxy. He adopted Leninism without surrendering Western Marxism. Although he devoted much of his later career to erasing its traces, the Hegel of consciousness and subjectivity indelibly marked his Marxism.

II

Compared to that of Lukács, Korsch's impact was limited. Yet its modesty owed more to his political trajectory than to his theoretical oeuvre. If Lukács and Korsch politically and theoretically intersected in 1923, henceforth their paths rapidly diverged. By 1926 the Communist party had expelled Korsch. Lukács never ceased to practice self-criticism – half feigned, half real – to shore up his position in the Communist party,[39] but Korsch began a long and isolated reevaluation of Marxism.[40] By the time of his death in 1961, he had been forgotten.

Yet this is a political fact, not a judgment on the quality of his work. His *Karl Marx* (1938) is outstanding (and remains ignored).[41] His theoretical labors continually stimulated and sustained those outside of Marxist orthodoxy. In the United States he worked peripherally with the Frankfurt School; the possibility of a major collaborative project, although broached, was not realized.[42] Bertolt Brecht considered Korsch his teacher and continuously sought his advice.[43] Korsch partly inspired what may be the best American book on Marxism from these years. Sidney Hook attended Korsch's lectures in 1928–1929, and his *Towards the Understanding of Karl Marx* (1933) thanked Korsch and testified to his thought.[44] Yet Korsch's isolation was palpable, as even T. W. Adorno noted after meeting him in the late 1930s.[45]

Like *History and Class Consciousness*, although smaller in size and conception, Korsch's *Marxism and Philosophy* was a philosophical work that was received as political heresy. The book echoed the general philosophical themes of Western Marxism. Marxism was not simply a political economy but a critique, and a critique included a philosophical confrontation with the "intellectual (ideological) structure of society." Vulgar Marxists deemed philosophy obsolete, surpassed by political economy; this was a fundamental misinterpretation. Marxism must be as multidimensional as is the social reality, and this required alertness to the ideological glue that bound society together. Korsch called for "intellectual action" and drew a parallel with Marx's statements on the relationship of political to economic action. "Just as political action is not rendered unnecessary by the economic action of a revolutionary class, so intellectual action is not rendered unnecessary by either political or economic action."[46]

As with *History and Class Consciousness*, the passions that *Marxism and Philosophy* stirred implied that beyond the pure philosophical horizon smoldered a political fire. Its size or extent was barely visible, since Korsch surrendered fewer clues than did Lukács. This partly reflected a contracting political universe. Lukács's undisguised "left" communism thrived in 1919–1921. In those years "left" communism was a reality, openly discussed and denounced. By 1923–1924, when Korsch emerged an oppositional Marxist, less was tolerated. Moreover, their respective positions within the communist movement differed radically. Lukács belonged to a minority faction in a small exiled Communist party. Korsch was a Communist party representative in the Reichstag for the most important party outside of the Russian and edited the German Communist party's (KPD) major theoretical journal. Like all activity in the KPD, his conduct and writings were closely monitored.

Korsch's early development and writings offer less interest and drama than those of Lukács. What has been said of Lukács's transformation from aesthete to Communist party member – "his conversion took place in the interval between two Sundays"[47] – cannot be said of Korsch. Not a sudden leap but a gradual development led the independent student Socialist before World War I into the Communist party. Korsch joined the SPD in 1912 and the opposition (Independent Social Democrats, USPD) to the SPD in 1919. He followed the majority of the USPD into the KPD in 1920.[48]

For his political and theoretical contributions, the most important experience seems to have been his years in England between 1911 and 1914, when he admired and adhered to the Fabian Society. For Korsch, the Fabian Society provided an Archimedean point from which to criticize standard German Marxism. Unlike the Germans, the Fabians did not believe that socialism would arrive without a practical activism and an ethical idealism – a *Geist der Tat.*[49] Moreover, the Fabians did not establish a political party but a "spiritual center" (*geistig Zentrum*).

Korsch's phrase "practical socialism" summarized the lessons he drew from the Fabians. The term did not do justice to its content, however. Korsch placed practical socialism squarely in opposition to orthodox and scientific Marxism. Orthodox Marxism posited that not only the economic preconditions but the socialist society itself would ripen on the "capitalist tree," one day falling to the ground. Practical socialism, conversely, is "no scientific socialism." It is "more than science, it is the creative will and preparation to action."[50]

The German October (1923) set the scene for Korsch's political role and heresies. After the 1921 March Action this was the next (and last) offensive of the KPD. The economic and political situation seemed propitious as the furious inflation of 1923 devasted much of the middle and working classes. The Russians, in particular Trotsky, nourished hopes of an imminent German revolution. The leaders of the KPD, Heinrich Brandler and August Thalheimer, although less convinced, let the Russians outwit, overrule, or convince them. If the planning and Russian participation were more extensive than in the March Action, the result was the same: utter failure because of bungling and lack of mass support.[51] The German October survived as a major issue in the subsequent factional battles of the KPD and the Comintern. It merits several lines in the histories of threats to the German state.[52]

The German October led to a change of leadership of the KPD. Brandler and Thalheimer, stained with a disaster, became a liability to Grigori Zinoviev, leader of the Comintern. In addition, in their post-mortum Brandler and Thalheimer charged that the Comintern failed to accurately gauge the objective conditions.[53] This was unacceptable to Zinoviev. Linking Brandler to Trotsky, who had just openly criticized the Soviet leadership,[54] Zinoviev commanded, "We must have a change in leadership [of the KPD]."[55] He threw his support to a new and left leadership of Ruth Fischer and Arkadi Maslow. Zinoviev, Fischer, and

Maslow agreed on at least one point, but a crucial one at the time: The Comintern did not misappraise the objective conditions, but Brandler and Thalheimer misled and misorganized the revolution.

This constellation of forces defined the field in which Korsch assumed a political role: an unstable alliance between the new left leadership of Fischer and Maslow, and the Comintern directed by Zinoviev.[56] The alliance was unstable because the left leadership of the KPD tended toward "left" communism, challenging orthodox Leninism.[57] For instance, Maslow had already been identified as a "left" Communist, and his transgressions were serious enough to gain Lenin's reproach.[58] A special committee had even been invoked to examine his record.[59]

Yet clarity is cheap after the events. Initially, many "left" Communists believed or hoped that they fought on the same side as the Comintern against reformism and social democracy; like Lukács, they tried to reconcile local autonomy and independence with iron discipline and centralization. By the end of 1923 most "left" Communists, chastised by the events, had discarded these illusions and hopes. For Fischer and Maslow, however, these illusions remained alive for the next two years.

The fragility, if not impossibility, of this Comintern–"left" pact was not completely obscure, however. Zinoviev, in fact, perceived more accurately than the left the risks of the alliance. From the very beginning he warned of leftism and ultra-leftism. This warning assumed a regular form. Zinoviev distinguished in the left between the responsible proletarian elements and irresponsible intellectuals.[60] On these grounds Korsch was targeted as an intellectual guilty of ultra-leftism.

The Ninth Party Congress of the KPD (April 1924) sealed the victory of the left in the wake of the German October. Zinoviev's letter to the Congress (March 26, 1924) already distinguished the responsible from the irresponsible leftists. The former were profoundly revolutionary workers who emerged from the masses. "The other current is represented by a group of leaders from the intelligentsia" and is characterized by "empty revolutionary phraseology."[61]

In addition to the letter to the Ninth Congress, Zinoviev fired off a series of messages on the dangers of the "left" intellectuals. At the end of March 1924, Zinoviev (and Nikolai Bukharin) wrote to several party members warning of tendencies in the party irreconcilable with bolshevism. These included tendencies to exit from the trade unions, renounce the united front, and "retreat to the perspective of Rosa Luxemburg in the organizational question" – all "left" positions. More damaging, some groups in the party had spoken of a "crisis in the Comintern." "Do not let yourself be lulled by sweet phrases that the ultra-left tendency is very weak."[62] In very similar terms, Zinoviev wrote to Fischer and Maslow. "Do not imagine that the ultra-left does not represent a serious force." The banner of Rosa Luxemburg is raised, the united front attacked, and there is talk of a "so-called 'crisis' in the Comintern."[63] A correspondent of Maslow reported that Zinoviev was troubled by the left "academics."[64]

It was in this atmosphere charged by accusations of ultra-leftism and suspicion of intellectuals that two works by Marxist philosophers appeared, Lukács's *History and Class Consciousness* and Korsch's *Marxism and Philosophy*. Lukács, although fast covering his tracks, was easily identified as part of an ultra-left. Korsch, in an "Afterwards instead of a Forwards" appended to an early edition of *Marxism and Philosophy*, expressed his solidarity with Lukács. He noted that while he was completing his book, Lukács's book was published and that Lukács's book, which is "based on a broader philosophical foundation, touches at many points on the questions raised here; as I presently see the matter I am pleased to state my fundamental agreement with him."[65]

On the eve of the Fifth World Congress of the Communist International (June 1924), an issue of *Internationale* (edited by Korsch) appeared containing "Lenin and the Comintern" back-to-back with an article by Boris (Roninger) on the program of the Comintern. Both caused stirs as ultra-left provocations. In the same issue Korsch reviewed several books, including Lukács's *History and Class Consciousness* and Bukharin's *Historical Materialism*. Here Korsch stepped on some Marxist toes. He criticized Béla Kun, Lukács's opponent in the Hungarian party, for crassly attacking Lukács's book; and he suggested that Bukharin advocated "a specifically bourgeois method of science."[66] Boris, who was already tainted by ultra-leftism,[67] transgressed not only because he also attacked Bukharin but because he completely defended Luxemburg; and he did not exempt Lenin from criticism.[68] For these critical essays and reviews to appear in the premier theoretical journal of the KPD on the eve of the Fifth World Congress was interpreted as a direct assault on Comintern politics.

The Fifth Congress opened in June with a leading address by Zinoviev. His earlier letters presaged his pronouncements on the KPD. He attacked the ultra-left, specifically naming Lukács and Korsch, as intellectuals and professors. "This theoretical revisionism cannot be allowed to pass with impunity."[69] He relegated to Bukharin the full response to Boris. Fischer sought to parry the blow by disassociating Korsch from Boris. "When Korsch and Boris are named in the same breath . . . when Comrade Korsch is thrown into the same pot as Boris . . . this the German Party will not allow."[70]

To be sure, Korsch's infractions do not seem especially grave; yet in the atmosphere of Marxist law and order, they sufficed to identify him as a renegade. He trespassed on both political and philosophical property. As editor of the *Internationale* he criticized the Comintern and opened its pages to other critics. His *Marxism and Philosophy*, although tactically uncontroversial, smacked of the historical Hegel; moreover, for those slow to make the connections, Korsch openly stated his solidarity with Lukács, who had already been branded a "left" Communist.[71]

During the next months the left leadership of Fischer and Maslow succumbed to – or embraced – the Comintern position; they became eager Bolshevizers, sniffing out Luxemburgism and ultra-leftism. Maslow himself replied to Boris's article,[72] and the Central Committee of the party formally condemned it.[73]

The rest of the story can be told briefly. Korsch moved increasingly toward the left opposition, and Fischer and Maslow increasingly toed the Comintern line; they hunted for left deviations, or what Fischer called "The West European Theoretical school," meaning Korsch and Lukács. "We will not tolerate theoretical deviations, nor make any concessions to the West European 'theoretical school', even when it acts as Leninist."[74] In this period, Korsch was several times identified as part of the radical opposition.[75]

These maneuvers culminated in the Tenth Party Congress of the KPD (July 1925). Although this nominally reaffirmed the victory that Fischer and Maslow had obtained at the previous Congress, it signaled their downfall. Again Zinoviev sent a letter to the Congress claiming progress against an ultra-left, although a fever still existed. He named

Korsch as part of this left.[76] Yet Zinoviev's alliance with Fischer and Maslow no longer served a purpose. Only weeks after the Tenth Party Congress, Zinoviev turned decisively against them. This shift only appears to be one more obscure change of direction in the Comintern, if the nature of the alliance from the beginning is missed. It was always unstable, and this was clearer to Zinoviev than to Fischer and Maslow. Despite their conversion to enthusiastic Bolshevizers, they remained tainted as intellectuals with links to the left opposition. They were convenient allies only after the debacle of the German October.

The German party was discussed by the Executive Committee of the Comintern in the middle of August 1925, only weeks after the Tenth Party Congress. What Zinoviev stated then rings partly true. He originally supported Fischer and Maslow "reluctantly," as the best opponents to Brandler; moreover, he had always distinguished between the "good proletarian elements" and the intellectuals in the left.[77] These discussions, which included members of the German party, announced the changing of the guard. Word did not reach the party at large until Zinoviev's "open letter" was published in the main party newspaper, *Die Rote Fahne*, on September 1, 1925.[78] The "open letter" called for the cashiering of Fischer and Maslow – the most direct intervention of the Comintern into the KPD to date.

The "open letter" charged that Fischer and Maslow not only failed to resist but coquetted with the ultra-left. The brunt of the attack fell on Maslow since he stood closer to the ultra-left than did Fischer. "Comrad Maslow sought to oppose a 'pure' 'left' specifically 'West European' Communism to the 'opportunism' of Leninism." The letter commanded: "The entire German Party, above all the best comrades . . . have the duty to break with the relationship that Fischer-Maslow Group has established between the party and the Comintern."[79]

Zinoviev's "open letter" caused "sensation and panic" in the party.[80] Few had anticipated that the left leadership of Fischer and Maslow, anointed by Zinoviev, would be so unceremoniously discharged. It did not take long for the party to vote them out. Within days of the "open letter," district meetings of the party were called. Korsch no longer minced his words. At the district meeting in Frankfurt on September 9, Korsch denounced the "red imperialism" of the Comintern.[81]

Heinz Neumann, an early favorite of Stalin, not only attacked Korsch for his remarks but published a long critique of Maslow. In his denunciation, he summarized the heresy: The overriding challenge to Leninism was what he called the "West European deviation." "The 'West European deviation' is the root error, which since Rosa Luxemburg's death runs through our whole party history. It is the common characteristic and the unmistakable sign of all deviations from revolutionary Marxism, from Leninism, which have appeared in our ranks." Neumann included in this list the KAPD, Levi, and the more recent ultra-leftists.[82]

The rest of Korsch's development need not be recounted here; it conformed to a logic and to his past. He next affiliated with a left opposition within the Communist party and formed a group called the "decisive left."[83] In this capacity he presented an analysis of the Soviet Union and the Comintern. The Soviet Union ceased to be revolutionary and "disrupted" the "identity" between its national interests and the imperatives of the international revolutionary movement. The program he penned ended by demanding that "the long promised internal party democracy be realized."[84] Shortly after this program he was expelled. Politically he maintained affiliation with a series of workers' council organizations, first in Germany and later in the United States. One of his last letters (1956) affirmed his loyalty to "another dream: to theoretically restore the 'ideas of Marx' that today are seemingly annihilated . . ."[85]

III

A philosophical denunciation of Lukács and Korsch seconded the political barrage. Yet the fissure within Marxism was evident: Each denunciation proceeded separately and barely alluded to the other. The charges mounted by Zinoviev and Comintern subalterns enunciated political, not philosophical, violations. The critique advanced by the orthodox philosophers stayed clear of explicit politics.

Nevertheless, the philosophers did not simply stumble upon Lukács and Korsch: A political label hung on them. Abram Deborin, the dean of Soviet philosophers, stated that Lukács had "disciples" and led "a whole tendency," which included Korsch.[86] Jan Sten, another Deborinite, put it more plainly. Philosophically Lukács represents an "idealistic distortion," a reversion to an "old-Hegelian idealism."

"This philosophy . . . reveals in certain of its theses a direct relationship with the left-wing childhood diseases with which political practice is fraught."[87] Yet these were political allusions on the margins of the philosophical encounter.

To those familiar with the canons of Soviet Marxism or official dialectical materialism, the philosophical critiques of Lukács rehearsed basic tenets. They merit attention, however, because they illustrate dramatically the two Hegelian traditions; here they directly clashed. Deborin and his "school" constituted the philosophical offensive against Lukács. In the Soviet context, they were known, and finally condemned, as Hegelians, although they harbored no sympathy for Lukács. This is puzzling only if the divergences between the two Hegelian traditions are surrendered. From a Russian and scientific Hegelianism, the Deborinites discerned and rejected in Lukács a historical Hegelianism. As in the earlier debates, the evaluation of Engels and the dialectic of nature signaled the breach.

In accord with scientific Hegelianism, the Deborinites proposed the universality of the dialectic, exactly what Lukács challenged. For Lukács, and the historical Hegelians, society and history marked the outer borders of dialectics. Within these boundaries, consciousness and subjectivity, foreign to pure nature and physical matter, were indigenous. For the Deborinites, subjectivity and consciousness receded before the universal and objective laws of development. Dialectics encompassed not only history but nature itself. It is to be recalled that Lukács criticized Engels on these grounds: "Following Hegel's mistaken lead" Engels had extended dialectics to nature and lost the critical relationship between subject and object.[88]

In his critique of Lukács, as well as elsewhere, Deborin reaffirmed the main principles of orthodox Marxism. He designated Marxism a total system, a "unified closed Weltanschauung" that governed the whole of reality.[89] "The form of the dialectic encompasses the whole of reality; since dialectics set forth the general teaching of the laws of movement and the forms of movement of all being, the natural sciences must also be penetrated by it."[90] Pure nature is not outside dialectics but "is itself dialectical." Dialectics merged into a theory of the objective unfolding of laws. An ally of Deborin, Ladislau Rudas, accused Lukács of "subjective idealism." Inasmuch as Lukács restricted dialectics to society he reduced it to a human creation; and worse, this implied that "the dialectic is not an objective law, independent from men, but a subjective law of men."[91]

On these issues Deborin insisted that Marx and Engels did not differ. "Marx and Engels are in the same way 'guilty' of the application of the dialectic to nature . . . not Engels but Lukács himself distorts the teachings of Marx."[92] Engels's *Dalectics of Nature*, only recently published (1925), proved to Deborin not only the validity of the dialectic of nature but its legitimization by Hegel.[93]

The Deborinites dominated only briefly as the official philosophers in the Soviet Union. They lost favor and were charged with the same sins of which they had charged Lukács: Hegelianizing Marxism. The irony of these charges hinted at a truth: Hegelian Deborinites demonstrated not only the divergence between two Hegelian traditions, but their fate indicated a convergence beyond the divergence. With Engels and the dialectic of nature as the red flags, the two traditions fought. Yet finally they both shared something: loyalty to Hegel and the independence of philosophy. This spanned the traditions and, to the Soviet guardians of thoughts, smacked of subversion.

Initially, during the 1920s, the Deborinites gained ascendancy in the conflict with philosophers known as the "mechanists."[94] The Russian mechanists represented a rough-and-ready Marxism, which advocated purging all philosophy from Marxism in favor of the natural sciences. It was advanced most enthusiastically by S. Minin in an article entitled "Overboard with Philosophy!" (1922). For Minin, philosophy itself was the evil, totally extraneous to Marxism. "Philosophy is a prop of the bourgeoisie." Science belonged to the proletariat, but "no kind of philosophy" did. "Away with the 'dirty linen' of philosophy. We need science, only science, simply science."[95]

Against crude efforts by the mechanists to liquidate philosophy and reduce Marxism to a natural science, the Deborinites rallied to the autonomy and supremacy of philosophy. Precisely on this point Deborin appealed to Engels and Hegel; the natural sciences did not dispense with, but required, philosophy. While seeking to avoid the implication of dictating results to natural scientists, the Deborinites situated philosophy above the natural sciences; it interpreted the findings of the natural sciences. Engels effectively supported the Deborinites on this issue: He said that regardless of the naiveté of the natural scientists, they were necessarily dominated by philosophical concepts. For Deborin, this justified the project of encompassing nature within a total dialectical philosophy.[96]

Theoretically this approach stood within scientific Hegelianism, and politically it served the Deborinites well – for awhile. In the first years of the Russian Revolution, the independence of the natural scientists was threatening; they were suspected of harboring bourgeois sympathies. For this reason the defense of the autonomy, even priority, of natural science by the mechanists was suspect; it shored up, not challenged, the fiefdom of the natural scientists. Official policy during the 1920s, especially during the years of Deborin's supremacy (1928–1931), sought to "undermine the ideological autonomy of natural scientists."[97] Insofar as the Deborinites elevated philosophy to a theoretical throne they were convenient allies. Marxist philosophy interpreted, and perhaps commanded, the natural scientists. By 1929 the mechanists had been officially condemned and the Deborinites awarded the philosophical loot, key research posts and journals. The official condemnation accused the mechanists of "objectively obstructing the penetration of the natural sciences by the methodology of dialectical materialism."[98]

Yet the victory of the Deborinites was brief; their links to a Hegelian tradition ensured their downfall. They valued Hegel too highly and balked at completely subordinating philosophy to the party commands: So ran the charges against them. In the heat of the conflict one of the Deborinites proclaimed: "Yes! We are Hegelians! Everything great in modern history has been in one way or the other connected with Hegel's name."[99] Stalin intervened and coined a term for Deborinite thought, "Menshivizing idealism."[100]

Mark Borisovich Mitin, the newly annointed philosopher, handled the presentation. The critics of Lukács's Hegelian idealism were indicated in the same court. Mitin noted that Deborin's institute spent three or four years studying only Hegel's *Logic*. This produced a "'Hegelianization' of materialism, of Marxism."[101] Mitin announced the liquidation of all autonomous philosophy. He applied with enthusiasm the notion of "partyness" or partisanship, which subordinated philosophy to the practical imperatives of the party. The new phase of philosophy must emphasize the "Leninist principle of the partyness of philosophy, the natural sciences, and the sciences generally." This would be "the best antidote against the present strong and bold tendencies of revisionism in Marxist philosophy – its idealistic Hegelian perspective – beginning with Lukács and ending with the Deborin group . . ."[102]

In the Soviet Union Marxism corroded into a series of bald pronouncements and principles. In Europe the defeats of the revolutions reinforced the dominion of orthodoxy and branded Western Marxism: Making only occasional forays into political economy and tactics, Western Marxism retreated to aesthetics, philosophy, and psychoanalysis. Unorthodox Marxists were eased out and expelled from the communist parties. *History and Class Consciousness* and *Marxism and Philosophy* presaged these developments but were still drenched in the past. They breathed in an atmosphere of political choices and possibilities, as the doors banged shut.

5

The subterranean years

In the mid-1920s the story breaks off and up into separate pieces and chapters. Stalinism as a world phenomenon, the onset of fascism, World War II, and the Cold War more than sufficed to repress or frighten into silence unorthodox Marxists. Yet a Western Marxism did not evaporate; its paths can be followed through these decades until the late 1950s, when it reemerged, again political and public.

The scattering and decentralization of Western Marxism lends an arbitrariness to the examination of particular individuals or groups. In Italy, France, Germany, and elsewhere, groups and grouplets, traditions, and currents persisted that finally coalesced into a viable – if unsuccessful – alternative to Soviet and orthodox Marxism.

I

The fate of Western Marxism in Italy requires some additional comments. In surveying the development of Western Marxism, simple patterns are seductive. If these fail, the opposite approach is equally tempting: to find only "special cases" and to arrive at no general conclusions. In many respects, Italy was a special case, at least in regard to the roots and impact of Western Marxism. Nowhere else did the Western Marxists – the Frankfurt School, or Pannekoek and Gorter, or Merleau-Ponty and Sartre – participate in the mainstream of Marxism. Yet Italian Marxism incorporated Antonio Gramsci. The resiliency and independence of Italian communism in the current period is partly due to this fact (or accident?).

The process by which Gramsci became anointed and official has provoked endless controversy.[1] To some it entailed the domestication of Gramsci, a falsification of his thought; the opponent of official Marxism is palmed off as the exponent. Yet Italian Marxism is shaped by more than a trick; it bears the scars of the political conflict between Gramsci and Amadeo Bordiga.

By virtue of his roots in Italian Hegelianism, his advocacy of factory councils, his analysis of intellectuals and culture, and his critique of mechanical Marxism, Gramsci is deemed a prime adherent of Western Marxism. For instance, in a neat case of theoretical symmetry, Lukács and Gramsci dissected in similar terms Nikolai Bukharin's *Historical Materialism*, once a basic text of Soviet Marxism.[2] Yet Gramsci did not become a pariah, the fate of Lukács or Korsch, but the effective leader of the Italian Communist party and spokesman for the Comintern. Bordiga has attracted less interest, especially outside Italy; but he became the dissident and opponent of the Comintern. Lenin identified Bordiga, not Gramsci, as the "left" Communist.

Narrow links bind Bordiga to the other "left" Communists, however; they derived from a rejection of parliamentary tactics but did not extend to a theory of organization. For Bordiga and his "abstentionists" (or boycottists), parliamentarism smacked of reformism and opportunism. His repudiation of elections, however, was based in a rigorous and disciplined party, not, as with other "left" Communists, in antiauthoritarian proletarian organizations. Bordiga represented obdurate Leninism. "*We favor the strong and centralized Marxist political party that Lenin speaks of; indeed, we are the most fervent supporters of this idea.*"[3]

"Left" communism, then, encompassed widely divergent positions. Unlike other "left" Communists, Bordiga, consistent with his inflexible Leninism, vigorously opposed factory councils. For Bordiga, the councils, by shifting struggles to the economic units, minimized the decisive importance of forming the Leninist political party.[4] Some of the mystery of Italian Marxism stemmed from this constellation of programs. Gramsci not only finally gained the upper hand in the Communist party but championed factory councils. To be sure, Gramsci did not always defend the councils, and when (and if and how much) he renounced them forms part of the Gramsci controversy.

The relationship of Bordiga and his followers to the wider European "left" communism can be illustrated by his journal, *Il Soviet*. Like

Kommunismus, it served as a forum for "left" Communists, publishing Pannekoek, Lukács, Pankhurst, and others.[5] In this sense there was solidarity and agreement within a European "left" communism. Yet Bordiga did not hide his differences with the other "left" Communists on organization. This is clear, for example, from his comments on the formation of the German Communist Worker's party (KAPD). Bordiga sympathized with the German Communist party (KPD) central committee, not the split of the "left" communist KAPD. Although Bordiga concurred with some of the tenets of the KAPD, he nevertheless saw it through Leninist glasses as a syndicalist deviation. If his group and the KAPD agreed on abstentionism from elections, their abstentionism "differed" from ours.[6]

Bordiga's position can be crystallized by examining *Il Soviet* in regard to Lukács's "Question of Parliamentarianism," discussed in the previous chapter. In this resolutely "left" communist essay, which had provoked Lenin's ire, Lukács wrote off the terrain of parliamentary politics as exclusively bourgeois and only "defensive" for the proletariat. *Il Soviet* serialized this essay and noted that this translation (from *Kommunismus*) "constitutes an extremely valuable contribution to the questions of parliamentarianism and corresponds in the greatest degree to our position."[7]

The last part of Lukács's essay, however, developed the notion of workers' councils as the "true index" of the proletarian revolution. "Their mere existence points the way forward beyond bourgeois society." For Lukács, councils served as the authentic field of proletarian activity. In reaching this part of the serialization, Bordiga and the editors had a change of heart. The serialization closed with another editorial note, this time qualifying that this "interesting study" corresponds "only in part" to our view. "We do not accept, in fact, the considerations in the last part, for reasons which would be superfluous to repeat."[8]

Nevertheless, the narrow links between Bordiga and the other "left" Communists cannot be dismissed; it is hardly fortuitous that Bordiga was driven into the opposition. Bordiga challenged Soviet Marxism more openly, if less profoundly, than did Gramsci, and the critique that Bordiga mounted shared many features with Western Marxism.[9] In the Enlarged Executive of the Comintern in 1926 Bordiga did not mince words. He said that the Russian model of revolution lacked universal applicability.[10] The stable bourgeois state apparatus of the West was "unknown in Russian history."[11] Bordiga's heresy was quickly answered. Bukharin indicated its roots. "We have heard similar objections in 1921 from the Renegade Paul Levi, who continually maintained that we mechanically transferred the 'Russian experience' onto Western Europe."[12]

The complexity of Italian Marxism was such that Bordiga became the opponent and Gramsci, at least nominally, the defender of the Comintern.[13] Against Gramsci, Bordiga argued that a "crisis" in the Comintern existed, as well as a "fundamental defect in the internal method of work." Unlike Gramsci, Bordiga rejected the slogan and reality of Bolshevization: "It signifies an artificial and mechanical transposition to the Western parties of methods which were specific to the Russian party. With Bolshevization, an attempt is being made to resolve questions, which are political with formulae of an organizational character."[14] In the Enlarged Executive he denounced the "regime of terror" conducted against Comintern opponents. This "mania of self-destruction must stop."[15]

II

In France, as discussed previously, the late development of a Western Marxism corresponded to the "lateness" of an indigenous Hegelian literature. Once this literature was established, the works of Maurice Merleau-Ponty and Jean-Paul Sartre retrieved and invigorated a Western Marxism in the post–World War II years. Merleau-Ponty's *Sense and Non-Sense* (1948)[16] and *Adventures of the Dialectic* (1955),[17] and Sartre's "Materialism and Revolution" (1946)[18] (and to a lesser extent his *Being and Nothingness* [1943]), as well as their journal, *Les Temps modernes*, signified a vital French Western Marxism.

Other eddies of Western Marxism surfaced, notably around the journals *Socialisme ou barbarie* (1949–1965) and *Arguments* (1956–1962). The former served as the vehicle for writings of Claude Lefort and Cornelius Castoriadis[19] and the latter for Henri Lefebvre. *Arguments* also presented the first French translations of Lukács and Korsch. Lefebvre's career in France recapitulates the general development of Western Marxism.

Lefebvre left the French Communist party only after 1956, but his earlier activities and writings betrayed a commitment to unorthodox Marxism. He belonged to a group called "Philosophies," which briefly (1925–1926) formed an alliance with the surrealists.[20] With Norbert Guterman he translated Hegel, Lenin's Hegel notebooks, and early Marx. He also wrote with Guterman a book that represented a high point of French Western Marxism in this earlier period, *La Conscience mystifiée*.

Published in 1936, the title itself hints of *History and Class Consciousness*. In many respects it was a French *History and Class Consciousness* rewritten in the context of the struggle against fascism.[21] Yet Lukács goes unmentioned in the text. As Lefebvre explained later, aware of the heresy of Lukács's book, he (or, more precisely, they) avoided references to it.[22] One of the ideas that Lefebvre and Guterman introduced in the book, "the critique of daily life," sustained much of Lefebvre's later work.[23] Norbert Guterman, though perpetually self-effacing, should not go unnoticed; he is one of few real international representatives of Western Marxism. He collaborated and translated with Lefebvre. Later in the United States he worked with the Frankfurt School. He wrote with Leo Lowenthal of the Frankfurt School *Prophets of Deceit* (1949), a volume in a series edited by Max Horkheimer.[24]

III

By its impact, productivity, and originality, the Frankfurt School, including Max Horkheimer, T. W. Adorno, and Herbert Marcuse, belongs in the first ranks of Western Marxism. Although frequently derided as isolated and ineffectual in its exile, one of the very few seminal American contributions to Western Marxism, Paul Baran and Paul Sweezy's *Monopoly Capital* (1966), bears its imprint. The heresy of *Monopoly Capital* is often missed, and its links to Western Marxism are usually ignored.

To the conventional Marxist concept of "surplus value" Baran and Sweezy added that of "surplus." This was not a minor revision. It appended a critical, almost a moral, dimension to an economic concept; and it allowed them to discuss features of everyday life – sexuality, modes of consumption, and so on – that escaped a flat economic approach. "Surplus" sought to register the difference between the present arrangement of society and a rational one. The last chapter of

Monopoly Capital, "The Irrational System," resounds with moral denunciation. The concept itself derived from Baran's earlier *Political Economy of Growth* (1957), where it was rooted in Horkheimer's concept of "objective reason."[25] Baran had studied in Frankfurt and had remained close to Marcuse and Lowenthal. According to Sweezy, Baran was "profoundly and permanently influenced" by his Frankfurt association.[26]

In any case, the ties between the Frankfurt School and Western Marxism do not need belaboring. The "Frankfurt School" refers to the Institute of Social Research in Frankfurt, where Max Horkheimer brought together a series of original and incisive thinkers.[27] The institute itself was designed to promote an independent Marxism equally distant (or close) to academic specialization and party imperatives.[28] Much of its inspiration, as well as its financial backing, came from Felix Weil.

A net of personal and political relationships, centering on Weil, bound together the figures of Western Marxism and the Frankfurt School. In 1921 Korsch published a volume by Weil; some years later Korsch was charged with forming with Weil (and Boris Roninger) a dissident faction within the Communist party.[29] In 1922 Weil convoked a Marxist study group in which both Korsch and Lukács participated, as well as others who played a role in the Frankfurt School: Friedrich Pollock and Karl Wittfogel.[30]

At the same time discussions proceeded among Weil, Pollock, and Max Horkheimer on the possibility of founding an institute to study Marxism that would be affiliated to a university but freed from the usual academic pressures. With caution or foresight, the projected name of Institute of Marxism was scrapped for the more acceptable Institute of Social Research. Financial backing by Weil's father enabled the Institute to open in 1924, as an affiliate of Frankfurt University. After the tenure of Carl Grünberg, Max Horkheimer became the director in 1931 and commenced *Zeitschrift für Sozialforschung* (1932–1941) (its last two volumes were titled *Studies in Philosophy and Social Science*).[31]

The chapters of the Frankfurt School span too many decades, and include too many people and projects, to summarize here. Yet the frequent charge that it betrayed Marxism by fleeing politics is historically blind: It was in flight, but from nazism. The participants of the

Frankfurt School were scattering almost as soon as they came together under Horkheimer's directorship. Among his first acts Horkheimer established a bureau in Geneva and investigated opening other offices outside of Germany.[32] Only months after the Nazis attained power in January 1933, the Institute was closed and its library seized. Horkheimer, Pollock, and Marcuse had already left. The second volume of their journal was published in exile in Paris.[33]

If their flight from nazism is obvious, it is often ignored in evaluating the politics of the Frankfurt School. For independent left-wing exiles, the possibilities of political intervention, already checked by Stalinization, further diminished. Nor are the charges that the Frankfurt School failed to develop a theory or organization, if not a practical politics, to the point. These charges succumb to the bewitchment of words: Out of a theory of a proletarian organization springs a revolutionary organization. Nothing is more scholastic than disputes on the correct line of the proletariat when the proletariat has been silenced.

To be sure, references to nazism cannot answer all questions of the Frankfurt School's relationship to political parties and organizations. It would be difficult to argue, for instance, that before 1933 Adorno's thought tended toward a practical political idiom and that nazism blocked this development. Without exile and fascism, however, the projectory of Horkheimer's or Marcuse's thought might have been very different.

Suggestions of the political dimension of their work are not difficult to uncover. The imperatives of exile dictated that the politics be expressed covertly – until the 1960s, when Marcuse emerged as a public and political thinker. That Horkheimer's most forthright political sentiments were published under a pseudonym or in privately circulated manuscripts testified to the fragility of his situation. In 1934 he published *Dämmerung*, a collection of notes and aphorisms, under the name Heinrich Regius. The first sentence summarized it succinctly: "This book is obsolete."[34] He explained that "problems like that of the cultural politics of the Social Democrats, bourgeois literature which sympathizes with the revolution, the academic presentation of Marxism, formed an intellectual world which has now disappeared."[35]

Horkheimer sharply attacked in *Dämmerung* bourgeois intellectuals and sympathizers to socialism. He remarked that when "literary radicals" bemoaned that capitalism had stabilized "they were never as downcast as when they related some personal misfortune." If they are knowledgeable about revolutionary theory "they lack expertise in questions relating to the time revolution will break out. This time depends upon the will of men. But that is not the same in one who leads the life of the intellect . . . and one to whom everything is denied."[36] Several passages read as defenses of the Communist party. However inadequate a revolutionary leadership, it does not "negate the fact that it is the head of the struggle." Criticism of this leadership from the "outside" is unacceptable; it fails to grasp the real options. "Bourgeois criticism of the proletarian struggle is a logical impossibility." "The revolutionary career is not a series of banquets and a string of honorific titles, nor does it hold the promise of interesting research or professor's salaries," wrote Professor Horkheimer.[37]

Yet *Dämmerung* was hardly an advertisement for the Communist party, and Horkheimer attached a note to this passage observing the disjunction between proletarian leadership and moral character. He resolved this only by questions: "Does the 'higher level' of the bourgeois critics, their more acute moral sensibility, not in part result from the fact that they keep away from the real political fight? . . . Do the better educated have any good reason to damn those who are actually involved in this struggle?" Another section expanded on the fateful disjunction between the political imperatives and human preconditions of socialism.

In a passage entitled "The Impotence of the German Working Class" Horkheimer put some of his theoretical cards on the table. "The capitalist process of production has thus driven a wedge between the interest in socialism and the human qualities necessary to its implementation. That is the new element." These devolved on separate groups and parties; the Communist party and the Social Democrats no longer combined both. The Communist party relied on authority and the Social Democrats renounced Marxism. The wedge fatally wounded Marxist theory:

> Loyalty to materialist doctrine threatens to become a mindless and contentless cult of literalism and personality unless a radical turn soon occurs. At the same time, the materialist content, which means knowledge of the real world, is the possession of those who have become disloyal to Marxism. It is therefore also about to lose its only distinguishing characteristic, its existence as knowledge.[38]

These reflections defined the Frankfurt School for the next decades: Marxists without a party or a proletariat faced a party and a proletariat without Marxism. Neither an act of will nor theoretical brilliance escaped this dilemma; and the situation did not improve. Horkheimer's next and most political writings belong to the darkest period of World War II. "The Authoritarian State," "Reason and Self-Preservation" and "The Jews and Europe" were written in the period 1939–1941. Each exuded the atmosphere of those years: the defeat of the Spanish Republic, the Nazi–Soviet pact, and the fall of France. Two were published in a privately circulated volume dedicated to Walter Benjamin, who, fleeing nazism, committed suicide in 1940.[39]

The terseness and compressed tension of these essays defy summary; they suggest, moreover, the existence of "two" Horkheimers. One Horkheimer directed the Institute of Social Research, writing prefaces and broad programmatic essays on critical theory; he worked to establish the academic legitimacy of a Western Marxism. The other Horkheimer occasionally took off his tie to use the "direct language of libertarian communism."[40] "Reason and Self-Preservation" and "The End of Reason" closed with words that Rosa Luxemburg made famous: "The progress of reason that leads to its self-destruction has come to an end; there is nothing left but barbarism or freedom."[41]

No microscope is necessary to find the links to a "left" communism in "The Authoritarian State"; Horkheimer expressly appealed to the tradition of workers' councils:

> The often cited political immaturity of the masses behind which party bureaucrats like to hide is in reality nothing but skepticism towards the leadership. The workers have learned that they have nothing to expect from those who called them out from time to time, only to send them home again, but more of the same – even after a victory . . . The theoretical conception which, following its first trailblazers, will show the new society its way – the system of workers' councils – grows out of praxis. The roots of the council system go back to 1871, 1905, and other events. *Revolutionary transformation has a tradition that must continue.*[42]

"The Authoritarian State," although hardly addressed to the proletariat, was permeated by Western Marxism and "left" communism. Horkheimer treated the party itself as a deadening bureaucratic structure; the large working-class organizations imitated the states they were combating. Like the captains of industry, the working-class leaders used the purse, and sometimes force, to eliminate internal opposition; they kept the masses "under strict discipline" and tolerated "spontaneity" only when preplanned. They sought not "the democracy of councils" but "work, discipline and order."[43]

Like Lukács, Horkheimer criticized the evolutionary interpretation of socialism. The laws of capitalism do not guarantee socialism or freedom. The idea of Marxists as the "midwives" of history, simply attending its natural course, degraded revolution to "mere progress" of the existing society. Rather the break in history rests on the actions of the subject that cannot be totally commanded. "The Authoritarian State" was published with Walter Benjamin's "Theses on the Philosophy of History." Benjamin also wrote of the "leap" out of history.[44] The prognosis, however, was bleak. "Not only freedom," explained Horkheimer, "but also future forms of oppression are possible." Moreover, "sociological and psychological concepts are too superficial to express what has happened to revolutionaries in the last few decades: their will toward freedom has been damaged." The hope was dim but real: "The eternal system of the authoritarian state, as terrible as the threat may seem, is no more real than the eternal harmony of the market economy."[45]

For decades the Frankfurt School spoke to few; yet it was not simply a personal failing if their language and concepts lacked political impact. The situation of homeless German Jewish exiles did not encourage boldness. When the conditions changed in the late 1950s, the language of the theory also changed, most emphatically with Marcuse. His path toward politics can be charted even at its most distant point, his prefaces and postscripts to his books on Hegel.

The Preface to *Hegels Ontologie und die Theorie der Geschichtlichkeit* (Hegel's Ontology and the Theory of Historicity) (1933), his first book on Hegel, declared his intention of establishing fundamental principles of "historicity."[46] The Preface to the first edition of *Reason and Revolution: Hegel and the Rise of Social Theory* (1941) sought to demonstrate that Hegel's ideas were hostile to fascism; and it closed citing Hegel: America may be the "land of the future."[47] A 1954 Epilogue, later dropped, to *Reason and Revolution* expressed another mood. "The defeat of Fascism and National Socialism has not arrested the trend towards totalitarianism. Freedom is on the retreat." His 1960 Preface announced: "From this stage on, all thinking that does not testify to an awareness of the radical falsity of the established forms of life . . . is not merely immoral; it is false.''[48] The threat of atomic destruction, the waste of resources, mental impoverishment, and brute force define the universe of discourse and action; in this universe, dialectical thought is critical and subversive.

To orthodox Marxists, the Frankfurt School remained a scandal; it never severed its links to German idealism and historicism; it criticized the fetish of science; it stayed clear of proletarian organizations; it was too interested in culture, psychoanalysis, and subjectivity; and, most damning of all, it lacked successes but not pessimism.

Yet pessimism is not only a personal choice or quirk; it is drenched in a heartless past. A cheerful Marxism is already suspect; it whitewashes the past in the name of a red future. What must be recognized is that to Western Marxists and the Frankfurt School the desperate hope of the dialectic had not been realized; nor could the pain and suffering of the past simply be added to the bill of the bourgeoisie. Marxists were implicated, and sometimes responsible. The shadow that accompanies Marxism is cast by this reality.

Late in Lukács's long career he denounced Adorno and other Marxist intellectuals for their pessimism and distance from revolutionary organizations. He charged that they preferred to remain in what he called the "Grand Hotel Abyss," a beautiful hotel where one could contemplate the void in first-class comfort.[49] The designation has enjoyed a certain vogue. It inferred that Marxist intellectuals without a party of the proletariat lacked verve and commitment.

If Lukács is allowed this denunciation, others who enthusiastically repeat it should not forget the few choices and options of the time. The risks were not only of falling in the front lines but of liquidation in the back rooms. While Lukács survived in Moscow in the 1930s and 1940s, others were less fortunate. Even Béla Kun, Lukács's bitter opponent in the Hungarian party, was arrested in 1938. To denounce the refugees in the Hotel Abyss without recognizing that the hotels on the street of Marxism were not only far apart but often firetraps is to mislead the traveler. Any guide that is more than a public relations ploy must scrutinize and evaluate all the available accommodations.

If the Hotel Abyss can symbolize Western Marxism in the 1930s and 1940s, the Hotel Lux can symbolize Soviet Marxism. Unlike the Hotel Abyss, the Lux was not a metaphor but a hotel housing foreign Communists who resided in Moscow. A detailed guide book might mention that the Lux offered a special service: Visitors were often spared the annoyance of checking out. Many foreign Communists were arrested in their rooms in the Lux.[50]

The guide might also include individuals' accounts of the accommodations. Heinz Neumann, the sharp critic of Korsch and Maslow, and the reliable servant of the Comintern, stayed at the Lux until arrested there in 1937. His wife recalled that at the end of the search of their room Neumann told her, "Don't cry." The secret police (GPU) leader then ordered, "That's enough. Get a move on, now." "At the door," she remembered, "Heinz turned and strode back, took me in his arms again and kissed me. 'Cry then,' he said. 'There's enough to cry about.' "[51] Neumann never returned. Along with other German Communists, in one of the infamous deals of history, his wife was delivered by the Russians to the Nazis during the Soviet–Nazi pact.[52]

6

Class unconsciousness

The monotony of defeat and self-destruction compelled Western Marxists to reevaluate the relationship of history and nature. Initially, they kept distant from the natural sciences for devaluing the new and unique in history; this devaluation condemned Marxism to improving, not undoing, the past. Yet the uniform defeat of the European revolutions and the barbarism of fascism exacted a toll. The hope of a liberating breakthrough dimmed. Moreover, Marxists were not only victims but victimizers. To Walter Benjamin's words that the "bourgeoisie never ceased to be victorious" could be added: Marxists never ceased to bury each other and the revolution. The subordination of history to bleak repetition tempered the efforts to rescue it from nature.

I

The Western Marxists, especially the theorists of the Frankfurt School, adopted a negative vision of nature. This vision is not to be confused with the classic ethos of entrepreneurial capitalism, which eyed nature only as stuff to be exploited and subdued. Rather nature, even before and outside of human exploitation, was racked by violence and pain. Nature mutely testified to ceaseless horror, perpetual cycles of silent suffering. "Nature" and "natural" lost their benign and innocent quality; the natural in nature was also violent and unnatural. Big fish eat little fish, although, Marcuse noted dryly, "it may not seem natural to the little fish."[1] History harbored a hope to escape from the eternal repetition of nature and even, in its most utopian formulations, to liberate nature. "The creatures too, must become free," said Marx citing Thomas Münzer.[2]

Unnoticed by the scientific Marxists, the negative vision of nature informed Marx and Engels's ideas of the "natural" laws of capitalism. They derided the myth of a serene and happy nature; instead "open warfare" and the "bitterest competition" suffused nature.[3] The laws of nature reflected its unfreedom, the dominion of perpetual repetition. What Marx wrote of his own method – it examined social movements as processes of "natural history" – derived from this interpretation of nature.[4] History could be treated as natural, subjugated to natural laws, exactly to the degree that it was unfree and repetitious. The laws of history were tokens of the absence of freedom and consciousness. Engels wrote that the natural laws of capitalism were "based on the unconsciousness of the participants."[5]

The earliest writings of the Frankfurt School reexamined the relationship of history and nature. Marcuse noted in 1930 that the posthumous publication of *The Dialectics of Nature* justified Lukács's polemic against Engels, because Engels's book clearly demonstrated the superficiality of a dialectic of nature. If Marcuse subscribed to Lukács's formulations on the "duality" of nature,[6] Adorno challenged the conventional antithesis of nature and history. Critical thought surmounted this antithesis, Adorno wrote in "The Idea of Natural History" (1932), and examined the interpenetration of nature and history. "Historical being" must be pursued to the point where it devolves into nature. Conversely, where nature seems most natural, most completely itself, its historical dynamic must be disclosed. To execute this project, Adorno retrieved the concept of second nature.[7]

The concept of second nature recurred throughout the writings of the Frankfurt School. According to Horkheimer, it originated in Democritus, who protested Aristotle's belief that the qualification to rule or serve was determined at birth, by nature. Democritus argued that the qualification was informed by education, which constituted a "second-nature."[8] Although the concept was known to Hegel and other thinkers, it assumed a decisive importance for Lukács. Second nature encompassed the social world of the bourgeoisie, a "rigid and strange" universe, "the charnel-house of long-dead interiorities."[9]

Second nature expressed and compressed the paradox of capitalism, which decimated the "natural" relations of feudalism to fabricate new "natural" relations.[10] The bourgeoisie fought under the banner of natural rights and laws. The belief that private property and capitalism itself accorded with nature served as a powerful weapon. The illusion of its natural arrangement ordained capitalism for perpetuity.

Second nature was not biology but history that congealed into nature; it congealed because it was imprisoned in the dungeons of repetition. Second nature signified the dialectic of history, which was not a dialectic but a dynamic of ineluctable cycles. The vocabulary of "natural laws" in Marx bespoke more accurately a vocabulary of second nature. Insofar as determinism and necessity dominated history and nature, the laws of nature and history converged; they registered the lack of choice. To the point that there were natural laws of history, history was unliberated, a second nature. "Society is irrational," wrote Marcuse, "precisely in that it is governed by natural laws."[11]

Yet the distinction between first and second nature cannot be lost. The Western Marxists did not soften their opposition to a dialectic of nature; this dialectic obliterated the differences between nature and history. Second nature as frozen history was still a product of humanity, whereas nature was not. The blind and fateful laws of history were ultimately grounded in human institutions. This was the difference, as Marx noted, between the "work" of a bee and the work of a man; the latter included conscious purpose.[12]

History was and was not natural. It was historical because it was made by men and women who consciously and freely controlled their actions. It was natural because it was still enacted unconsciously; it still participated in recurring cycles of suffering that were intrinsic to nature but extrinsic to history. "The natural laws of history," wrote Adorno, "are ideology so far as they are hypostatized as unchangeable givens of nature. But they are real as the law of movement of the unconscious society."[13]

The idea of the unconscious society was familiar to Lukács, but in *History and Class Consciousness* it was closely associated with reification. Reification was a form of unconsciousness, a form specific to capitalism. The capitalist commodity structured the consciousness of society by burying the human and historical relations under neutral and quantitative relations: This was the primal bourgeois myth that repelled insight. The activity of labor appeared as an exchange of equilavencies. Yet to speak of reification was also to speak of class consciousness. The power of Lukács's analysis rested not simply on charting the parameters of reification but in plotting its dissolution by a class-conscious proletariat.

The concept of second nature did not replace reification, but the Frankfurt School's preference for it incorporated several decades of historical experience. Between *History and Class Consciousness* (1923) and Adorno and Horkheimer's *The Dialectic of Enlightenment* (1947) lay too many cemeteries. Second nature recorded the defeats and the doubts; it testified to an unfreedom that preceded, and perhaps survived, capitalism. Nor did second nature, like reification, infer the imminence of class consciousness. In an abridged formulation, reification was the unconsciousness specific to capitalism, or reification was the capitalist form of second nature. Second nature was the form of unconsciousness of an unliberated humanity.

II

To shift from reification to second nature, from class consciousness to class unconsciousness, threatens the concreteness of Marxism. History may be bartered for abstractions. Yet abstractions are not inevitably neutral and blank. Marx incisively demonstrated the opposite. The effacement of diversity is not natural; it testifies to historical violence. The loss of specificity is specific to advanced societies. "The most general abstractions arise only in the midst of the richest possible concrete development, when one thing appears common to many, to all."[14]

Class unconsciousness is not simply class unconsciousness; it is the ingredient and product of historical forces and institutions. It requires a theory that goes beyond its borders. Class unconsciousness cannot simply be explained by itself, by its own internal logic or illogic, as if classes lacked insight because of the absence of consciousness. To remain locked within its borders is to ignore that class consciousness refers to a class and that class refers, finally, to men and women enmeshed in social relations.

The fact of class unconsciousness is not new to Marxists. In the 1890s the emergence of revisionism and reformism within Marxist parties challenged theorists of various stripes. Visible and invisible reformism jettisoned the revolutionary vocabulary and goals of Marxism for incremental changes. For contemporary observers, Marxists and non-Marxists, the task was not simply to refute revisionism but to explain its diffusion.

The term "class unconsciousness" was not adopted, but the theorists grappled with a similar problem: to explain why (sectors of) the working class did not gravitate toward revolution but toward reformism, jingoism, and militarism. Observers sought an explanation not of the formation but of the siphoning off of class consciousness. The German Social Democrats (SPD), by far the largest Marxist party, expressed the tendencies of reformism most dramatically and often served as the locus of examination.

The explanations of a broad reformism in the SPD covered the spectrum from its class composition to its psychological character.[15] Those outside, or against, the dominant Marxist parties frequently advanced the most compelling hypotheses; those inside tended to discount the phenomenon, attributing it to marginal factors. Although these theories cannot be accepted almost a century later, no reformulation of class unconsciousness can afford to ignore them.

Little agreement existed on reformism. The facts were clear, but the first conceptual step prompted disputes. How did one measure revolutionary class consciousness or its absence? Did its public spokesmen represent more profound invisible sentiments? or nothing more than themselves? How did one evaluate (massive) votes for the Marxists? or the party itself in relation to the class? Did reformism of the former imply reformism of the latter? Did the social composition of the party differ from the class? If so, did it matter?

To many French and Italian observers, reformism seemed exclusively rooted in the German party and character. Charles Andler, who had previously announced the "decomposition" of Marxism, charged in 1912 that the German party, in surrendering to "colonialism, militarism, perhaps capitalism,"[16] was imperialist by instinct. Others aired similar suspicions. The Dutch anarchist Ferdinand Nieuwenhuis raised the specter of the "Germanization" of the working-class movement in his *Socialism in Danger* (1897). He characterized German socialism as authoritarian and bureaucratic.[17] Robert Michels, the greatest observer and critic of German socialism, agreed that the "Germany hegemony of international socialism" threatened to spread "verbal radicalism" and factual opportunism.[18]

If ignored by orthodox Marxists, the anarchist critiques of the German Social Democrats were often prescient. Nieuwenhuis discerned the discipline and slavishness that infused the Social Democrats. Conceding that discipline was necessary, he noted that at a certain point it vitiated autonomy and independence.[19] Moreover, the party organization itself created a layer of dependents less interested in revolution than job security, an idea Michels later expanded upon.[20]

The Polish revolutionary Jan W. Machajski advanced a provocative "critique of Marxism on Marxist grounds."[21] For Machajski, European Social Democracy was composed of a new "class" of "intellectual workers." This "class" was less committed to transferring the wealth of capitalism to the proletariat than intensifying capitalist development. Machajski discerned the ethos of industrialism that imbued Marxism, eclipsing a revolutionary consciousness. "Marxist doctrine preaches class struggle only against a handful of plutocrats" but harbors "the most sentimental affection" for the progress of bourgeois society. Marxists fetishize productivity in the name of science in order to justify their own "class" position.[22]

That the Social Democrats allowed or encouraged bourgeois adherents offered an explanation for the weakening of class consciousness and the growth of revisionism. This line of analysis was pursued by both anarchists and conservative sociologists. An internal opposition (*Die Jungen*) to the SPD mounted this critique; they argued that the party had been "de-proletarianized" by an influx of petty-bourgeois elements that controlled the leadership.[23] Some sociologists drew similar conclusions from the massive votes for the SPD; they attributed the votes not simply to the proletariat but to the bourgeoisie voting for the working-class party, which was no longer the party of the working class.[24]

The two most forceful and coherent statements approached reformism from opposite directions. According to the theory of the "aristocracy of labor," a segment of the working class, by virtue of high wages, lost interest in revolution and gravitated toward opportunism. In one form or another, this theory entered the lexicon of orthodox Marxism, providing a materialist explanation of persistent reformism.[25] The other approach delved less into the composition of the class than into the composition of the proletarian party; it argued that as the party of the proletariat swelled into a bureacracy it smothered revolutionary consciousness.

Engels informally employed the theory of labor aristocracy to explain the passivity of the English working class. Later Lenin's *Imperialism* approved it for orthodox Marxism. The "super profits" of imperialism allowed some countries to bribe and corrupt a segment of the working class by high wages; opportunism and revisionism were rooted in this economic reality.[26] More recently Arghiri Emmanuel enlarged the theory to include the entire working class of the advanced capitalist countries:

> To explain a historical fact that has endured for nearly a century by the corruption of the leaders and the deception of the masses is, to say the least, hardly in conformity with the method of historical materialism . . . It is not the conservatism of the leaders that has held back the revolutionary elan of the masses . . . it is the slow but steady growth in awareness by the masses that they belong to privileged exploiting nations.[27]

The attraction of the theory of labor aristocracy resides in its dissatisfaction with ad hoc explanations of reformism. It insists on the basic economic relations; yet this insistence is also a weakness. The theory corrodes into economic reductionism, already visible in Emmanuel's analysis. The concept is distended until it loses coherence. The absence of class consciousness is a flat economic fact.

The inadequacy of a theory of labor aristocracy is evinced by its counter-logic; it implicitly postulates that nonaristocratic working class is revolutionary. The labor aristocracy theory is inextricably linked to its opposite, the theory of immiseration. Despite (and because of) all discussions on the subject, it is difficult to maintain that a (relatively or absolutely) impoverished working class is automatically revolutionary.[28] Insofar as the labor aristocracy/immiserations theories translate bald economic relations directly into class consciousness (or its absence) they remove a linchpin of Western Marxism and return to orthodoxy.

Michels in *Political Parties* offered an incomparable phenomenology of reformism in the SPD.[29] To be sure, he was finally less interested in the Marxist parties than in a general theory of organization; the former was simply proof and example of the latter. Nonetheless, his texts remain suggestive – and ignored by Marxists. The tendency was to judge him instantly obsolete or applicable only to competing parties. In 1928 Lukács reviewed the second edition of *Political Parties*. He tried to write off Michels as only applicable to the SPD. Michels did not illuminate the dissipation of class consciousness; rather he was both a victim and expression of Social Democratic revisionism. The theory of labor aristocracy served to refute Michels. He "wants to give a general sociology of party life and he gives at best a descriptive presentation of the development of opportunism in Social Democracy in the imperialist period under the influence of the rise and growth of the aristocracy of labor." Lukács judged severely: Michels was "worthless."[30]

Yet Michels may have the last word. The histories of the Communist parties, in and out of power, do not simply refute Michels. "The struggle carried on by the socialists against the parties of the dominant classes," announced Michels, "is no longer one of principle, but simply one of competition. The revolutionary party has become a rival of the bourgeois parties for the conquest of power." The international labor movement, "increasingly inert as the strength of its organization grows," "loses its revolutionary impetus"; it becomes "sluggish, not in respect of action alone, but also in the sphere of thought."

According to Michels, the revolutionary organization, "ever greedy for new members," fattens from the means into the goal. The qualities initially required to facilitate the revolution – subordination, cooperation, discretion, propriety of conduct – serve to consolidate the organization. Yet Michels did not simply provide a justification for the renunciation of revolution. The physiognomy of explicit reformism did not escape his eye. In a telling phrase he labeled reformism "the socialism of non-socialists with a socialist past."[31]

III

A theory of class unconsciousness remains unwritten and is perhaps unwritable; it may circumscribe too many historical experiences and disconnected situations. Yet to lose the phenomenon by a series of discrete explanations sabotages a critical Marxism. The absence of class consciousness is explained away by working-class aristocracy, nationalism, racism, and so on. These partial explanations may be akin to pre-Copernican astronomy: each new sighting is fit into an essentially false map by adding circles. The point, however, is to reconceive the entire endeavor.

In recent years efforts have been renewed to rethink the weakness, absence, or quiescence of class consciousness. Theories of mass culture, advertising, affluence, and legitimization – to name just several – have taken their place beside older approaches of labor aristocracy, nationalism, and racism.[32] That they remain partial does not mean they are inaccurate, nor that they suffice. Non-Marxists tend to multiply the factors until the phenomenon dissipates in a cloud of graphs and charts; and Marxists veer between ad hoc explanations that write off the reality and a reductionism that tags behind it.

The identification of class consciousness with success, and its absence with defeat, has not lost its allure; it has encouraged the imitation of successful political struggles. Yet a defeat is not identical to the absence of class consciousness; nor is a silent class necessarily an unconscious one. The gun and the rack are tried-and-true means to quiet an unruly class: This should not be minimized. Crowded prisons and morgues from South Africa to Paraguay testify that this remains a favorite tool of authoritarian power.

Nevertheless, the power of society passes beyond deadly violence; it dwells within social and human relations. An obedient class eyes not only the security police but its social security and health benefits. Acceptance and political withdrawal may not only be encouraged and commanded but also inbred, a second nature. If tomorrow the economic order disintegrates, the revolutionary class may rally to the reaction. The myth that the proletariat is simply biding its time, that despite all appearances it is revolutionary in heart and mind, has drugged Marxists for too long.

The mystique of success generates the fiction of defeat. Setbacks and losses are chalked off as unreal or momentary. The absence of class consciousness is a ploy, an illusion of bourgeois commentators or the excuse of rootless intellectuals; or it is ascribed to a combination of factors that cannot endure. The orthodoxy is preserved by belittling the phenomenon, deferring to the myth of a steadily growing class-conscious proletariat.

Endless studies on income level and positions in the class structure participate in this myth. The boldest Hegelians would be shamed by the

Marxists arguing that the proletariat has enlarged as an economic reality but (momentarily) shrunk as a political presence. The complete disjunction between the economic reality and the political appearance cannot be sustained interminably; at a certain point, the absence of a political and class consciousness forces a reconsideration of its economic and extraeconomic sources. Class unconsciousness cannot be explained simply by false consciousness or by a fatter paycheck. The dialectic trick is to keep everything in view. A one-eyed theory of class unconsciousness is still half blind.

A final and significant objection: A theory of class unconsciousness simply reverses all the bad Hegelianism of Lukács. Theories of class unconsciousness or consciousness are remnants of a Hegelianism that cannot be proved; neither classes nor groups attain consciousness. A valid social theory must simply dispense with the idea of historical consciousness or unconsciousness.

There is no convincing response to this objection; logic is threadbare here. Instances can be matched against counter-instances; and doubtlessly the cases of decisive class consciousness are as frequent as the happy pages of history. The argument does not rest on frequency, however; a single instance suffices. It rests on a theory of the historical process. Even the darkest theories of class unconsciousness are grounded in an idea of humanity creating itself: no longer victim but subject of history. In the recesses of the blackest pessimism pulsates a secret optimism.

Journal abbreviations used in notes

AfSz	*Archiv für Sozialwissenschaft und Sozialpolitik*
BGDA	*Bibliographie zur Geschichte der deutschen Arbeiterbewegung*
CJPST	*Canadian Journal of Political and Social Theory*
GCFI	*Giornale Critico dello Filosofia Italiana*
IRSH	*International Review of Social History*
IWK	*Internationale wissenschaftliche Korrespondenz zur Geschichte der deutschen Arbeiterbewegung*
J. Cont. H.	*Journal of Contemporary History*
MOS	*Movimento Operai e Socialista*
RSC	*Rivista di Storia Contemporanea*
VfZ	*Vierteljahrsheft für Zeitgeschichte*

Notes

Introduction

1 K. Marx, *Theories of Surplus Value*, Part 1 (Moscow, 1969), p. 387.
2 See Bernie Fels, "The Academy and Its Discontents," *Telos*, 40 (Summer, 1979), pp. 173–176.
3 See the incisive essay by Hans Magnus Enzensberger, "Tourists of the Revolution," *The Consciousness Industry* (New York, 1974).
4 Victor Serge, *Memoirs of a Revolutionary 1901–1941* (Oxford, 1978), p. 367.
5 F. Engels, *The Peasant War in Germany* (Moscow, 1956), p. 138.
6 Fernando Claudin, *The Communist Movement from Comintern to Cominform* (Harmondsworth, 1975), pp. 36–40.
7 I have dealt with some of the economic–political issues in "The Politics of the Crisis Theory," *Telos*, 23 (Spring, 1975), pp. 3–52.
8 Perry Anderson, *Considerations on Western Marxism* (London, 1976).
9 *Social Amnesia: A Critique of Conformist Psychology from Adler to Laing* (Boston, 1975).

1. Conformist Marxism

1 Georg Lukács, "What Is Orthodox Marxism?" *Political Writings 1919–1929* (London, 1972), pp. 27, 26.
2 Central Committee of the CPSU (B.) 1938, ed., *History of the Communist Party of the Soviet Union (Bolsheviks): Short Course* (Calcutta, 1968), pp. 297–298.
3 Bertram D. Wolfe, "Khrushchev's Secret Report to the Twentieth Congress," *Khrushchev and Stalin's Ghost* (New York, 1957), p. 124.
4 Charles Bettelheim, "Letter of Resignation" and "The Great Leap Backward," *Monthly Review*, XXX/3 (July–August, 1978), pp. 9–13 and 37–

130. See the responses, especially that by Arthur MacEwan, "Comments on China since Mao," *Monthly Review*, XXXI/1 (May, 1979), pp. 44-48.

5 Bettelheim, "The Great Leap Backward," pp. 38, 98.

6 C. Bettelheim, *Cultural Revolution and Industrial Organization in China* (New York, 1974), pp. 9-10. The book "relies heavily on material I gathered during my stay in China in August and September 1971" (p. 7).

7 C. Bettelheim, "Formes et méthodes de la planification socialiste et niveau de développement des forces productives" (1964), *La Transition vers l'économie socialiste* (Paris, 1968), pp. 129-152.

8 Ernesto "Che" Guevara, "La planificación socialista, su significado" (1964), *El socialismo y el hombre nuevo* (Mexico City, 1977), pp. 386-395. A brief summary of "Che's" criticism of Bettelheim can be found in Michael Lowy, *The Marxism of Che Guevara* (New York, 1973).

9 C. Bettelheim, "On the Transition between Capitalism and Socialism," with a reply by Paul Sweezy, *Monthly Review*, XX/10 (March, 1969), pp. 1-19. This text is included in Bettelheim and Sweezy, *On the Transition to Socialism* (New York, 1971).

10 C. Bettelheim, *Class Struggles in the USSR: First Period: 1917-1923* (New York, 1976), pp. 15, 10.

11 For a fine analysis see Ralph Miliband, "Bettelheim and the Soviet Experience," *New Left Review*, 91 (May-June, 1975), pp. 57-66. Cf. Carmen J. Sirianni's review in *Socialist Review*, 36 (Nov.-Dec., 1977), pp. 143-160.

12 For another Bettelheim debate, where he demonstrates his mastery of Althusserian lingo, see "Preface to the French Edition by Charles Bettelheim," in Arghiri Emmanuel, *Unequal Exchange* (New York, 1972), pp. 343-356.

13 Maurice Merleau-Ponty, *Humanism and Terror* (Boston, 1969), p. xxxiii.

14 Gérard Chailland, *Revolution in the Third World* (New York, 1978), pp. 39-50.

15 See Debray's self-critical comments in his *A Critique of Arms*, Vol. 1 (New York, 1977), p. 225.

16 Louis Althusser, *Lenin and Philosophy* (New York, 1971), p. 93.

17 L. Althusser, *Essays in Self-Criticism* (London, 1976), p. 71.

18 L. Althusser and Etienne Balibar, *Reading Capital* (New York, 1970), p. 8.

19 Althusser, *Essays*, p. 68.

20 Ibid., p. 146.

21 Although defenders of the faith maintain that "North American resistance to the work of Althusser is . . . ideological" (Terry Eagleton, response to a review of his *Marxism and Literary Criticism*, in *Clio*, VII [1978], p.

323), Americans, along with the English and French, have written penetrating critiques. In a class by itself is E. P. Thompson's wild and extraordinary *The Poverty of Theory* (London, 1978); this reached me during the final stages of this manuscript, too late to fully consider or utilize. Brian Singer provides a fine discussion in his review of Rancière's *La Leçon d'Althusser* in *Telos*, 25 (Fall, 1975), pp. 224-233. Other critiques include Paul Piccone, "Structuralist Marxism?" *Radical America*, III/5 (Sept., 1969); Richard P. Appelbaum, "Born Again Functionalism? A Reconsideration of Althusser's Structuralism," *Insurgent Sociologist*, IX/1 (Summer, 1979), pp. 18-33; Raymond Aron, *D'une Sainte Familie à l'autre* (Paris, 1969); Pierre Vilar, "Marxist History, a History in the Making: Towards a Dialogue with Althusser," *New Left Review*, 80 (1973), pp. 65-106; Norma Geras, "Althusser's Marxism," *New Left Review*, 71 (1972), pp. 57-86; Alex Callinicos, *Althusser's Marxism* (London, 1976) and the review by Tom Good in *Telos*, 30 (Winter, 1976), pp. 226-230; and Miriam Glucksmann, *Structuralist Analysis in Contemporary Social Thought* (London, 1974).

22 See the chapter "Marxism Is not a Historicism" in Althusser and Balibar, *Reading Capital*, pp. 119-144.

23 From the glossary of *For Marx* (New York, 1970) with "corrections and interpolations" by Althusser, pp. 250, 257.

24 Nicos Poulantzas, *Fascism and Dictatorship* (London, 1974), p. 359. For a good critical appraisal see Anson G. Rabinbach, "Poulantzas and the Problem of Fascism," *New German Critique*, 8 (1976), pp. 157-170. Cf. Martin Plaut, "The Problem of Positivism in the Work of Nicos Poulantzas," *Telos*, 36 (Summer, 1978), pp. 159-167; Salvador Giner and Juan Salcedo, "The Ideological Practice of Nicos Poulantzas," *Archives européennes de sociologie*, XVII (1976), pp. 344-365; Amy Bridges, "Nicos Poulantzas and the Marxist Theory of the State," *Politics and Society*, IV (1974), pp. 161-192; and Simon Clarke, "Marxism, Sociology and Poulantzas' Theory of the State," *Capital and Class*, 2 (Summer, 1977), pp. 1-31.

25 Althusser, *For Marx*, p. 9. Cf. "Note to the English Edition," in Althusser and Balibar, *Reading Capital*, p. 8.

26 Althusser, *Lenin and Philosophy*, p. 189.

27 Althusser, *Essays*, p. 36.

28 K. Marx, *Class Struggles in France 1848-1850* (New York, 1964), p. 33.

29 K. Marx, "Inaugural Address of the International Working Men's Association" (1864), *First International and After*, ed. D. Fernbach (New York, 1974), p. 78.

30 Stanley M. Elkins, *Slavery*, 3rd ed. (Chicago, 1976). (First edition 1959.)

31 Bruno Bettelheim, *The Informed Heart* (New York, 1971); and Hannah Arendt, *Eichmann in Jerusalem* (New York, 1965). It is hardly accidental that these books are themselves theoretically related. Elkins's book leans heavily on the essay that was later incorporated into *The Informed Heart*, Bettelheim's "Individualism and Mass Behavior in Extreme Situations" (1943).

32 See the survey of the literature on the "integration" of the working class in John H. Goldthorpe, D. Lockwood, F. Bechhofer, and J. Platt, *The Affluent Worker in the Class Structure* (Cambridge, 1969), pp. 1–29.

33 For an outsider it is necessary to be intrepid to wade into the vast and passionate debate on slavery. Elkins (and Frank Tannenbaum) have been attacked for years; this is partly due to the utilization or misutilization of Elkins by the Moynihan Report; see Lee Rainwater and William L. Yancey, *The Moynihan Report and the Politics of Controversy* (Cambridge, Mass., 1967). Inasmuch as blacks or the black family were seen as passive victims, the rejoinders emphasized the elements of resistance and autonomous culture. See *The Debate over Slavery: Stanley Elkins and His Critics*, ed. Ann J. Lane (Urbana, Ill., 1971). Herbert G. Gutman's *Black Family in Slavery and Freedom 1750–1925* (New York, 1977) takes as its point of departure the Moynihan Report and is an effective reply, arguing on behalf of a distinct black culture. On these grounds Gutman criticizes Eugene D. Genovese's *Roll, Jordan, Roll: The World the Slaves Made* (New York, 1975) for slighting slave culture (pp. 303–326). Whether Genovese represents, or is made to represent, an opposite position remains a question. George Rawick and Evelyn Brooks Barnett provide two thoughtful, and contrasting, discussions of Gutman's book in "A Symposium on Herbert Gutman's *The Black Family . . .* ," *Radical History Review*, IV/2–3 (Summer–Spring, 1977), pp. 76–101. See also George P. Rawicks's *From Sundown to Sunup* (Westport, Conn., 1973) for an important discussion of the issues, esp. pp. 95–121. One final note here: Elkins is far from finished; his "The Two Arguments on Slavery" (1975) included in the 3rd ed. of *Slavery* is apposite.

34 See Reuben Ainsztein, *Jewish Resistance in Nazi Occupied Eastern Europe* (New York, 1974). Cf. Jacob Robinson, *And the Crooked Shall Be Made Straight: The Eichmann Trial, the Jewish Catastrophe and Hannah Arendt's Narrative* (New York, 1965); and Terrence des Preis, *The Survivor: An Anatomy of Life in the Death Camps* (New York, 1970).

35 The fundamental work, which has inspired many, often lesser, efforts, is E. P. Thompson's *The Making of the English Working Class* (London, 1963).

36 From a burgeoning literature see Sheila Rowbotham, *Women, Resistance and Revolution* (New York, 1972).

37 Perry Anderson, *Lineages of the Absolutist State* (London, 1974), p. 11.

38 Andrei Zhdanov, *Problems of Soviet Literature: Reports and Speeches at the First Soviet Writers' Congress* (1934) (New York, n.d.), p. 20. Cf. Kenneth E. Harper, "Controversy in Soviet Literary Criticism on the Doctrine of Socialist Realism," Ph.D. dissertation, Columbia University, 1950; Eduard J. Brown, *The Proletarian Episode in Russian Literature 1928–1932* (New York, 1953); and Hermann Ermolaev, *Soviet Literary Theories 1917–1934* (Berkeley, Calif., 1963).

39 K. Marx, "Preface to the French Edition," *Capital*, trans. B. Fowkes (New York, 1977), p. 104.

40 One example: Walter Kaufmann, *Hegel: A Reinterpretation* (Garden City, N. Y., 1966), pp. 157–158. The transition from a Hegelian to a positivist science is developed in Herbert Schnädelbach, *Erfahrung, Begründung und Reflexion: Versuch über den Positivismus* (Frankfurt, 1971). See also the classic work of Edmund Husserl, *The Crisis of European Sciences* (Evanston, Ill., 1970).

41 See Paul Thomas, "Marx and Science," *Political Studies*, XXIV (1976), pp. 1–23; and Pier A. Rovatti, *Critica e scientificità in Marx* (Milan, 1975).

42 Marx, *Capital*, p. 161. Marx employs the term "science," not *Wissenschaft*, here: K. Marx, *Kapital*, in Marx/Engels, *Werke*, Vol. 23 (Berlin, 1963), p. 83.

43 K. Marx, *The Poverty of Philosophy* (New York, 1963), p. 126. The term in the original French text is again "science": K. Marx, *Misère de la philosophie* (Paris, 1964), p. 433.

44 K. Marx, "Conspectus of Bakunin's *Statism and Anarchy*," *First International and After*, p. 337.

45 K. Marx, "Konspekt," in Marx/Engels, *Werke*, Vol. 18 (Berlin, 1969), pp. 635–636.

46 The term "positivism" poses many problems; some restrict positivism to Comte and his direct followers. See W. M. Simon, *European Positivism in the Nineteenth Century* (Ithaca, N.Y., 1963), p. 3. Yet the Vienna Circle, with few or no links to Comte, adopted the term "logical positivism." See A. J. Ayer, "Introduction," in *Logical Positivism*, ed. A. J. Ayer (New York, 1959); and, in the same volume, Moritz Schlick, "Positivism and Realism." Cf. Gustav Bergmann, *The Metaphysics of Logical Positivism* (Madison, Wisc., 1967), pp. 1–16. Others, such as Popper, who might be situated within the history of positivism, reject the term; see his "Reason

or Revolution?" in T. W. Adorno et al., *The Positivist Dispute in German Sociology*, trans. Glyn Adey and David Frisby (London, 1976), pp. 288–300. Yet what Popper himself presents as the substance of his agreement with the Vienna Circle suffices to include him within the currents of positivism. "I still feel very much at one with the Vienna Circle"; and he mentions in particular the distinction Carnap drew between "the way in which mathematicians and scientists proceed" and the "depressing ways of the philosopher" (K. Popper, *Unended Quest* [La Salle, Ill., 1976], p. 89). This confirms Albrecht Wellmer: "Popper's criterion features the tendency proper to the positivist theory of science: that is, the intention to make scientific empiricism the unique, consciously applied law of scientific research" (A. Wellmer, *Critical Theory of Society* [New York, 1971], p. 19). In general I follow Leszek Kolakowski's definition: "Positivism is a collection of prohibitions concerning human knowledge, intended to confine the name of 'knowledge' (or 'science') to those operations that are observable in the evolution of the modern sciences of nature" (L. Kolakowski, *The Alienation of Reason: A History of Positivist Thought* [Garden City, N.Y., 1961], p. 9). Compare this with: "One of the tenets of positivism is *methodological monism,* or the idea of the unity of scientific method . . . A second tenet is the view that the exact natural sciences, in particular mathematical physics, set a methodological ideal or standard which measures the degree of development and perfection of all other sciences, including the humanities" (Georg Henrik von Wright, *Explanation and Understanding* [Ithaca, N.Y., 1971], p. 4). Cf. the discussion in D. G. Charlton, *Positivist Thought in France during the Second Empire 1852–1870* (London, 1959).

47 Gertrud Lenzer, ed., *Auguste Comte and Positivism* (New York, 1975), pp. 65, 75. On Comte see Otwin Massing, *Fortschritt und Gegenrevolution: Die Gesellschaftslehre Comtes in ihrer sozialen Funktion* (Stuttgart, 1966); and Oskar Negt, *Strukturbeziehungen zwischen den Gesellschaftslehren Comtes und Hegels* (Frankfurt, 1964).

48 Hans Hahn, Otto Neurath, and Rudolf Carnap, "The Scientific Conception of the World: The Vienna Circle" (1929), in Otto Neurath, *Empiricism and Sociology* (Dordrecht, 1973), pp. 309, 306.

49 K. Marx, *The 18th Brumaire of Louis Bonaparte* (New York, 1963), p. 15.

50 Marx, *Capital,* p. 493.

51 Hahn, Neurath, and Carnap, "The Scientific Conception," pp. 306, 309–310.

52 The Hegel literature is vast. See James Schmidt, "Recent Hegel Literature," *Telos,* 46 (Winter, 1980–1981), pp. 113–147. Some helpful works

are: Hans Radermacher, "Hegel und der Positivismus," in *Aktualität und Folgen der Philosophie Hegels*, ed. O. Negt (Frankfurt, 1970); Theodore Litt, *Hegel* (Heidelberg, 1953); José M. Ripalda, *The Divided Nation: The Roots of a Bourgeois Thinker: G. W. F. Hegel* (Assen, 1977); Otto Pöggler, *Hegels Idee einer Phänomenologie des Geist* (Munich, 1973); Andries Sarlemign, *Hegel's Dialectic* (Dordrecht, 1975); Wolfgang Bonsiepen, *Der Begriff der Negativität in den Jenaer Schriften Hegels* (Bonn, 1977).

53 W. Kaufmann, ed., *Hegel: Texts and Commentary* (Garden City, N.Y., 1966), p. 60.

54 W. Wallace, trans., *Logic of Hegel* (London, 1963), p. 304.

55 Ibid., p. 187.

56 Kaufmann, ed., *Hegel: Texts and Commentary*, p. 58.

57 Wallace, trans., *Logic of Hegel*, p. 55.

58 Popper, *Unended Quest*, pp. 115–116.

59 K. Popper, *The Open Society and Its Enemies*, Vol. 2 (New York, 1967), pp. 32–33. The quotation is from Schopenhauer.

60 Joseph Stalin, *Dialectical and Historical Materialism* (New York, 1940).

61 V. I. Lenin, *Collected Works*, Vol. 38, *Conspectus of Hegel's Book "The Science of Logic"* (Moscow, 1963), p. 180. See the discussion in Raya Dunayevskaya, *Philosophy and Revolution* (New York, 1973), pp. 95–120.

62 Althusser, *Essays*, p. 116.

63 See generally "Marxism Is Not a Historicism," in Althusser and Balibar, *Reading Capital*, pp. 119–144.

64 Althusser, "Introduction" (1965), *For Marx*, p. 35.

65 Althusser, "Preface to *Capital*" (1969), *Lenin and Philosophy*, p. 93.

66 Ibid., pp. 103, 95. "A Hegelian-evolutionist conception . . . disappears 99 per cent in *Capital*" (p. 103).

67 Ibid., pp. 95, 94.

68 K. Marx, "Montesquieu LVI," *Neue Rheinische Zeitung* (January 21, 1849), in Marx/Engels, *Collected Works*, Vol. 8 (New York, 1977), p. 266.

69 For a critique of Soviet accounts see Boris Nicolaievsky, "Towards a History of the Communist League 1847–1852," *IRSH*, I (1956), pp. 234–253.

70 Marx's actions and politics in regard to the Cologne working-class movement and the Communist League have been subject to much controversy. Part of the dispute concerns the authenticity of a deposition made by Peter Röser, president of the Cologne Association of Workers. He reported, "Both Marx and Schapper . . . are opponents or even enemies as soon as it comes to the methods by which communism is to be attained.

The supporters of Schapper and Willich want communism introduced at the present stage of development, if necessary by force of arms... To Marx, communism is possible only as a result of an advance in education and general development; in one of his letters he addressed to us he distinguished four phases through which it will be necessary to pass before it is achieved" (B. Nicolaievsky and Otto Maenchen-Helfen, *Karl Marx* [Harmondsworth, 1976], p. 416). The full text of Röser, and further discussion, can be found in Werner Blumenberg, "Zur Geschichte des Bundes der Kommunisten: Die Aussagen des Peter Gehardt Röser," *IRSH*, IX (1964), pp. 81–122. Cf. Fritz Brügel, "Zur Geschichte des Kölner Arbeitervereins," *Die Gesellschaft*, VII (1930), pp. 112–116. That this was Marx's position, if not his words, is confirmed by the minutes of the meeting of the League in 1850. In an oft-cited passage, Marx attacked Willich and Schapper: "While we say to the worker: you must pass through 15, 20, 50 years of civil war in order to change the relations, in order to make yourself capable of power, you say instead: We must *immediately* come to power or, we can stay asleep" ("Sitzung der Zentralbehörde vom 15. September 1850," in Marx/Engels, *Werke*, Vol. 8, p. 598). Cf. Nicolaievsky and Maenchen-Helfen, *Karl Marx*, p. 231. On Willich, see Loyd D. Easton, *Hegel's First American Followers* (Athens, Ohio, 1966), pp. 159–203.

71 Cited in Hans Stein, *Der Kölner Arbeiterverein (1848–1849)* (Cologne, 1921), p. 97. On Gottschalk see Ernst Czóbel, "Zur Geschichte des Kommunistenbundes," *Grünberg Archiv*, XI (1925), pp. 299–335; David McLellan, *Karl Marx* (New York, 1977), pp. 195–197; Edmund Silberner, *Moses Hess: Geschichtes seines Lebens* (Leiden, 1966), pp. 283–286; and P. H. Noyes, *Organization and Revolution: Working Class Associations in the German Revolutions of 1848–1849* (Princeton, N.J., 1966). The "we" in the quotation is misleading: Gottschalk was a doctor. For a careful reconstruction of the events and issues, see Hal Draper, *Karl Marx's Theory of Revolution*, Vol. 2, *Politics and Social Class* (New York, 1978).

72 K. Marx, "The Future Results of British Rule in India" (1853), in *Karl Marx on Colonialism and Modernization*, ed. S. Avineri (Garden City, N.Y., 1969), pp. 132–139.

73 Marx, *Capital*, pp. 617, 618.

74 V. I. Lenin, *Collected Works*, Vol. 3, *The Development of Capitalism in Russia* (Moscow, 1964), p. 596.

75 Bulgakov, as cited in Arthur P. Mendel, *Dilemmas of Progress in Tsarist Russia: Legal Marxism and Legal Populism* (Cambridge, Mass., 1961), p. 140.

76 Struve, as cited in Shmuel Galai, *The Liberation Movement in Russia 1900–1905* (Cambridge, 1973), p. 85. Cf. Richard Kindersley, *The First Russian Revisionists: A Study of Legal Marxism in Russia* (Oxford, 1962); Richard Pipes, *Struve: Liberal on the Left 1870–1905* (Cambridge, Mass., 1970) and his Introduction to P. von Struve, "La Théorie marxienne de l'évolution sociale," *Etudes de marxologie*, VI (1962), pp. 105 ff.; Bastiann Wielenga, *Lenins Weg zur Revolution: Eine Konfrontation mit Sergej Bulgakov und Petr Struve im Interesse einer theologischen Besinnung* (Munich, 1971); Solomon M. Schwarz, "Populism and Early Russian Marxism on Ways of Economic Development of Russia," in *Continuity and Change in Russian and Soviet Thought*, ed. E. J. Simmons (Cambridge, Mass., 1955); and Andrzej Walicki, *The Controversy over Capitalism* (London, 1969).

77 The text is included in Hélène Carrère d'Encausse and S. R. Schram, eds., *Marxism and Asia* (London, 1969), p. 126. Cf. Georges Haupt and M. Reberioux, eds., *La Deuxième Internationale et l'orient* (Paris, 1967), esp. pp. 79–94. For a summary of the debate on colonialism at Stuttgart (1907) see Julius Braunthal, *History of the International*, Vol. 1, *1864–1914* (New York, 1967), pp. 318–319. For a good discussion of the issues see Horace B. Davis, *Nationalism and Socialism* (New York, 1973). Davis attacks Abraham Ascher's "Imperialists within German Social Democracy prior to 1914," *Journal of Central European Affairs*, XX (1961), pp. 397–422. Cf. Max Victor, "Die Stellung der deutschen Sozialdemokratie zu den Fragen der auswärtigen Politik (1869–1914)," *AfSz*, 60 (1928), esp. pp. 147–179.

78 Marx, *Capital*, pp. 476–478.

79 Recently attempts have been made to retrieve Marx's critique of technology and the division of labor. See Harry Braverman, *Labor and Monopoly Capital* (New York, 1974); and my review, which elaborates some of the remarks in these pages, in *Telos*, 29 (Fall, 1976), pp. 199–207. See also David F. Noble, *America by Design: Science, Technology and the Rise of Corporate Capitalism* (New York, 1977). Herbert Marcuse has made a celebrated interpretation of technology specific to capitalism; see William Leiss, "Technological Rationality: Marcuse and His Critics," *The Domination of Nature* (New York, 1972), pp. 199–212.

80 Lenin, "The Taylor System – Man's Enslavement by the Machine," in *Collected Works*, Vol. 20, p. 153.

81 V. Lenin, "The Immediate Tasks of the Soviet Government," *Selected Works in Three Volumes*, Vol. 2 (Moscow, 1970), p. 663. See Ulysses Santamaria and Alain Manville, "Lenin and the Problem of the Transition," *Telos*, 27 (Spring, 1976), pp. 79–96; Rainer Traub, "Lenin and

Taylor," *Telos,* 37 (Fall, 1978), pp. 82–92; Kendall E. Bailes, "Alexei Gastev and the Soviet Controversy over Taylorism, 1918–24," *Soviet Studies,* XXIX/3 (July, 1977), pp. 373–394; F. J. Fleron and L. J. Fleron, "Administrative Theory as Repressive Political Theory: The Communist Experience," *Telos,* 12 (Summer, 1972), pp. 63–92; and F. J. Fleron, ed., *Technology and Communist Culture* (New York, 1977).

82 J. Stalin, "The Foundations of Leninism," in *The Essential Stalin,* ed. B. Franklin (Garden City, N. Y., 1972), p. 186. According to Robert Tucker, Bukharin originated this formulation (R. Tucker, *Stalin as Revolutionary 1879–1929* [New York, 1973], p. 318).

83 For the wider impact of Taylorism see Charles S. Maier, "Between Taylorism and Technocracy: European Ideologies and the Vision of Industrial Productivity," *J. Cont. H.,* V (1970), pp. 27–62. Cf. Paul Devinat, *Scientific Management in Europe* (Geneva, 1927).

84 Some years ago Andre G. Frank sparked a debate reexamining the terms and realities of development and underdevelopment; see especially "The Development of Underdevelopment" and "Sociology of Development," in his *Latin America: Underdevelopment or Revolution* (New York, 1969), pp. 3–94. Later contributions include Immanuel Wallerstein, ed., *World Inequality* (Montreal, 1975); Arghiri Emmanuel, *Unequal Exchange* (New York, 1972); and Samir Amin, *Accumulation on a World Scale,* 2 vols. (New York, 1974).

85 Marx, *Capital,* p. 91.

86 For a survey see David S. Landes, *The Unbound Prometheus: Technological Change and Industrial Development in Western Europe from 1750 to the Present* (Cambridge, 1972), pp. 242–358.

87 Cited in and see Wolfgang Mommsen, *Max Weber und die deutsche Politik 1890–1920,* 2nd ed. (Tübingen, 1974), pp. 114–115. Cf. W. Mommsen, *Max Weber: Gesellschaft, Politik und Geschichte* (Frankfurt, 1974).

88 Max Weber, in *Schriften des Vereins für Sozialpolitik,* Vol. 125, *Verhandlungen der Generalversammlung in Magedburg, 1907* (Leipzig, 1908), pp. 298–300. Cf. Dieter Lindenlaub, *Richtungskämpfe im Verein für Sozialpolitik,* Vol. II (Wiesbaden, 1967).

89 Oswald Spengler, *The Decline of the West,* one-volume edition (London, 1959), Vol. 2, pp. 460–463.

90 Ivan Illich, *Medical Nemesis: The Expropriation of Health* (London, 1975).

91 O. Spengler, "Prussianism and Socialism," in *Selected Essays,* ed. D. O. White (Chicago, 1967), pp. 95, 99, 100. This position contrasting Prussian to English socialism was not unique to Spengler; it reached back to Fichte

and forward to Sombart; see Werner Sombart, *Deutscher Sozialismus* (Berlin, 1934), which juxtaposes German to proletarian socialism; the latter is the theory of Marx and industrialization. Cf. Ernst Stutz, *Oswald Spengler als politischer Denker* (Bern, 1958), which locates Spengler within a twentieth-century "conservative revolution." For predecessors see Hans J. Schoeps, *Vorläufer Spenglers* (Leiden, 1955). Cf. Anton M. Koktanek, *Oswald Spengler in seiner Zeit* (Munich, 1968).

92 See my "A Falling Rate of Intelligence?" *Telos*, 27 (Spring, 1976), pp. 141–146.

93 Marx, *Capital*, p. 769.

94 "We have tried on the one hand to refrain from all system-making and all barack-room communism" ("A Circular of the First Congress of the Communist League to the League Members, June 9, 1847," in Marx/Engels, *Collected Works*, Vol. 6 [New York, 1976], p. 598). Although Marx and Engels did not write this, it was probably written under Engels's supervision, and it referred to his "Draft of a Communist Confession of Faith," in *Collected Works*, VI, pp. 96–103. See also Marx's denunciation of "baracks-communism" in "Ein Komplott gegen die IAA," in Marx/Engels, *Werke*, Vol. 18, p. 425.

95 K. Marx, "Critique of Hegel's Philosophy of Right: Introduction," in *Early Writings*, ed. Q. Hoare (New York, 1975), p. 244.

96 William Morris, "Communism," *Prose, Verse, Lectures and Essays*, ed. G. D. H. Cole (London, 1948), pp. 660–661.

97 William Morris, "The Worker's Share of Art," *Selected Writings and Designs*, ed. A. Briggs (Harmondsworth, 1962), p. 143. E. P. Thompson in his 1976 Postscript to *William Morris* (London, 1977) puts the issue well: "The Romantic tradition is not to be defined only in terms of its traditional, conservative, 'regressive,' 'escapist' and 'utopian' characteristics – and hence to be seen as a continual undertow threatening to draw Morris back to 'subjectivism' and 'idealism' " (p. 779). Cf. Michael Levin, "Marx and Romanticism," *Political Studies*, XXII (1974), pp. 400–413.

98 See David Gross, "Marxism and Utopia: Ernst Bloch," in *Towards a New Marxism*, ed. B. Grahl and P. Piccone (St. Louis, Mo., 1973), p. 86. Cf. Maynard Solomon, "Marx and Bloch," *Telos*, 13 (Fall, 1972), pp. 68–85; Oskar Negt, "Ernst Bloch – The German Philosopher of the October Revolution," *New German Critique*, 4 (Winter, 1975), pp. 3–16; Jürgen Habermas, "Ernst Bloch – A Marxist Romantic," *Salmagundi*, 10–11 (Fall–Winter, 1969–1970), pp. 311–325; Douglas Kellner and Harry O'Hara, "Utopia and Marxism in Ernst Bloch," *New German Critique*, 9

(Fall, 1976), pp. 11–34; and Helmut Reinicke, *Materie und Revolution: Eine materialistisch-erkenntnistheoretische Untersuchung zur Philosophie Ernst Bloch* (Kronberg Taunus, 1974).

99 E. Block, *Durch die Wüste* (Frankfurt, 1964), p. 35. (First edition 1923.)

100 E. Bloch, *Geist der Utopie* (Frankfurt, 1973), p. 305. (First edition 1918.)

101 André Breton, "Legitimate Defense" (1926), in Breton, *What is Surrealism? Selected Writings*, ed. F. Rosemont (New York, 1978), pp. 39–40. "I really fail to see – some narrow-minded revolutionaries notwithstanding – why we should refrain from supporting the Revolution, provided we view the problems of love, dreams, madness, art and religion from the same angles they do" (Breton, "Second Manifesto of Surrealism," *Manifestoes of Surrealism* [Ann Arbor, Mich., 1972], p. 140). See generally Maurice Nadeau, *The History of Surrealism* (New York, 1965). Cf. Herbert Gershman, *The Surrealist Revolution in France* (Ann Arbor, Mich., 1968), pp. 80–116; J. H. Mathews, *Towards the Poetics of Surrealism* (Syracuse, N.Y., 1976). Robert S. Short provides the conventional interpretation of the incompatibility of surrealism and Marxism "The Politics of Surrealism 1920–1936," in *Left-Wing Intellectuals between the Wars 1919–1939*, ed. W. Laqueur and G. L. Mosse (New York, 1966), pp. 3–26.

102 Gareth S. Jones, "The Marxism of the Early Lukács," *New Left Review*, 70 (Nov.–Dec., 1971), p. 44. Cf. Alvin W. Gouldner, "The Two Marxisms," *For Sociology* (New York, 1973), pp. 425–462. This was expanded into Gouldner's final work, *The Two Marxisms* (New York, 1980), which appeared too late for me to consider. In spirit and argument it is frequently close to this book.

103 J. Henrich von Heiseler, ed., *Die 'Frankfurter Schule' im Lichte des Marxismus* (Frankfurt, 1970), p. 51.

104 Lucio Colletti, *From Rousseau to Lenin* (New York, 1972), pp. 111–140, 233. Colletti himself is sometimes difficult to take seriously: "The only way in which Marxism can be revived is if no more books like [my] *Marxism and Hegel* are published . . ." (L. Colletti, "A Political and Philosophical Interview," *New Left Review*, 86 [July–August, 1974], p. 28).

105 Cited by Reich in his "What Is Class Consciousness?" (1934), in *Sex-Pol: Essays 1929–1934*, ed. L. Baxandall (New York, 1972), p. 350. For other criticisms by the Communists, see "Geschichte der deutschen Sex-Pol-Bewegung," *Zeitschrift für politische Psychologie und Sexualökonomie*, II (1935), pp. 64–70. See also Constantin Sinelnikov, "Early 'Marxist' Critiques of Reich," *Telos*, 13 (Fall, 1972), pp. 131–137.

106 Pierre Naville, *La Révolution et les intellectuels* (Paris, 1927), p. 136.

107 T. W. Adorno et al., *The Positivist Dispute in German Sociology* (London, 1976), pp. 55–56.
108 The charge of infantilism can be found in Engels's rebukes to the "Jungen," opponents of German Social Democratic orthodoxy; see Engels, "Antwort an die Redaktion der Sächsischen Arbeiter-Zeitung" (1890), in Marx/Engels, *Werke*, Vol. 22, pp. 68–70. See Dirk H. Müller, *Idealismus und Revolution: Zur Opposition der Jungen gegen den Sozial-demokratischen Parteivorstand* (Berlin, 1975); and Hans M. Bock, *Geschichte des 'linken Radikalismus' in Deutschland* (Frankfurt, 1976), pp. 24–73.
109 Jones, "The Marxism of the Early Lukács," p. 45.
110 Göran Therborn, "The Frankfurt School," *New Left Review*, 63 (Sept.-Oct., 1970), pp. 95–96.
111 Max Horkheimer, "The Authoritarian State" (1940), in *The Essential Frankfurt School Reader*, ed. A. Arato and E. Gebhardt (New York, 1978), p. 114, and in *Telos*, 15 (Spring, 1973).
112 Mary Douglas, *Natural Symbols* (New York, 1973), p. 100. Cf. her *Purity and Danger* (London, 1978).
113 Balibar, in *Reading Capital*, p. 207. I would have missed this revealing passage without E. P. Thompson's discussion of it in his *Poverty of Theory*, pp. 336–337.

2. The Marxism of Hegel and Engels

1 At least one partial exception, Austro-Marxism, requires a comment. It is a partial exception for two reasons. It is not clear to what extent Austro-Marxism embodied a coherent and unorthodox Marxism; and to the extent that it did, this was as much a result of its roots in German idealism as a whole as of its specific Kantianism. Its distance from II International Marxism is measured by Austro-Marxism's critique of Marxism as a simple materialism; Max Adler did not exempt Engels from criticism (see his *Marxistische Probleme* [Stuttgart, 1919], p. 85). The lack of distance is reflected in Adler's reiteration that dialectics is a method uncontaminated by material antagonisms. See for instance his "Marx und die Dialektik" (1908), reprinted in *Austromarxismus*, ed. H. J. Sandkühler and R. de la Vega (Frankfurt, 1970), pp. 120–139. The weakness of Adler is evinced in his full discussion of Engels in "Engels als Denker" (1920), reprinted in Max Adler, *Marx und Engels als Denker*, ed. T. Meyer (Frankfurt, 1972). See Herbert Marcuse's critique of Adler's Kantianism: "Transzendentaler Marxismus?" *Die Gesellschaft*, VII (1930), pp. 304–326. For a critical discussion see Aldo Zanardo, "Aspetti del socialismo neo-Kantiano in

Germania negli anni della crisi del Marxismo," *Annali Feltrinelli*, III (1960), pp. 169 ff. Cf. Peter Heintel, *System und Ideologie: Der Austromarxismus im Spiegel der Philosophie Max Adlers* (Vienna, 1967). Austro-Marxism is currently enjoying a renaissance. See Sergio Amato, "Otto Bauer and Austro-Marxism," *Telos*, 40 (Summer, 1979), pp. 144–150; the collection *Austro-Marxism*, ed. T. Bottomore and P. Goode (Oxford, 1978); and Raimund Loew, "The Politics of Austro-Marxism," *New Left Review*, 118 (Nov.–Dec., 1979), pp. 15–51.

2 For some examples see Karl G. Ballestrem, *Die sowjetische Erkenntnismetaphysik und ihr Verhältnis zu Hegel* (Dordrecht, 1968). Max Werner designated Soviet Marxism a "renaissance of unrestricted Hegelianism," meaning that it sought a universal science of sciences; see his "Der Sowjetmarxismus," *Die Gesellschaft*, IV (1927), especially pp. 53–54; and Neil McInnes, *The Western Marxists* (London, 1972), pp. 130–150.

3 Joseph Stalin, *Dialectical and Historical Materialism* (New York, 1949), p. 5.

4 Cited in Alexandre Koyré, "Hegel en Russie," *Etudes sur l'histoire de la pensée philosophique en Russie* (Paris, 1950), p. 104.

5 Cited in Edward J. Brown, *Stankevich and His Moscow Circle* (Stanford, Calif., 1966), p. 106.

6 Michael Bakunin, "The Reaction in Germany," in *Russian Philosophy*, Vol. 1, ed. James M. Edie et al. (Chicago, 1965), pp. 403–404. See E. H. Carr, *Michael Bakunin* (New York, 1961), pp. 97–120.

7 Nicolas Berdyaev, *The Russian Idea* (Boston, 1962), pp. 39–40.

8 For a survey see James H. Billington, *The Icon and the Axe: An Interpretative History of Russian Culture* (New York, 1970), pp. 391–433.

9 Chernyshevskii is "half" an exception insofar as he was "half" a Populist. William F. Woehrlin argues in *Chernyshevskii* (Cambridge, Mass., 1971) that Chernyshevskii deviated from the Populists on many issues. See Chernyshevskii's discussion of Hegel in "Essays on the Gogol Period of Russian Literature" in his *Selected Philosophical Essays* (Moscow, 1953). Herzen distanced himself from Hegel to the degree that his disillusion with the West augmented. See Martin Malia, *Alexander Herzen and the Birth of Russian Socialism* (New York, 1965), pp. 378–379. For two rich surveys see Dmitrij Tschizewskij, "Hegel in Russland," in *Hegel bei den Slaven*, ed. D. Tschizewskij (Bad Homburg, 1961); and Boris Jakowenko, *Geschichte des Hegelianismus in Russland*, Vol. 1 (Prague, 1940), esp. pp. 208–259. Tschizewskij contests that the Slavophiles uniformly disregarded or despised Hegel. Obviously this can be overstated. Yet his major examples of Hegelian Slavophiles (K. Aksakov and J. Samarin) both eventually renounced Hegel. See Koyré, "Hegel en Russie," p. 170. Andrzej Walicki

in his *The Slavophile Controversy: History of a Conservative Utopia in Nineteenth-Century Russian Thought* (Oxford, 1975) also affirms that Hegel was nothing more than a brief ally of the Slavophiles: "The Slavophiles were the most serious and also the most consistent opponents of Hegelianism in Russia" (p. 288).

10 Nicolas V. Riasanovsky in *Russia and the West in the Teachings of the Slavophiles: A Study of Romantic Ideology* (Gloucester, Mass., 1965) emphasized the romantic and mystical roots of the Slavophiles; if anything, they turned to the later Schelling, not Hegel. Cf. Peter K. Christoff, *An Introduction to Nineteenth-Century Russian Slavophilism: A. S. Xomjakov* (The Hague, 1961). Christoff disagrees that Schelling was the exclusive source of the first Slavophiles; he also argues, however, that they, like Kireevsky, finally rejected Hegel; see his *An Introduction to Nineteenth-Century Russian Slavophilism: I. V. Kireevsky* (The Hague, 1972).

11 Guy Planty-Bonjour, *Hegel et la pensée philosophique en Russie 1830–1917* (The Hague, 1974), p. 99.

12 I. Dawydow, as cited in Jakowenko, *Geschichte des Hegelianismus in Russland*, p. 217.

13 As Belinsky said, "I will stick to my view: the fate of a subject, an individual, a personality is more important than the fate of the world and the weal of the Chinese emperor (viz., the Hegelian *Allgemeinheit*)" (Belinsky to V. P. Botkin [March 1, 1841], in Vissarrion G. Belinsky, *Selected Philosophical Works* [Moscow, 1956], p. 160). See Edward J. Brown, *Stankevich and His Moscow Circle*, pp. 83–114.

14 See Leonard Schapiro, *Rationalism and Nationalism in Russian Nineteenth Century Thought* (New Haven, Conn., 1967).

15 The populist social thinkers accented the subjective and distinct qualities of Russia that separated it from the West. See Alexander Vucinich, *Social Thought in Tsarist Russia* (Chicago, 1976). The populist sociologists were generally known as the "subjectivist" school. See Julius Hecker, *Russian Sociology* (London, 1934), esp. pp. 75–176. Cf. Richard Wortman, *The Crisis of Russian Populism* (London, 1967).

16 Nicholas Mikhailovsky, "What Is Progress?" in *Russian Philosophy*, Vol. 2, ed. J. M. Edie et al. (Chicago, 1969), p. 186. Cf. James Billington, *Mikhailovsky and Russian Populism* (Oxford, 1958).

17 Cited by Plekhanov in *Selected Philosophical Works*, Vol. 1, *The Development of the Monist View of History* (Moscow, 1974), p. 701.

18 Plekhanov, "For the Sixtieth Anniversary of Hegel's Death," *Selected Philosophical Works*, Vol. 1, pp. 401–426.

19 For the impact on Lenin and others see Samuel H. Baron, *Plekhanov* (Stanford, 1963), pp. 145–148.

20 Plekhanov, "For the Sixtieth Anniversary of Hegel's Death," p. 418.

21 Plekhanov, *The Development of the Monist View*, p. 639.

22 The followers of Peter Struve, the legal Marxist, were known as the "objectivists" (Richard Pipes, *Struve: Liberal on the Left* [Cambridge, Mass., 1970], p. 100). "The elimination of the individual from sociology is only a particular instance of the general tendency towards scientific knowledge" (Struve, as cited in Richard Kindersley, *The First Russian Revisionists: A Study of Legal Marxism in Russia* [Oxford, 1962], p. 113). Cf. Struve's "La Théorie marxienne de l'évolution sociale," *Etudes de marxologie*, VI (1962), pp. 105 ff.

23 See Andrzej Walicki, *The Controversy over Capitalism: Studies in the Social Philosophy of Russian Populists* (London, 1969).

24 "At the core of this method was the distinction Mikhailovsky drew between the study of nature and the study of human society" (Arthur P. Mendel, *Dilemmas of Progress in Tsarist Russia: Legal Marxism and Legal Populism* [Cambridge, Mass., 1961], p. 31).

25 See Friedrich Überweg, *Grundrisse der Geschichte der Philosophie*, Part Four, ed. K. Oesterreich (Berlin, 1916), pp. 281–282. Cf. Willy Moog, *Hegel und die Hegelsche Schule* (1930) (Nendeln, Lichtenstein, 1973); and Heinrich Levy, *Die Hegel-Renaissance in der deutschen Philosophie mit besonderer Berücksichtigung des Neukantianismus* (Leipzig, 1927).

26 Marx, "Postface to the Second Edition" (1873), *Capital*, Vol. 1 (New York, 1977), p. 102.

27 Gustav Mayer commented that the second generation of Marxists, with the exceptions of Labriola and Plekhanov, was educated not in Hegelian thought but in positivism and neo-Kantianism (G. Mayer, *Friedrich Engels: Eine Biographie*, Vol. 2 [The Hague, 1934], p. 448).

28 Poland could also boast a viable Hegelian tradition; see Bronislaw Baczko, "La Gauche et la droite hégéliennes en Pologne dans la première moitié du XIX siècle," *Annali Feltrinelli*, VI (1963), pp. 137–163. Not to be ignored, indeed to be explained, is English Hegelianism, which flowered and disappeared with few lasting consequences, except for Collingwood. See François Houang, *Le Néo-hégélianisme en angleterre* (Paris, 1954); Haralal Haldar, *Neo-Hegelianism* (London, 1927); and John H. Muirhead, *The Platonic Tradition in Anglo-Saxon Philosophy* (New York, 1931). The first important work of the English Hegelians was James H. Stirling's *The Secret of Hegel* (Edinburgh, 1898; first edition 1865). For turn-of-the-century Dutch Hegelians see Samuel Adrianus van Lutern, "Der Niederländische Hegelianismus," *Logos*, XIV (1925), pp. 240–257. Not to be forgotten is American Hegelianism. See especially *The Journal of Speculative Philosophy*, a small gold mine of nineteenth-

century American (and European) Hegelianism. Cf. the recent anthology edited by W. H. Goetzmann, *The American Hegelians* (New York, 1973).

29 Karl Rosenkranz, *Hegels Naturphilosophie und die Bearbeitung derselben durch den italienischen Philosophen A. Véra* (Berlin, 1868), p. 1.

30 Antonio Labriola, *Socialism and Philosophy* (Chicago, 1918), p. 56. Cf. A. Labriola, *Lettere a Engels* (Rome, 1949), pp. 141–142.

31 For a survey of the literature see Giuseppe Vacca, "Recenti studi sull'hegelismo napoletano," *Studi Storici,* VII (1966), pp. 159–210. Cf. Salvatore Onufrio, *Lo'stato etico' e gli hegeliani di Napoli* (Celebes Editore, 1972), pp. 29–52.

32 For a trenchant analysis of the Italian Hegelians see Paul Piccone, "From Spaventa to Gramsci," *Telos,* 31 (Spring, 1977), pp. 35–66. Piccone provides information on the political context of the splits in the Italian Hegelians. Cf. Pier C. Masini, "Bertrando Spaventa," *Revista Storica del Socialismo,* VI (1959), pp. 304 ff.

33 B. Spaventa, "Studii sopra la filosofia di Hegel," in Spaventa, *Unificazione nazionale ed egemonia culturale,* ed. G. Vacca (Bari, 1969), pp. 21–23.

34 Spaventa, "False accuse contro l'Hegelismo" (1851), *Unificazione nazionale,* pp. 95–96.

35 On Spaventa's relation to Hegel see generally Renato Bortot, *L'Hegelismo di Bertrando Spaventa* (Florence, 1968).

36 Cited in Teresa Serra, *Bertrando Spaventa* (Rome, 1974), p. 54. Serra also takes up the charges of subjectivism leveled at Spaventa. Cf. Italo Cubeddu, *Bertrando Spaventa* (Florence, 1964).

37 Cited in Giuseppe Vacca, *Politica e filosofia in Bertrando Spaventa* (Bari, 1967), p. 291. Landucci has claimed that Spaventa anticipates Lukács and contemporary French Hegelians; see his "Il giovane Spaventa fra hegelismo e socialismo," *Annali Feltrinelli,* VI (1963), pp. 647–707; and "L'hegelismo in Italia nell'età del Risorgimento," *Studi Storici,* VI (1965), pp. 597–628. For a criticism of a "left" interpretation of Spaventa see Teresa Serra, "Oltre la lettura idealistica di Bertrando Spaventa," *GCFI,* 53 (1974), pp. 175–202.

38 Vacca, *Politica e filosofia,* pp. 237–238.

39 Two anthologies of the Italian Hegelians are Guido Oldrini, ed., *Il primo hegelismo italiano* (Florence, 1969); and Augusto Guzzo and Armando Plebe, eds., *Gli hegeliani d'Italia* (Turin, 1953).

40 See Guido Oldrini, *Gli hegeliani di Napoli: Augusto Vera e la corrente ortodossa* (Milan, 1964), p. 90.

41 Rosenkranz, *Hegels Naturphilosophie,* p. 1. Cf. G. Oldrini, *La cultura filosofica napoletana dell'ottocento* (Rome, 1973).

42 Cited in Oldrini, *Gli hegeliani di Napoli*, p. 173.
43 Cited in Oldrini, *La cultura filosofica napoletana*, p. 427.
44 A. Véra, *Logique de Hégel*, translated with an Introduction and commentary by Véra (Paris, 1874), p. xv. (First edition 1859.)
45 Unlike Spaventa, Vera stood on the political right. See for instance his "La Souveraineté du peuple" (1848), *Mélanges philosophiques* (Paris, 1862), pp. 242–263.
46 Vera, as cited in Oldrini, *Gli hegeliani di Napoli*, pp. 169–170.
47 Quoted by Piccone in "From Spaventa to Gramsci," p. 60.
48 Oldrini, *Gli hegeliani di Napoli*, pp. 193–194.
49 Rosenkranz, *Hegels Naturphilosophie*, pp. 36, 107–129. Labriola was scandalized that Rosenkranz placed Vera at the center of Italian Hegelians, ignoring Spaventa. See Labriola's review of Vera's *Introduzione alla filosofia della storia* in his *Opere*, Vol. III, ed. L. Dal Pane (Milan, 1962), p. 274. For a sympathetic defense of Vera see Armando Plebe, *Spaventa e Vera* (Turin, 1954).
50 Labriola to Kautsky (Oct. 8, 1898), in Giuliano Procacci, "Antonio Labriola e la revisione del marxismo attraverso l'epistolario con Bernstein e con Kautsky," *Annali Feltrinelli*, III (1960), p. 317.
51 The best discussion of Labriola may be Eugenio Garin's Introduction to Labriola's *La concezione materialistica della storia* (Bari, 1967). The standard biography is Luigi Dal Pane, *Antonio Labriola* (1935) (reprinted Bologna, n.d.). See Bruno Widmar, "La giovinezza di Antonio Labriola," *Revista Storica del Socialismo*, III (1960), pp. 639–676.
52 A. Labriola, *Socialism and Philosophy* (Chicago, 1918), pp. 5–6.
53 Ibid., p. 96. "I have long lost the gift of repeating in writing the things which I used to express spontaneously, in ready and flexible speech, as fitted the occasion, pungent with side issues and full of references" (p. 146). See Croce's comments on Labriola as teacher and writer in "Come nacque e come morì il marxismo teorico in Italia (1895–1900)," *Materialismo storico ed economia marxistica* (Bari, 1961), p. 285.
54 Labriola to Engels (March 14, 1894), in A. Labriola, *Lettere a Engels* (Rome, 1949), p. 142.
55 Labriola, "Del socialismo," in Labriola, *Scritti politici 1886–1904*, ed. V. Gerratana (Bari, 1970), p. 185.
56 Labriola to Engels (Feb. 21, 1891), in Labriola, *Lettere a Engels*, p. 10. On the diffusion of Marxism in these years see E. J. Hobsbawm, "La diffusione del marxismo (1890–1905)," *Studi Storici*, XV (1974), pp. 241–269.
57 A. Labriola, *Essays on the Materialistic Conception of History* (Chicago, 1908), p. 13.

58 Labriola to Engels (June 13, 1894), in Labriola, *Lettere a Engels*, pp. 146-148.

59 Labriola to Kautsky (August 29, 1897), in Procacci, "Antonio Labriola e la revisione del marxismo," p. 312. He complained to Bernstein that *Die Neue Zeit* would never be a "critical review" (p. 319).

60 Labriola, *Socialism and Philosophy*, p. 100.

61 Ibid., p. 96.

62 Ibid., p. 101.

63 Ibid., p. 105.

64 Labriola, *Essays on the Materialistic Conception*, pp. 120-121.

65 Ibid., pp. 101-102.

66 Labriola, *La concezione materialistica*, p. 65.

67 A. Labriola, "Una risposta alla prolusion di Zeller" (1862), in Labriola, *Opere*, ed. F. Sbarber (Naples, 1972).

68 Labriola, *Socialism and Philosophy*, pp. 43, 87. The Italian "nel processo della praxis" becomes "practical process" in translation; see *La concezione materialistica*, p. 204.

69 Criticisms of Labriola have focused on his analysis of revisionism and colonialism. See Enzo Santarelli, *La revisione del marxismo in Italia* (Milan, 1974); and Giacomo Marramao, *Marxismo e revisionismo in Italia* (Bari, 1971). Marramao argues that Labriola and Kautsky were analogous figures. See also Nicola Badaloni, "Labriola politico e filosofo," *Critica Marxista*, IX (1971), pp. 16-35; Giovanni Mastroianni, "*I saggi* di Antonio Labriola," *Studi Storici*, VI (1965), pp. 329-341; and a reply: Augusto Guerra, "Determinismo e libertà nello storicismo di Antonio Labriola," *Studi Storici*, VI (1965), pp. 501-506.

70 Labriola, *Socialism and Philosophy*, pp. 77-78.

71 Labriola, *Essays on the Materialistic Conception*, p. 53.

72 Croce, *Materialismo storico*, p. 49. See Gian B. Bravo, "Friedrich Engels und Achille Loria," in *Friedrich Engels*, ed. H. Pelger (Hannover, 1971).

73 Ibid., p. 188.

74 Ibid., pp. 10, 112, 70.

75 Croce to Gentile (Nov. 23, 1898) in Giovanni Gentile, *Lettere a Benedetto Croce*, Vol. 1, ed. S. Giannantoni (Florence, 1972), p. 140.

76 Labriola to Croce (Oct. 7, 1898), in Labriola, *Lettere a Benedetto Croce 1895-1904* (Naples, 1975), p. 301.

77 Sorel, writing to Croce in 1899, mentioned that Bernstein had said he had been "inspired, to a certain extent, by your work" ("Lettere di Georges Sorel a B. Croce," *La Critica*, XXV [1927], p. 311). Bo Gustafsson, who meticulously reconstructs all the influences on Bernstein, finds many parallels between Croce and Bernstein; but "it is difficult to determine

with certainty the *specific* contribution of Croce" to Bernstein's revisionism. See B. Gustafsson, *Marxismus und Revisionismus: Eduard Bernsteins Kritik des Marxismus und ihrer ideengeschichtlichen Voraussetzung* (Frankfurt, 1972), p. 211.

78 See Croce's comments in *Materialismo storico*, p. 143.

79 Labriola to Croce (March 3, 1898), in *Lettere a Benedetto Croce*, p. 269.

80 Labriola to Croce (Dec. 31, 1898), ibid., p. 323. See "Author's Postscript to the French Edition" (1898), *Socialism and Philosophy*, pp. 164–178.

81 See H. S. Harris's very sympathetic discussion of Gentile's fascism in his *The Social Philosophy of Giovanni Gentile* (Urbana, Ill., 1966), p. 220.

82 Marramao considers Gentile's contribution to be decisive for Italian Marxism; see his *Marxismo e revisionismo*, pp. 175–195.

83 V. I. Lenin, *Karl Marx* (Peking, 1976), p. 59.

84 For the Spaventa–JaJa–Gentile relationship see Manlio di Lalla, *Vita di Giovanni Gentile* (Florence, 1975). A brief discussion of JaJa can be found in Anna Rosa Leona, *Il pensiero filosofico di Donato JaJa* (Bari, 1972).

85 Gentile, as cited in Harris, *The Social Philosophy of Giovanni Gentile*, p. 40.

86 Gentile, as cited in Ugo Spirito, *Giovanni Gentile* (Florence, 1969), p. 65.

87 At least this is what Gentile, based on a letter from Croce, wrote to JaJa: Gentile to JaJa (Oct. 1, 1898), in *Carteggio*, Vol. 1, ed. Maria Sandirocco, (Florence, 1962), pp. 185–186.

88 G. Gentile, *Opere*, Vol. XXVIII, *La filosofia di Marx* (1899) (Florence, 1955), p. 119.

89 For a critical discussion of Gentile's interpretation of Marx see Alberto Signorini, *Il giovane Gentile e Marx* (Milan, 1966).

90 K. Marx, "Theses on Feuerbach," in *Writings of the Young Marx on Philosophy and Society*, ed. L. D. Easton and K. H. Guddat (Garden City, N.Y., 1967), p. 400.

91 Gentile, *La filosofia di Marx*, pp. 87, 72, 76, 78.

92 For a survey of twentieth-century French Hegelian thought and its relationship to Marxism, see Mark Poster, *Existential Marxism in Post-War France* (Princeton, N.J., 1977); John Heckman, "Hyppolite and the Hegel Revival in France," *Telos*, 16 (1973), pp. 128–145. See also George Lichtheim, *Marxism in Modern France* (New York, 1968), pp. 82–102; H. Stuart Hughes, *The Obstructed Past: French Social Thought in the Years of Desperation* (New York, 1969), pp. 190–226; Jean Duvignaud, "France: The Neo-Marxists," in *Revisionism*, ed. L. Labedz (New York, 1962); and Daniel Lindenberg, *Le Marxisme introuvable* (Paris, 1975).

93 Oldrini effectively rebuts the view that Hegel was unknown in nineteenth-century France; yet he admits that most French treatments were deriva-

tive and inferior; see Guido Oldrini, "La prima penetrazione 'ortodossa' dello hegelismo in Francia," *Annali Feltrinelli*, VI (1963), pp. 621–646. See also Roberto Salvadori, *Hegel in Francia* (Bari, 1974), which punctures the claim that Hegel in France commences with Kojève and Hyppolite. Cf. Marcel Régnier, "Hegelianism and Marxism," *Social Research*, 34 (1967), pp. 31–47. Bernhard Knoop's *Hegel und die Franzosen* (Stuttgart, 1941) contains relevant information, within a Nazi framework.

94 Cousin's knowledge was based on conversations and letters with Hegel, not a reading of the German texts; see the study by Alfred Cornelius, *Die Geschichtslehre Victor Cousins unter besonderer Berücksichtigung des hegelschen Einflusses* (Geneva, 1958).

95 Karl Rosenkranz, *Hegel als deutscher Nationalphilosoph* (Leipzig, 1870), p. 297.

96 A. Véra, *Essais de philosophie hégélienne* (Paris, 1864), p. vi.

97 Lucien Herr, "Hegel," in *La Grande Encylopédie*, Vol. 19 (Paris, n.d.), p. 1002.

98 George Noël, *La Logique de Hegel* (1897) (Paris, 1967), p. v.

99 Wahl can be credited as the first modern French Hegelian; his existential interpretation focused on *The Phenomenology of Mind*; see his *Le Malheur de la conscience dans la philosophie de Hegel* (1929) (Paris, 1951). The book included an extract on the "unhappy consciousness" from *The Phenomenology*. According to Hyppolite, this text constituted the "first shock" in the renaissance of Hegel in France (Jean Hyppolite, "Discours d'introduction," *Hegel-Studien*, Beiheft 3 [1964], pp. 11–13). Cf. R. Salvadori, *Hegel in Francia*, pp. 85–233.

100 A. Koyré, "Rapport sur l'état des études hégéliennes en France," in *Verhandlungen des Ersten Hegelkongresses* (1930), ed. B. Wiegeusma (Tübingen, 1931), pp. 80 ff.

101 Koyré, "Hegel en Russie" (1936), pp. 103–170. In the prefatory note to this essay Koyré mentioned that he had assisted "for some years" in the "renaissance in Hegelianism" (*Etudes sur l'histoire de la pensée philosophique en Russie* [Paris, 1950], p. 103). See also Jean Wahl, "Le Role de A. Koyré dans le développement des études hégéliennes en France," *Hegel-Studien*, Beiheft 3 (1964), pp. 15–26.

102 A. Kojève, "Entretien par Gilles Lapouge," *La Quinzaine littéraire*, No. 53 (July 1–15, 1968), p. 19.

103 Lefebvre and Guterman made the first French translations of Marx's *Economic and Philosophical Manuscripts* and translated Hegel in 1938. See Chapter 5 for a more detailed discussion.

104 A. Breton, "Surrealist Situation of the Object" (1935), *Manifestoes of Surrealism* (Ann Arbor, Mich., 1972), p. 259.

105 See Franklin Rosemont, "Introduction," in A. Breton, *What Is Surrealism? Selected Writings* (New York, 1978), pp. 33–34.

106 The French Hegelians uniformly rejected Hegel's philosophy of nature. Herr judged it the least satisfactory part of the system; Koyré thought it arid; Kojève judged it unfortunate. See Salvadori, *Hegel in Francia*, p. 73.

107 The parallels are intriguing. The first-named (Herr and Labriola) were the most committed Socialists; the second-named (Andler and Croce) were the least political and nearly antisocialist; the last-named (Sorel and Gentile) represented the most active "subjective" orientation, and both were tarnished by fascism. For a rebuttal to the charges of Sorel's fascism, however, see John L. Stanley, "Introduction," in Sorel, *From Georges Sorel* (New York, 1976).

108 The period did witness other attempts to interpret the relationship of Hegel to Marx. See for example Leopold Leseine, *L'Influence de Hegel sur Marx* (Paris, 1907). Although conventional, it does note divergences between Marx and Engels; it also includes an annotated appendix that lists other commentaries on Marx and Hegel (pp. 218–242).

109 Labriola to Croce (April 4, 1898), in Labriola, *Lettere a Benedetto Croce*, p. 276.

110 B. Croce, "Prefazione" (1899), *Materialismo storico*, p. lx.

111 See "Lettere di Georges Sorel a B. Croce," which Croce published in *La Critica* in many installments, commencing with Vol. XXV (1927), pp. 38 ff. For a discussion of the links between Sorel and Croce see Neil McInnes, "Les Débuts du marxisme théorique en France et en Italie (1880–1897)," *Etudes de marxologie*, No. 102 (1960), pp. 5–50. Cf. James H. Meisel, *The Genesis of Georges Sorel* (Ann Arbor, Mich., 1951).

112 See Harvey Goldberg, *The Life of Jean Jaurès* (Madison, Wisc., 1962), pp. 62–64.

113 Herr, "Hegel," pp. 997–1003.

114 Charles Andler, *Vie de Lucien Herr* (Paris, 1932), p. 59.

115 Herr's *La Révolution sociale*, as cited in Daniel Lindenberg and Pierre-André Meyer, *Lucien Herr: Le Socialisme et son destin* (Paris, 1977), pp. 308–309.

116 Georges Sorel, "La crisi del socialismo," *Critica Sociale*, VIII (1898), pp. 134–138.

117 G. Sorel, "Préface," in Saverio Merlino, *Formes et essence du socialisme* (Paris, 1898), p. ii.

118 Sorel, "Necessity and Fatalism in Marxism" (1898), *From Georges Sorel*, p. 128.

119 Jean Deroo, *Le Renversement du matérialisme historique: L'Expérience*

de Georges Sorel (Paris, n.d., 1936?), p. 160. Cf. Michael Freund, *Georges Sorel* (Frankfurt, 1972). (First edition 1932.)

120 Sorel to Croce (June 10, 1907), "Lettere di Georges Sorel a B. Croce," *La Critica,* XXVI (1928), p. 103.

121 Sorel to Croce (June 28, 1910), ibid., p. 341.

122 Yvonne Kapp, *Eleanor Marx,* Vol. 2 (New York, 1976), p. 446. See W. O. Henderson, *The Life of Friedrich Engels,* Vol. 2 (London, 1976), pp. 657 ff.

123 Harmut Mehringer, "Friedrich Engels als politscher Mentor der deutschen Sozialdemokratie," in *Debatte um Engels,* Vol. 1, ed. H. Mehringer (Reinbek bei Hamburg, 1973), pp. 22–46.

124 Engels to Kautsky (April 1, 1895), in K. Marx and F. Engels, *Selected Correspondence,* ed. S. Ryazanskaya (Moscow, 1965), p. 486. See Bo Gustafsson, *Marxismus und Revisionismus,* pp. 68 ff.

125 Gustafsson, *Marxismus und Revisionismus,* p. 90.

126 According to W. O. Henderson, Engels's pamphlet *Socialism: Utopian and Scientific* was one of the most widely read socialist texts at the end of the nineteenth century; see his *Life of Friedrich Engels,* Vol. 2, pp. 591, 599. Reliance on Engels as authoritative extended to the academic literature; Stammler considered Engels more reliable because he was more systematic (Rudolf Stammler, *Wirtschaft und Recht nach der materialistischen Geschichtsauffassung* (Leipzig, 1914), p. 36. (First edition 1896.)

127 "Engels was directly responsible for the evolutionism and accommodationism of the Second International" (Norman Levine, *The Tragic Deception: Marx contra Engels* [Santa Barbara, Calif., 1975], p. 183).

128 Predrag Vranicki provides a good discussion of Engels in *Storia del marxismo,* Vol. I (Rome, 1972), pp. 217–255. Cf. George Lichtheim, *Marxism* (New York, 1965), pp. 244–258; Iring Fetscher, *Marx and Marxism* (New York, 1971), pp. 162–172; Donald C. Hodges, "Engels' Contribution to Marxism," *Socialist Register 1965,* ed. Ralph Milliband (New York, 1965), pp. 297–310; Leonard Krieger, "Introduction," in Engels, *The German Revolutions* (Chicago, 1967), pp. ix–xxxi; Alfred Schmidt, *The Concept of Nature in Marx* (London, 1971), pp. 52–61; Heinz-Dieter Kittsteiner, "'Logische' und 'historisch': Über Differenzen des Marxschen und Engelsschen System der Wissenschaft," *IWK,* XIII (1977), pp. 1–47.

129 Engels, *Anti-Dühring: Herr Eugen Dühring's Revolution in Science* (New York, 1970), pp. 154–155.

130 See Gustav A. Wetter, *Die Umkehrung Hegels: Gründzuge und Ursprünge der Sowetphilosophie* (Cologne, 1963); and Karl G. Balles-

trem, *Die sowjetische Erkenntnismetaphysik und ihr Verhältnis zu Hegel* (Dordrecht, 1968). Both Wetter and Ballestrem argue on behalf of a Hegel–Engels–Soviet philosophical tradition. Cf. Z. A. Jordan, *The Evolution of Dialectical Materialism* (New York, 1967). One example of the dependence on Engels is Lenin's *Materialism and Empirio-criticism*. "Though Lenin mentions the name of Marx scores of times, there is only one three sentence quotation from the philosophical writings of Marx in the entire book" (Bertram Wolfe, *Three Who Made a Revolution* [New York, 1964], p. 512).

131 G. Lukács, *History and Class Consciousness* (London, 1971), pp. 3, 24.

132 "It was Lukács and to a lesser extent Korsch . . . who drove the first effective wedge between the theory of Marx and that of Engels" (Gareth S. Jones, "Engels and the Genesis of Marxism," *New Left Review*, 106 [Nov.–Dec., 1977], p. 80). Comments depreciating Engels in comparison to Marx were not uncommon in the 1890s. See for example Ernest Seillière, *Littérature et morale dans le parti socialiste allemand* (Paris, 1898), p. 310.

133 For a discussion of Szabó see Chapter 4. Szabó's own critique may have been inspired by Sorel. Szabó, who had syndicalist leanings, visited Paris and was in touch with French syndicalists. See János Jemnitz, "La Correspondance d'Ervin Szabó avec les socialistes et syndicalistes de France (1904–1912)," *Le Mouvement social*, 52 (July–Sept., 1965), pp. 111–119.

134 B. Croce, *What Is Living and What Is Dead of the Philosophy of Hegel* (London, 1915). (First Italian edition 1906). Engels, "who has in recent times been much known and discussed in Italy . . . , reduced philosophy by equating it to the positivist sciences" (pp. 206–207).

135 The following illustrates that national traditions constrict studies of Marxism: In a two-volume German anthology on Engels, Mondolfo is not mentioned once; see Marmut Mehringer and Gottfried Mergner, eds., *Debatte um Engels*, 2 vols. (Reinbek bei Hamburg, 1973).

136 F. Engels, *Socialism, Utopian and Scientific* (Peking, 1975), p. 69.

137 Gentile, "Una critica del materialismo storico" (1897), in *La filosofia di Marx*, p. 39.

138 Gentile to JaJa (Nov. 14, 1897), in *Carteggio*, Vol. 1, p. 65.

139 Gentile, *La filosofia di Marx*, pp. 125–126.

140 Croce, *Materialismo storico*, pp. 81–82.

141 Labriola to Croce (Dec. 31, 1898), in Labriola, *Lettere a Benedetto Croce*, pp. 323–324.

142 Sorel to Croce (Dec. 27, 1897), "Lettere di Georges Sorel a B. Croce," *La Critica*, XXV (1927), p. 51. He regretted that "our friend" Labriola had

followed Engels (April 1, 1898, Ibid., p. 108). Sorel also had a tiff with Gentile about Engels. See Gentile, *La filosofia di Marx*, pp. 127–128.

143 G. Sorel, "Is There a Utopia in Marxism" (1899), *For Georges Sorel*, p. 130.

144 Ibid., p. 141.

145 Charles Andler, *Les Origines du socialisme d'état en allemagne* (Paris, 1897), p. 6.

146 C. Andler, "Introduction historique et commentaire," *Le Manifeste communiste* (Paris, 1901), p. 139.

147 See Ernest Tonnelat, *Charles Andler* (Paris, 1937), p. 87.

148 Sorel's *The Decomposition of Marxism* (1908) is included in Irving L. Horowitz's *Radicalism and the Revolt against Reason: The Social Theories of Georges Sorel* (Carbondale, Ill., 1968), pp. 201–254. "Ten years ago . . . Andler announced that the moment had come to write the history of the decomposition of Marxism" (p. 215).

149 Another fragment can be found in his review of Labriola: "La Conception matérialiste de l'historie d'après M. Antonio Labriola," *Revue de métaphysique et de morale*, V (1897), pp. 644–658.

150 C. Andler, "Frédéric Engels: Fragment d'une étude sur la décomposition du marxisme," *Revue socialiste*, 58 (1913), pp. 387–388.

151 C. Andler, "Frédéric Engels: Fragment d'une étude sur la décomposition du marxisme," *Revue Socialiste*, 59 (1914), pp. 59, 74–75, 70.

152 Thomas G. Masaryk's major contribution to Marxism, *Die philosophischen und sociologischen Grundlagen des Marxismus*, appeared in 1899 (reprinted Osnabrücke, 1964). Whatever its faults, it was encyclopedic in scope; perhaps because of its size – nearly 600 pages – it was not widely discussed. In Labriola's judgment "the book discusses an infinite number of things, but it never gets to the real point" (Labriola, "Concerning the Crisis of Marxism," *Socialism and Philosophy*, p. 199). Labriola despised Masaryk for promoting the term and idea of a "crisis" of Marxism. Some years prior to the book, several of Masaryk's articles had been published as a pamphlet entitled "The Philosophical and Scientific Crisis of Contemporary Marxism." (See Erazim Kohák, "T. G. Masaryk's Revision of Marxism," *Journal of the History of Ideas*, XXV [1964], pp. 519–542; this includes the text of Masaryk's pamphlet.) To Labriola, a "crisis" of Marxism was an utter mystification insofar as in Italy Marxism "fights for its very existence" (A. Labriola, "A Propos du Livre de Bernstein," *Le Mouvement socialiste*, May 1 [1899] p. 456). Masaryk did in fact associate himself with Bernstein; he wrote in a footnote, "While correcting this final chapter Bernstein's book [*Die Voraussetzung des Sozialismus*] reached

me. I can say only it fully confirms my diagnosis" (*Die philosophischen und sociologischen Grundlagen*, p. 590); and he wrote to Bernstein that he was "pleased" that their books were parallel (cited in Gustafsson, *Marxismus und Revisionismus*, p. 313). In any case, Masaryk did seriously pursue the divergences between Engels and Marx. An abridged translation of the book has appeared: *Masaryk on Marx*, ed. Erazim V. Kohák (Lewisburg, Pa., 1972). See also Antonie van den Beld, *Humanity: The Political and Social Philosophy of Thomas G. Masaryk* (The Hague, 1975). Van den Beld attacks Labriola's criticism of Masaryk (pp. 99-100).

153 My only knowledge of Brzozowski derives from Leszek Kolakowski, *Main Currents of Marxism: Its Rise, Growth and Dissolution*, Vol. II (London, 1978), pp. 215-239. It seems likely that the source for his critique of Engels was also Sorel. "There was not a single concept, vision or method which, in the transfer from Marx's mind to Engels, did not become completely different, and indeed diametrically opposite as far as the philosophical nature of concepts is concerned" (Brzozowski in 1910, as cited by Kolakowski, pp. 223-224). For Szabó see footnote 133, this chapter, and Chapter 4.

154 Arturo Labriola, *Studio su Marx* (Naples, 1926), p. 36. This is a reprinting (and a retitling) with only typographical corrections of his 1908 *Marx nell'economia e come teorico del socialismo*. See generally Dora Marucco, *Arturo Labriola e il sindicalismo rivoluzionario in Italia* (Turin, 1970).

155 Labriola, *Studio su Marx*, pp. 35-36, 123.

156 For this reason partisans of Antonio Labriola have often claimed that Mondolfo is his rightful successor; see Luigi Dal Pane, *Antonio Labriola nella politica e nella cultura italiano* (Turin, 1975), p. 459; and Noberto Bobbio, "Introduzione," in Mondolfo's *Umanismo di Marx 1908-1966* (Turin, 1968), pp. xxiii-xlviii.

157 There are substantial discussions of Mondolfo in Enzo Santarelli, *La revisione del marxismo in Italia* (Milan, 1977); and G. Marramao, *Marxismo e revisionismo*.

158 Mondolfo, "Feuerbach e Marx" (1909), in *Umanismo di Marx*, p. 9.

159 Ibid., pp. 70, 63.

160 Eugenio Di Carlo, "La dialettica engelsiana," *Revista di Filosofia*, VIII (1916), pp. 352-368.

161 R. Mondolfo, "Chiarimenti su la dialettica engelsiana," *Revista di Filosofia*, VIII (1916), p. 702. This reply is also an appendix to the reprinting of Mondolfo, *Il materialismo storico in Federico Engels* (1912) (Florence, 1973), but it lacks this passage and some footnotes.

162 Mondolfo, *Il materialismo storico in Federico Engels*, pp. 3-4, 294.

163 Croce, *What Is Living and What Is Dead*, p. 164.

164 Mondolfo, *Il materialismo storico in Federico Engels*, p. 18.
165 Heinrich Heine, *Religion and Philosophy in Germany* (Boston, 1959), p. 123.

3. From philosophy to politics

1 My disagreements with Perry Anderson's *Considerations on Western Marxism* (London, 1976) should be evident from the Introduction and preceding chapters. For two good critical reviews see Richard D. Wolff in *Monthly Review*, XXX/4 (Sept., 1978), pp. 55–64; and Jeffrey Herf in *Socialist Revolution*, 35 (Sept.–Oct., 1977), pp. 129–144. Cf. Alvin W. Gouldner, *The Two Marxisms* (New York, 1980), pp. 159–162.
2 Karl Korsch, *Marxism and Philosophy* (London, 1970), p. 106. *Marxismus und Philosophie*, ed. E. Gerlach (Frankfurt, 1966), p. 50.
3 "It is absolutely incontestable that on a world scale the open revolutionary struggle of the proletariat for power is at present passing through a stoppage, a slowing down in tempo" (Leon Trotsky, "Theses on the International Situation and the Tasks of the Comintern" [1921], *The First Five Years of the Communist International*, Vol. 1 [London, 1973], p. 312).
4 At the time *Materialism and Empirio-criticism* appeared (1909), during the onslaught against the followers of Ernst Mach and Richard Avenarius, Plekhanov was a political opponent; yet he was the philosopher Lenin valued the most. Because of this embarrassment, Lenin worked energetically to separate philosophical from political disputes. As he explained to Gorky, "In the Summer and Autumn of 1904 Bogdanov and I reached a complete agreement, as Bolsheviks, and formed the tacit block, which tacitly ruled out philosophy as a neutral field." The embarrassment was compounded by Bogdanov being not only Lenin's close political ally but a prime philosophical offender. For this reason Lenin wanted to preserve the political agreement while excluding the grave philosophical differences. "*Proletary* must remain absolutely neutral towards all our divergences in philosophy and not give the reader *the slightest grounds* for associating the Bolsheviks, as a trend . . . with empirio-criticism or empirio-monism." See *Lenin and Gorky: Letters, Reminiscences, Articles* (Moscow, 1973), pp. 32–33. It was in this period that Lenin protested to *Die Neue Zeit* when it mentioned that the philosophical disputes in the Russian party were also political disputes. "This philosophical controversy is not a factional one . . . Both factions contain adherents of two philosophical trends" ("Statement of the Editors of *Proletary*," in V. Lenin, *Collected Works*, Vol. 13 [Moscow, 1962], p. 447). The point here is only that where politics and philosophy seem to present no problem – in Lenin – there is a tangled relationship. Although Lenin was convinced that Machist doctrine was

"ridiculous, harmful, philistine, fideist," he could also write: "I say *separate* the fight from the faction. Of course, such a separation, on living persons, is rather difficult and painful" (*Lenin and Gorky*, pp. 38–40). Not only was it difficult, it did not turn out to be feasible. One of the best accounts of these events is in David Joravsky, *Soviet Marxism and Natural Science* (London, 1961), pp. 24–44. Cf. Manuel Sacristán, "Lenin e la filosofia," *Critica Marxista*, IX (1971), pp. 87–118. On Bogdanov see Dietrich Grille, *Lenins Rivale: Bogdanov und seine Philosophie* (Cologne, 1966); and for a partial rebuttal of Grille, see George Katkov, "Lenin as Philosopher," in *Lenin: The Man, the Theorist, the Leader*, ed. L. Schapiro and P. Reddaway (New York, 1967). See also A. A. Bogdanov in *Makers of the Russian Revolution: Biographies of Bolshevik Leaders*, ed. G. Haupt and J.-J. Marie (Ithaca, N.Y., 1974), pp. 286–292; Bertram Wolfe, *Three Who Made a Revolution* (New York, 1964), pp. 501–517; and Robert S. Cohen, "Machists and Marxists: Bogdanov and Lenin," in *Ernst Mach*, ed. R. S. Cohen, Boston Studies in the Philosophy of Science (Dordrecht, 1970), pp. 156–160. For an account of Lenin's attitude see Nikolay Valentinov's memoir, *Encounters with Lenin* (London, 1968), pp. 205–243.

5 Norman O. Brown, *Life against Death* (Middletown, Conn., 1970), p. 1.

6 Lukács, *History and Class Consciousness* (London, 1971), p. 299.

7 The first edition of the collected words ceased when its editor, Paul Frölich, was expelled from the Communist party in 1928. See Iring Fetscher's "Postscript" to Paul Frölich's *Rosa Luxemburg* (London, 1972).

8 Gilbert Badia notes that efforts to reconcile Lenin and Luxemburg have increased since the death of Stalin; see his *Rosa Luxemburg* (Paris, 1975), pp. 321 ff.

9 For example, Norman Geras, *The Legacy of Rosa Luxemburg* (London, 1976).

10 On Levi, see generally Charlotte Beradt, *Paul Levi* (Frankfurt, 1969). Cf. Helmut Gruber, "Paul Levi and the Comintern," in *International Communism in the Era of Lenin*, ed. H. Gruber (Greenwich, Conn., 1967), pp. 391–406.

11 See E. H. Carr, *The Bolshevik Revolution 1917–1923*, Vol. 3 (Middlesex, 1966), p. 128.

12 Branko Lazitch and Milorad M. Drachkovitch, *Lenin and the Comintern*, Vol. 1 (Stanford, Calif., 1972), p. 194.

13 See the figures in Hermann Weber, *Die Wandlung des deutschen Kommunismus*, Vol. 1 (Frankfurt, 1969), pp. 361–394.

14 See especially Richard Lowenthal, "The Bolshevisation of the Spartakus League," in *International Communism*, ed. D. Footman, St. Antony's Pa-

pers, No. 9 (London, 1960), pp. 23-71. Cf. Albert S. Lindemann, *The "Red Years": European Socialism versus Bolshevism 1919-1921* (Berkeley, Calif., 1974), p. 274.

15 John M. Cammett, *Antonio Gramsci and the Origins of Italian Communism* (Stanford, Calif., 1967), p. 153. Cf. Gaetano Arfé, *Storia del socialismo italiano 1892-1926* (Turin, 1965).

16 Levi addressed the Congress at Livorno; yet his public prouncements and his private conduct diverged. Publicly he called for a split, and privately he worked to prevent one. See Luigi Cortesi, *Il socialismo italiano fra riforme e rivoluzione* (Bari, 1969), pp. 795 ff. In his remarks he stated that the German party did not believe in preserving unity at all costs; and that moments arrive in party life in which it is necessary to separate from former comrades. See Paul Levi, "Il saluto del Partito communista unificato di Germania," *Resoconto stenografico del XVII Congresso Nazionale del Partito Socialista Italiano*, Livorno 15-20 (Jan., 1921) (Milan, 1962), pp. 16-17.

17 See Levi's published report, "Der Parteitag der italienischen Partei," *Die Rote Fahne*, No. 37 (Jan. 23, 1921). This is anonymous, but the reply by "P. B." (Karl Radek) identified Levi as the author (P. B., "Die Spaltung der italienischen sozialistischen Partei und die Kommunistische Internationale," *Die Rote Fahne*, No. 41 [Jan. 26, 1921].)

18 P. Levi, "Der Beginn der Krise in der Kommunistischen Partei und Internationale" (delivered February 24, 1921), excerpts in *International Communism*, ed. Gruber, pp. 304-309.

19 "Report of Comrade Levi to the Executive Committee of the Third Internationale on the Italian Party Congress" (Jan. 20, 1921) and "Session of the *Zentrale* with the Representatives of the Executive Committee for Germany" (Jan. 28, 1921). These are private statements, both published in *The Comintern: Historical Highlights*, ed. M. M. Drachkovitch and B. Lazitch (New York, 1966), pp. 280, 295-296.

20 Levi, "Beginning of the Crisis," in *International Communism*, ed. Gruber, p. 306. Levi was vulnerable on a key point: He himself had helped split the USPD. He maintained, however, that this was a very different matter from splitting the Italian Socialist party; the former was an "organic" split and created a mass revolutionary party; the latter was artificial and destroyed a mass revolutionary party. The USPD has recently received detailed attention; see Hartfrid Krause, *USPD* (Frankfurt, 1975); David W. Morgan, *The Socialist Left and the German Revolution: A History of the German Independent Socialist Democratic Party, 1917-1922* (Ithaca, N.Y., 1975); and Robert F. Wheeler, *USPD und Internationale* (Frankfurt, 1975).

21 Levi, "The Beginning of the Crisis in the Communist Party and International," in *International Communism*, ed. Gruber, pp. 308, 305. Cf. Beradt, *Paul Levi*, pp. 46–47.
22 Levi believed that after the establishment of a European proletarian state, the Comintern should be relocated in the West. This was essentially Luxemburg's position. See Levi's "Wir und die Exekutive," *Die Rote Fahne*, No. 59 (Feb. 5, 1921). Cf. "Zur Aktion und Organisation der Kommunistischen Internationale," *Die Rote Fahne*, No. 53 (Feb. 2, 1921).
23 For the statement of those resigning, which included Klara Zetkin, see "Sitzung des Zentralausschlusses," *Die Rote Fahne*, No. 98 (Feb. 28, 1921). See "EECI Resolution on the Resignation of Five Members from the Central Committee of the German Communist Party" (March, 1921), in *Communist International 1919–1943*, ed. J. Degras (London, 1956), pp. 211–212. Cf. "Die Executive der KI zur italienischen Frage," *Die Rote Fahne*, No. 165 (April 14, 1921).
24 Lazitch and Drachkovitch, *Lenin and the Comintern*, Vol. 1, p. 512.
25 The March Action was a "turning point in the history both of German Communism and of Soviet policy" (Carr, *The Bolshevik Revolution*, Vol. 3, p. 336). See generally Werner T. Angress, *Stillborn Revolution: The Communist Bid for Power in Germany 1921–23* (Princeton, N.J., 1963). By surgically separating the March Action from the Comintern, Perry Anderson in "The Antinomies of Antonio Gramsci," *New Left Review*, 100 (Nov.–Jan., 1976–1977), pp. 56–58, seeks to exonerate Lenin and Trotsky. In fact, the March Action was partly engineered by the Comintern and unopposed by Lenin and Trotsky; and they both endorsed the expulsion of Levi for his public criticism of the March Action. See Lazitch and Drachkovitch, *Lenin and the Comintern*, pp. 518–527. Whether Lenin approved the action in advance is questionable. For one bit of evidence see the testimony of Bernhard Reichenbach, who recorded that Lenin reversed himself on the March Action under the influence of Klara Zetkin. See B. Reichenbach, "Moscow 1921: Meeting in the Kremlin," *Survey*, No. 53 (Oct., 1964), pp. 16–22.
26 P. Levi, "Brief an Lenin" (Feb. 27, 1921), in Levi, *Zwischen Spartakus und Sozialdemokratie*, ed. C. Beradt (Frankfurt, 1969), p. 41.
27 Die Zentrale der VKPD, "Paul Levi aus der Partei ausgeschlossen," *Die Rote Fahne*, No. 169 (April 16, 1921). For a brief period, after it united with part of the USPD, the German Communist party (KPD) was called the United German Communist party (VKPD).
28 Undated letter cited in Lazitch and Drachkovitch, *Lenin and the Comintern*, p. 512. Levi made the same points in *Was ist das Verbrechen? Die Märzaktion oder die Kritik daran?* Speech at the May 4, 1921, meeting of

the central committee of the VKPD (Berlin, 1921). Appealing to Luxemburg, he argued that the social relations in Western Europe and Russia differed. In the former the proletariat faced a "fully developed bourgeosie" and required an open mass party that could not act on orders of a central committee (pp. 18–21). For another statement see his "Der Parteitag der VKPD," *Unser Weg (Sowjet)*, III/18–19 (1921), p. 236.

29 P. Levi, "Unser Weg: Wider den Putschismus" (1921), in *Zwischen Spartakus und Sozialdemokratie*, pp. 70–71. A second edition appeared in the same year with a new Foreword replying to criticisms of Ernst Meyer (Paul Levi, *Unser Weg*, Zweite Auflage [Berlin, 1921]).

30 Levi, "Brief an Lenin," p. 38.

31 Levi, "Unser Weg," p. 90.

32 R. Luxemburg, "Organizational Questions of Russian Social Democracy" (1904), in *Selected Political Writings*, ed. D. Howard (New York, 1971), p. 306.

33 Levi, "Vorwort und Einleitung zu Rosa Luxemburg 'Die russische Revolution,'" in *Zwischen Spartakus und Sozialdemokratie*, pp. 128–129.

34 Ibid., p. 134.

35 Levi in 1924, as cited in Beradt, *Paul Levi*, pp. 59–60.

36 "Politische Abrechnung" (1905), in R. Luxemburg, *Internationalismus und Klassenkampf: Die polnischen Schriften*, ed. J. Hentze (Neuwied, 1971), p. 285.

37 "Vorwort zu dem Sammelband 'Die polnische Frage und die sozialistische Bewegung'" (1905), ibid., p. 215. "Men make their own history, but they do not make it just as they please" is the standard English translation (K. Marx, *The 18th Brumaire of Louis Bonaparte* [New York, 1963], p. 15). It reads in German "Die Menschen machen ihre eigene Geschichte aber sie machen sie nicht aus freien Stücken." The German translation of Luxemburg's Polish reads "Die Menschen machen ihre Geschichte nicht aus freien Stücken, aber *sie machen ihrer eigene Geschichte.*"

38 For one discussion of the economic issues see my "The Politics of the Crisis Theory," *Telos*, 23 (Spring, 1975), esp. pp. 22–29.

39 Arnold Reisberg denounces as anticommunist the interpretation of a Luxemburg-Lenin antagonism; he stresses the rapprochement of Luxemburg and Lenin after 1905, and he cites from a letter of Luxemburg welcoming the Russian Revolution; see his *Lenins Beziehungen zur deutschen Arbeiterbewegung* (Berlin, 1970), pp. 87 ff, 361–362. Norman Geras in his *The Legacy of Rosa Luxemburg* (London, 1976) belittles her critique of Lenin. J. P. Nettl also places little importance on it; see his *Rosa Luxemburg*, Vol. 1 (London, 1966), p. 294.

40 See Dietrich Geyer, "Die russische Parteispaltung im Urteil der deutschen

Sozialdemokratie," *IRSH*, III (1958), pp. 195–219, 418–444. Cf. Claudie Weill, *Marxistes russes et social-démocratie allemande 1898–1904* (Paris, 1977); and Peter Lösche, *Der Bolschewismus im Urteil der deutschen Sozialdemokratie 1903–1920* (Berlin, 1967).

41 See Georg W. Strobel, *Die Partei Rosa Luxemburgs, Lenin und die SPD* (Wiesbaden, 1974), pp. 433–436. Cf. Feliks Tych, "Georg W. Strobels Geschichte der polnischen Sozialdemokratie und ihrer Beziehungen zur SPD und SDAPR," *IWK*, XII/2 (1976), pp. 217–227.

42 K. Kautsky, "Eine neue Strategie" and "Die Aktion der Mass" in *Die Massenstreikdebatte*, ed. A. Grunenberg (Frankfurt, 1970), pp. 153–190 and 233–263.

43 R. Luxemburg, "Die Theorie und die Praxis" (1909–1910), *Gesammelte Werke*, Vol. 2 (Berlin, 1972), p. 401. Cf. "The Mass Strike, the Political Party and the Trade Unions," in *Rosa Luxemburg Speaks*, ed. M.-A. Waters (New York, 1970), esp. pp. 202–207.

44 R. Luxemburg, "Blanquismus und Sozialdemokratie" (1906), in *Internationalismus und Klassenkampf*, pp. 302–303. Yet she retained her reserve vis-à-vis the Bolsheviks. See her comments to the 1907 RSPD Conference in "Parteitag der Sozialdemokratischen Arbeiterpartei Russlands . . . 1907 in London," *Gesammelte Werke*, Vol. 2, pp. 205–233.

45 See Lelio Basso, *Rosa Luxemburgs Dialektik der Revolution* (Frankfurt, 1969), pp. 117 ff.

46 Luxemburg, "Social Reform or Revolution," in *Selected Political Writings*, p. 85.

47 Luxemburg, "Nachbetractungen zum Parteitag" (1898), *Gesammelte Werke*, Vol. 1, Part 1, p. 253. See Peter Strutynski, *Die Auseinandersetzungen zwischen Marxisten und Revisionisten in der deutschen Arbeiterbewegung um die Jahrhundertwende* (Cologne, 1976), pp. 116 ff.

48 V. Lenin, "One Step Forward, Two Steps Back," *Selected Works in Three Volumes*, Vol. 1 (Moscow, 1970), pp. 426–427.

49 Luxemburg, "Organizational Questions of Russian Social Democracy" (1904), in *Selected Political Writings*, pp. 288–290.

50 R. Luxemburg, *The Russian Revolution*, ed. B. D. Wolfe (Ann Arbor, Mich., 1961), p. 71.

51 Luxemburg, "Organizational Questions of Russian Social Democracy," p. 291.

52 See Peter Lösche, *Der Bolschewismus im Urteil der deutschen Sozialdemokratie 1903–1920*, pp. 204–205; Julius Braunthal, *History of the International*, Vol. 2, *1914–1943* (New York, 1967), pp. 163–165; Weber, *Die Wandlung des deutschen Kommunismus*, Vol. 1, pp. 28–29; and the Introduction by Hermann Weber to *Der Gründungsparteitag der KPD* (Frankfurt, 1969), pp. 38–39.

53 Luxemburg, *The Russian Revolution*, pp. 28-30.
54 Ibid., pp. 78-79.
55 Korsch, *Marxism and Philosophy*, p. 106.
56 H. Gorter, "Die marxistische Revolutionäre Arbeiterbewegung in Holland" (1922), reprinted in Herman de Liagre Böhl, *Herman Gorter* (Nijmegen, 1973), pp. 274-275.
57 Herman Gorter, *Der historische Materialismus*, trans. from Dutch by A. Pannekoek (Stuttgart, 1921), p. 128. (First edition 1908.)
58 See in general S. Schurer, "Anton Pannekoek and the Origins of Leninism," *The Slavonic and East European Review*, 41 (1963), pp. 327 ff.; Erik Hansen, "Crisis in the Party: *De Tribune* Faction and the Origins of the Dutch Communist Party," *J. Cont. H.*, 11 (1976), pp. 43-64; Paul Mattick, "Anton Pannekoek 1873-1960," in Pannekoek, *Lenin as Philosopher* (London, 1975); G. Mergner, ed., *Gruppe Internationale Kommunisten Hollands*, (Reinbek bei Hamburg, 1971); Hans Bock, "Zur Geschichte und Theorie der Höllandischen Marxistischen Schule," Introduction to A. Pannekoek and H. Gorter, *Organisation und Taktik der proletarischen Revolution*, ed. H. Bock (Frankfurt, 1969); Serge Bricianer, *Pannekoek and the Workers' Councils* (St. Louis, Mo., 1978); Erik Hansen, "Dutch Social Democracy and Agrarian Policy 1894-1906," *Agricultural History*, 50 (1976), pp. 460-476; Paul Mattick, "La prospettiva della rivoluzione mondiale di Anton Pannekoek," *Annali Feltrinelli* XV (1973), pp. 344-363; and Cajo Brendel, "Die 'Gruppe Internationale Kommunisten' in Holland," *Jahrbuch Arbeiterbewegung*, ed. C. Pozzoli, II (1974), pp. 253-266.
59 Cited in Hansen, "Crisis in the Party," p. 52.
60 See Pannekoek's own account: A. P. [Anton Pannekoek], "The Social Democratic Party School in Berlin," *International Socialist Review*, VIII (1907), pp. 321-324. Cf. Dieter Fricke, "Die sozialdemokratische Parteischule (1906-1914)," *Zeitschrift für Geschichtswissenschaft*, V (1957), pp. 229-248; and Nicholas Jacobs, "The German Social Democratic Party School in Berlin 1906-1914," *History Workshop*, 5 (Spring, 1978), pp. 179-187. On Luxemburg's participation see J. P. Nettl, *Rosa Luxemburg*, Vol. 1 (London, 1966), pp. 388 ff.
61 Pannekoek to Kautsky (Nov. 2, 1906), as cited by Hans M. Bock in "Anton Pannekoek in der Vorkriegs-Sozialdemokratie," in *Jahrbuch Arbeiterbewegung*, ed. C. Pozzoli, Vol. 3 (1975), p. 112.
62 A. Pannekoek, "Massenaktion und Revolution" (1912), reprinted in *Die Massenstreikdebatte*, ed. A. Grunenberg (Frankfurt, 1970), pp. 266, 268.
63 Ibid., pp. 274, 284. In Lenin's "postmortem" of this debate, he generally agreed with Pannekoek. "In this debate it is Pannekoek, not Kautsky, who

represents Marxism" (*State and Revolution* [1919] [New York, 1943], p. 95).

64 A. Pannekoek, "Marxist Theory and Revolutionary Tactics" (1912), in *Pannekoek and Gorter's Marxism*, ed. D. A. Smart (London, 1978), pp. 58–61. Cf. A. Pannekoek, "Zum Schluss," *Die Neue Zeit*, XXXI/1 (1913), pp. 611–612.

65 For a brief survey of Dietzgen's thought see Predrag Vranicki, *Storia del Marxismo*, Vol. I (Rome, 1973), pp. 260–264. See also Loyd D. Easton, "Empiricism and Ethics in Dietzgen," *Journal of the History of Ideas*, XIX (1958), pp. 77–90; and Vittorio Ancarani, "La teoria della conoscenza nel primo Dietzgen (1866–1869)," *Annali Feltrinelli*, XVII (1976), pp. 137–164.

66 Dietzgen to Marx, as cited in K. Marx, *Letters to Kugelmann*, Preface by V. I. Lenin (New York, 1934), p. 56.

67 Marx to Engels (Nov. 7, 1868), in *Selected Correspondence*, ed. S. Ryazanskaya (Moscow, 1965), p. 217.

68 A. Pannekoek, "The Position and Significance of Joseph Dietzgen's Philosophical Works" (1902), Introduction to J. Dietzgen, *The Positive Outcome of Philosophy* (Chicago, 1906), p. 35. One of Dietzgen's most enthusiastic defenders was the German-American socialist Ernst Untermann; see his obsessive treatment in *Die logischen Mängel des engeren Marxismus: Georg Plechanow et alii gegen Josef Dietzgen* (Munich, 1910). Untermann, who also translated Labriola, was convinced they supplemented each other; see his "Antonio Labriola and Joseph Dietzgen" in Labriola's *Socialism and Philosophy* (Chicago, 1918). He juggled other contraries: Untermann also managed a gold mine. See Daniel Bell, *Marxian Socialism in the United States* (Princeton, N.J., 1967), p. 87.

69 Henriette Roland-Holst, *Josef Dietzgens Philosophie* (Munich, 1910).

70 For a discussion of Pannekoek and Dietzgen see John Gerber, "The Formation of Pannekoek's Marxism," in Bricianer, *Pannekoek and the Workers' Councils*, pp. 3–8. Cf. Cajo Brendel, *Anton Pannekoek, theoretikus van het socialisme* (Nijmegen, 1970), pp. 140 ff.

71 Pannekoek, "Joseph Dietzgen's Philosophical Works," p. 37. Cf. Pannekoek, "Dietzgens Werke," *Neue Zeit*, XXXI/2 (1913), pp. 37–47.

72 A. Pannekoek, "Dietzgenismus und Marxismus" (1910), reprinted in *Jahrbuch Arbeiterbewegung*, ed. C. Pozzoli, III (1975), pp. 131–132. A later discussion of Dietzgen by Pannekoek can be found in *Lenin as Philosopher* (1938) (London, 1975), pp. 34–44.

73 On the formation and life of the various bureaus and offices see James W. Hulse, *The Forming of the Communist International* (Stanford, Calif., 1964), pp. 152 ff.; Lazitch and Drachkovitch, *Lenin and the Comintern*,

Vol. 1, pp. 164–201; Piero Conti, "Le divergenze fra gli uffici europei del comintern (1919–1920)," *MOS*, XVIII (1972), pp. 133–192; Boris Nicolaievsky, "Les Premières Années de l'Internationale communiste: D'après le récit du 'camarade Thomas,'" *Contributions à l'histoire du Comintern* (Geneva, 1965), pp. 1–28.

74 H. Gorter, "Opportunism and Dogmatism," *Worker's Dreadnought*, June 26, 1920.

75 The Amsterdam Bureau lasted only several months before being shut down as "leftist." In that brief period it issued a bulletin and held a conference. For the conference see its own report, "Conference of the 3rd International," *Bulletin of the Sub-Bureau in Amsterdam of the Communist International*, No. 2 (March, 1920). The first bulletin opened with an announcement by H. Roland-Holst and contained a criticism of Zinoviev on the sensitive issue of parliamentarism. "The main lines laid down by the Moscow Secretariat have not since proved sufficient in all practical cases" ("Comment on Theses concerning Parliamentarism," *Bulletin of the Provisional Bureau in Amsterdam of the Communist International*, No. 1 [Feb., 1920]).

76 See Lazitch and Drachkovitch, *Lenin and the Comintern*, Vol. 1, pp. 200, 257.

77 For example, A. Pannekoek, "La Socializzazione," *Il Soviet*, III/9–10 (March 28, 1920); A. Pannekoek, "Lo sviluppo della rivoluzione mondiale e la tattica del communismo," *Il Soviet*, III/22 (Sept. 5, 1920). This article, which is discussed later, was translated from *Kommunismus*.

78 *Worker's Dreadnought* is generally neglected as a source of texts and information on "left" communism. It published, for instance, Luxemburg's "The Russian Revolution," including "How the Book Was Written" by Paul Levi (April 29, 1922, and subsequent issues). Even Lukács's writing appeared in its pages: "The Social Background of the White Terror," *Worker's Dreadnought*, Nov. 20, 1920. It published an early version of Gorter's "An Open Letter to Comrade Lenin" (Sept. 25, 1920, and subsequent issues) and the full text of the final version: "Open Letter to Comrade Lenin: An Answer to Lenin's Brochure . . ." (March 29, 1921, through June 11, 1921). James Klugmann called *Worker's Dreadnought* "remarkably well informed." See his *History of the Communist Party of Great Britain*, Vol. 1 (London, 1968), p. 20. Cf. Walter Kendall, *The Revolutionary Movement in Britain 1900–1921: The Origins of British Communism* (London, 1969). For some details of Sylvia Pankhurst and *Worker's Dreadnought* see David Mitchell, *The Fighting Pankhursts* (London, 1967), pp. 81 ff. See her *Soviet Russia as I Saw It* (London, 1921) for a very muted presentation of her differences with Lenin.

79 A letter from Pannekoek to the KAPD newspaper announced his general agreement: He differed, however, on the role of the factory councils ("Ein Brief des Genossen Pannekoek," *Kommunistische Arbeiter-Zeitung,* No. 112 (n.d.). For a history of the KAPD see especially Hans M. Bock, *Syndikalismus und Linkskommunismus von 1918–1923* (Meisenheim, 1969), pp. 225–262. See also his "Bericht über den Gründungsparteitag der KAPD, 1920," *Jahrbuch Arbeiterbewegung,* ed. C. Pozzoli, V (1977), pp. 185–242. Cf. Olaf Ihlau, *Die roten Kampfer* (Meisenheim, 1969), pp. 3 ff.; Bernard Reichenbach, "Zur Geschichte der Kommunistischen Arbeiter Partei Deutschlands," *Grünberg Archiv,* XIII (1928), pp. 117–143; Denis Authier and Jean Barrot, *La Gauche Communiste en allemagne 1918–1921* (Paris, 1976), pp. 159–165; Enzo Rutigliano, *Linkskommunismus e rivoluzione in occidente: Per una storia della KAPD* (Bari, 1974); and Fritz Kool's Introduction to *Die Linke gegen die Parteiherrschaft,* ed. F. Kool (Olten, 1970). The Rutigliano text is essentially an anthology; the Introduction by Kool is extremely well informed.

80 KPD, "Leitsätze des II Parteitages über kommunistische Grundsätze und Taktik" (1919), reprinted in *Der deutsche Kommunismus: Dokumente,* ed. H. Weber (Cologne, 1964), pp. 73–75.

81 For a statement by the KAPD see "Die Lehren des Generalstreiks," *Kommunistische Arbeiter-Zeitung,* No. 89 (April 19, 1920). The KPD initially opposed the general strike called by the socialist parties. "Do not move a finger for the democratic republic which is only a shabby mask for the dictatorship of the bourgeoisie" (KPD, "Aufruf der KPD während des Kapp-Putsches [1920]," in *Der deutsche Kommunismus: Dokumente,* p. 139). This position was not maintained or obeyed by many regional KPD organizations, however. For an important study and argument about the response to the Kapp Putsch see George Eliasberg, *Der Ruhrkrieg von 1920* (Bonn, 1974). Cf. Erhard Lucas, *Märzrevolution 1920,* 2 vols. (Frankfurt, 1973 and 1974). Lucas sharply criticizes Eliasberg in Vol. 2, pp. 197 ff. See also Barrington Moore Jr., *Injustice: The Social Bases of Obedience and Revolt* (White Plains, N.Y., 1978), pp. 328–353.

82 See the figures in Weber, *Die Wandlung des deutsche Kommunismus,* Vol. 1, pp. 39, 362.

83 Kommunistische Arbeiterpartei Deutschlands, "An das deutsche Proletariat," *Die Aktion,* April 17, 1920. Cf. "German Communist Workers' Party," *Worker's Dreadnought,* July 17, 1920; and "Bericht über den Gründungs Parteitag der Kommunistischen Arbeiterpartei Deutschlands," *Kommunistische Arbeiter-Zeitung,* No. 90 (April 23, 1920).

84 "Programm der Kommunistischen Arbeiter-Partei Deutschlands," *Die Aktion,* June 12, 1920. Similar analyses are reiterated in various KAPD publi-

cations. For instance, an article in the KAPD journal argued that the problem of the German revolution was not "technical" but "cultural." "We must . . . place ever more strongly in the forefront the struggle for the development of the self-consciousness [*Selbstbewusstseinsentwicklung*] of the proletariat" ("Einigung der Kommunistischen Parteien Deutschlands?" *Proletarier: Monatsschrift für Kommunismus* I/1 [1920], p. 7).

85 Die Redaktion, *Kommunismus* I/28–29 (1920), p. 976. The KAPD newspaper excerpted the essay, titling it "Das Problem der westeuropäischen Revolution," *Kommunistische Arbeiter-Zeitung*, No. 121 (n.d.).

86 Pannekoek, "World Revolution and Communist Tactics," *Pannekoek and Gorter's Marxism*, p. 97.

87 Ibid., p. 103.

88 A. Pannekoek, "Der neue Blanquismus" (1920), reprinted in Pannekoek and Gorter, *Organisation und Taktik*, pp. 120–121. The KAPD generally followed, or borrowed, these formulations on the distinction between Western Europe and Russia; the KAPD was also aware that the SPD emphasized the uniqueness of Western Europe. For that reason it demarcated its position from the Social Democrats. See "Grundzüge kommunistischer Politik: Die Bedingungen der westeuropäischen Revolution," *Kommunistische Arbeiter-Zeitung*, No. 147 (n.d.). At times their position did approach Slavic phobia; see in the KAPD monthly "Oesticher und westlicher Kommunismus," *Proletarier* I/1 (1920), pp. 9–11.

89 H. Gorter, "Offener Brief an den Genossen Lenin" (1920), in *Organisation und Taktik*, pp. 194, 224, 226. This was originally published by the KAPD. Cf. Communist Labor Party of Germany [KAPD], "A Manifesto of the German Anti-Parliamentarians," *Worker's Dreadnought*, Jan. 29, 1921. The most forceful counter-reply to Gorter (not to his pamphlet but to his presentation of views in the Executive Committee of the Communist International) belonged to Trotsky. For an abbreviated account of the session, where Gorter is identified as Comrade "Ch," see "Das Exekutive Komitee der Kommunistischen Internationale: Sitzung vom 24, November," *Die Kommunistische Internationale*, II/15 (1920), pp. 410–413. For Trotsky's full statement see his "On the Policy of the KAPD" (1920), reprinted in his *The First Five Years of the Communist International*, Vol. 1 (London, 1973), pp. 174–189. With supreme sarcasm Trotsky replied in the name of the "poor orphans of Eastern Europe" to Gorter's "edifying lecture" in the name of Western Europe. "Allow me to recall that many of us participated for a number of years in the Western European labor movement." Like Lenin in *"Left-Wing" Communism*, Trotsky defended the international significance and model of the Russian Revolution. "In analyzing our Russian conditions and in connecting them up with the march of the world

revolution we were not aided by an indigenous Russian theory" (pp. 174–177). Several points about Trotsky's counter-charges should be mentioned: Trotsky accused Gorter of approaching the world from an "English insular standpoint, forgetting about Asia and about Africa" and ignoring the "international character" of the revolution. In general Gorter was not guilty of this; see for example his "Der opportunismus in der niederlandischen Kommunistischen Partei" (1921), which defended an "international" perspective (reprinted in Kool, ed., *Die Linke gegen die Parteiherrschaft*, pp. 260–298). Moreover, an abdication of an international perspective does not inhere in Western Marxism; that is, the argument for the *specificity* of West European conditions does not necessarily conclude with the superiority of Western Europe or North America. Rosa Luxemburg is a case in point. Like Trotsky, she adopted an emphatic international view of the revolution, but she also objected to the Russian Revolution as the universal model; and she did so in the name of the specific conditions of Western Europe. This is also true for Pannekoek. His "World Revolution and Communist Tactics," which is probably the best Western Marxist text of the period, took careful note of international developments and came close to assuming – to use a later vocabulary – a Third World stance. For Pannekoek, the very difficulty of revolution in the "old" bourgeois countries shifted the arena to the newer regions. "The Russian Revolution is the beginning of the great revolt by Asia against the Western European capital" ("World Revolution and Communist Tactics," *Pannekoek and Gorter's Marxism*, p. 138). "The world revolution is not seen in its full universal significance if considered only from the Western European perspective" (p. 137). "The interests of Asia are in essence the interests of the human race." Consequently, Pannekoek defended, as did Lenin, movements of national liberation. Trotsky also charged that Gorter's belief that the working class had been "bourgeoisified" was "absolutely false and anti-revolutionary." However sharply Trotsky raised this issue, his reply rested on a single and slender theoretical reed: Only the labor aristocracy ("although rather large numerically") was "bourgeoisified" (p. 179). Beneath this "crust" lay the great mass of revolutionary workers. As discussed in Chapter 6, Western Marxism implicitly or explicitly challenged the concept of labor aristocracy.

90 Council communism and its variants – soviets, factory councils, workers' councils – have been criticized for political naiveté, failure to confront the reality of state power, fetish of factory labor and technology, and limited social base in skilled labor. The first two points were raised by Bordiga in his often cogent critique of Gramsci. Several recent discussions have pursued these points. See Carl Boggs, "Marxism, Prefigurative Communism

and the Problem of Workers' Control," *Radical America*, XI–XII (Nov., 1977–Feb., 1978), pp. 99–122, and his "Three Pannekoek Books," *Telos*, 42 (Winter, 1979–1980), pp. 169–181; Brian Peterson, "Workers Councils in Germany, 1918–1919: Recent Literature on the Rätebewegung," *New German Critique*, 4 (Winter, 1975), pp. 113–124; Sergio Bologna, "Class Composition and the Theory of the Party and the Origin of the Workers-Council Movement," *Telos*, 13 (Fall, 1972), pp. 3–27; Guido de Masi and Giacomo Marramao, "Councils and State in Weimar Germany," *Telos*, 28 (Summer, 1976), pp. 3–35; and Barrington Moore Jr., *Injustice*, pp. 275–315.

4. From politics to philosophy

1 Karl Horner [Anton Pannekoek] in *Proletarier*, 7–8 (1927), as cited in Serge Bricianer, *Pannekoek and Worker's Councils* (St. Louis, Mo., 1978), p. 231.

2 Major studies on the young Lukács have recently appeared in English, German, Italian, and French. See Andrew Arato and Paul Breines, *The Young Lukács and the Origins of Western Marxism* (New York, 1979); Jörg Kammler, *Politishe Theorie von Georg Lukács* (Darmstadt, 1974); Laura Boella, *Il giovane Lukács* (Bari, 1977); Michael Löwy, *Pour Une Sociologie des intellectuels révolutionnaires: L'Évolution politique de Lukács 1909–1929* (Paris, 1976). Other relevant studies include Georg H. R. Parkinson, *Georg Lukács* (London, 1977); Fritz J. Raddatz, *Georg Lukács* (Reinbek bei Hamburg, 1972); Antonia Grunenberg, *Bürger und Revolutionär: Georg Lukács 1918–1928* (Cologne, 1976); George Lichtheim, *Georg Lukács* (New York, 1970); Iring Fetscher, *Marx and Marxism* (New York, 1971); István Mészáros, *Lukács' Concept of Dialectic* (London, 1972); Morris Watnick, "Relativism and Class Consciousness: Georg Lukács," in *Revisionism*, ed. L. Labedz (New York, 1962); Andrew Arato, "Lukács' Path to Marxism," *Telos*, 7 (1971), p. 128–136; David Kettler, "Culture and Revolution: Lukács in the Hungarian Revolution of 1918," and Andrew Feenberg, "Reification and the Antinomies of Socialist Thought," both in *Telos*, 10 (1971), pp. 35–92 and 93–118; Andrew Arato, "Lukács' Theory of Reification," Paul Breines, "Praxis and Its Theorists: The Impact of Lukács and Korsch in the 1920s," and Paul Piccone, "Dialectic and Materialism in Lukács," all in *Telos*, 11 (1972), pp. 25–66, 67–103, and 105–133; Peter Ludz, "Der Begriff der 'demokratischen Diktatur' in der politischen Philosophie von Georg Lukács," in *Festschrift zum achzigsten Geburtstag von Georg Lukács*, ed. F. Benseler (Neuwied, 1965); and James Schmidt, "Lukács' Concept of Proletarian *Bildung*," *Telos*, 24 (1975), pp. 2–40.

3 G. Lukács, "Preface" (1962), *The Theory of the Novel* (Cambridge, Mass., 1971), pp. 12–17; "Vorwort," *Die Theorie des Romans* (Neuwied, 1963), pp. 10–11.
4 Cited in Tibor Hanak, *Lukács war anderes* (Meisenheim, 1973), p. 36.
5 G. Lukács, "Zur romantischen Lebensphilosophie: Novalis" (1907), in *Die Seele und die Formen* (Neuwied, 1971), p. 72.
6 G. Lukács, "Märchenvorträge in den Schulen" (1919), in Lukács, *Taktik und Ethik: Politische Aufsätze*, Vol. I (Darmstadt, 1975), p. 274. See the description in Frank Eckelt, "The Internal Policies of the Hungarian Soviet Republic," in *Hungary in Revolution 1918–1919*, ed. I. Völgyes (Lincoln, Neb., 1971), pp. 65–66.
7 Lukács, "Der Bolschewismus als moralisches Problem" (1918), *Taktik und Ethik*, pp. 27–33.
8 Lukács, "Eine kulturelle Pressfehde" (1919), *Taktik und Ethik*, p. 94.
9 K. Marx, "On the Jewish Question," in *Early Writings*, ed. Q. Hoare (New York, 1975), p. 233.
10 G. Lukács, "The Old Culture and the New Culture" (1919), in *Towards a New Marxism*, eds. B. Grahl and P. Piccone (St. Louis, Mo., 1973), pp. 21–30; see also the Introduction by Paul Breines, "Notes on Lukács' 'The Old Culture and the New Culture.' "
11 G. Lukács, "The Changing Function of Historical Materialism" (1919), *History and Class Consciousness*, trans. R. Livingstone (London, 1971), p. 249–252.
12 G. Lukács, "Tactics and Ethics," *Political Writings 1919–1929* (London, 1972), p. 15.
13 Ibid., p. 16; *Taktik und Ethik*, pp. 59–60.
14 "While I continued to support ultraleft tendencies on the great international problems of revolution . . . On the Hungarian front I followed Landler in advocating an energetic anti-sectarian line" ("Preface to the New Edition" [1967], *History and Class Consciousness*, p. xv).
15 Lichtheim calls Lukács "Szabó's disciple" (*Georg Lukács*, p. 36). Löwy stresses his role; see his *Pour Une Sociologie des intellectuels révolutionnaires*.
16 On Szabó see Oscar Jászi, "Erwin Szabo und seine Werke," *Grünberg Archiv*, X (1922), pp. 22 ff.; Zoltán Horváth, *Die Jahrhundertwende in Ungarn* (Neuwied, 1966), pp. 354 ff.; Kammler, *Politische Theorie von Georg Lukács*, pp. 60–65; Rudi Dutschke, *Versuch, Lenin auf die Füsse zu stellen* (Berlin, 1974), pp. 144–153.
17 Lagardelle to Szabó (Feb. 17, 1905), in János Jemnitz, "La Correspondance d'Ervin Szabó avec les socialistes et les syndicalistes de France (1904–1912)," *Le Mouvement social*, 52 (1965), p. 117.

18 Cited in and see the discussion in Tibor Süle, *Sozialdemokratie in Ungarn: Zur Rolle der Intelligenz in der Arbeiterbewegung 1899-1910* (Cologne, 1967), p. 95.
19 Szabó, as cited in F. Musci, *Die Kämpfe für die organisatorische Reform der Sozialdemokratischen Partei Ungarns (1900-1918)* (Budapest, 1975), p. 17.
20 See Jósef Révai, "Ervin Szabó et sa place dans le mouvement ouvrier hongrois," in *Etudes historiques* (*Studia Historica*), 10 (1955), pp. 137-138.
21 See Yvon Bourdet, "Georg Lukács im Wiener Exil (1919-1930)," in *Geschichte und Gesellschaft: Festschrift für Karl R. Stadler*, ed. G. Botz (Vienna, 1974). Bourdet stresses, unconvincingly, the theoretical affinity between Lukács and Austro-Marxism. In this regard see Tom Bottomore, "Introduction," in *Austro-Marxism*, ed. T. Bottomore and P. Goode (Oxford, 1978), p. 7.
22 These included articles by Pannekoek and Roland-Holst. The text by Pannekoek was discussed in Chapter 3. An essay by Roland-Holst developed an unconventional analysis, close to Lukács, within a conventional framework. The Communist party was viewed as extraneous, but necessary, to the working class. According to Roland-Holst, the Russian example possessed only limited validity in the West; she argued that the Communist party should not ratify its existence apart from the working class but dissolve into it. The article closed, "Communists work to prepare their own destruction." By this she meant that Communists worked to make themselves superfluous. See her "Die Aufgabe der Kommunistischen Partei in der proletarischen Revolution," *Kommunismus*, II (1921), p. 209. Between the original Dutch text published in 1920 and the German translation in 1921, much of the emphatic "left" statements were deleted. See Cajo Brendel, "Texthinweise," in H. Roland-Holst, *Die revolutionäre Partei* (Berlin, 1972), pp. xx-xxiii.
23 V. Lenin, "Kommunismus," *Collected Works*, Vol. 31 (Moscow, 1966), pp. 165-168.
24 Lukács, "Party and Class," *Political Writings*, p. 31.
25 Lukács, "The Question of Parliamentarianism," Ibid., pp. 53-63.
26 Kammler's *Politische Theorie von Georg Lukács*, the most detailed examination, dates the supremacy of the party in Lukács from the end of 1920 (p. 194). Grunenberg in *Bürger und Revolutionär* sees a change in the course of the whole of 1920 (pp. 137 ff.) but cites a decisive shift spurred by the March Action of the following year. Boella in *Il giovane Lukács* also cites a decline in councils from the end of 1920 (p. 126). Inasmuch as Lukács's position was slowly changing and he was working toward a syn-

thesis of centralization of the party and the ethos of workers' councils, many essays show signs of each; and many can be used as proof that he retained his "leftism" or embraced orthodox Leninism. For example, his "Massenstreik und Arbeiterräte in Deutschland" (1920), reprinted in Lukács, *Revolution und Gegenrevolution: Politische Aufsätze,* Vol. II (Darmstadt, 1976), explained that because of the "infantile disease," the revolutionary workers' movement has "not grasped and correctly evaluated the revolutionary meaning of workers' councils" (p. 85). He also asserted that "hitherto the revolutionary movement failed because the revolution had no leading party" (p. 83). Citations evenly stressing the party and the councils can be multiplied. Rudi Dutschke draws attention to a debate slightly later where Lukács was still suspicious of (over)centralization. Lukács defended relative autonomy for the Youth International and the Communist party, and he decried a mechanical transfer of the Russian model to the international youth movement. For this he was charged with syndicalism. See Dutschke, *Versuch, Lenin auf die Füsse zu stellen,* pp. 278–279. This volume reprints an attack on Lukács by B. Ziegler, "Doch 'Jugendsyndikalismus?' " pp. 343–347. Lukács's essays, "Partei und Jugendbewegung in Ungarn" (1921) and "Zur Frage von Partei und Jugend" (1921), are both in his *Organisation und Illusion: Politische Aufsätze,* Vol. III (Darmstadt, 1977). On the Youth International see E. H. Carr, *The Bolshevik Revolution, 1917–1923,* Vol. 3 (Harmondsworth, England, 1971), pp. 398–402.

27 From the March Action and the Paul Levi "case" Lukács drew the conclusion of "the necessity of centralization and discipline." See his "Paul Levi" (1921), *Organisation und Illusion,* pp. 11–15. In a Foreword from the same year to Luxemburg's "Mass Strike" he defended her repudiation of the idea that the party can "make" a revolution, adding that she did not deny the party: "On the contrary! She is the first – outside the Russians – who correctly recognized and classified the true role of the party: *leadership and direction of the spontaneous occurrences of the mass movement*" ("Vorwort zu Rosa Luxemburg: Massenstreik" [1921], *Organisation und Illusion,* pp. 95–96).

28 Lukács, "Selbstkritik" (1920), *Revolution und Gegenrevolution,* p. 45.

29 B. Kun, as cited by R. L. Tökés, "Béla Kun," in *Hungary in Revolution,* ed. I. Völgyes, p. 190.

30 B. Kun, as cited in Dutschke, *Versuch, Lenin auf die Füsse zu stellen,* p. 300.

31 For some details of the Hungarian dispute see Boella, *Il giovane Lukács,* pp. 152–156; and Kammler, *Politische Theorie,* pp. 222–229. That Kun was able to mount the charges of "syndicalism" and "Dutch Marxism"

against Lukács and Landler while advocating adventurism is a mystery. Part of the explanation may be because, to quote Lukács, Kun "was anxious to clear himself in Moscow eyes from the suspicion of leftist tendencies dating from the March Action" (Lukács, "The Politics of Illusion – Yet Again?" *Political Writings*, p. 118). This is generous. Kun's putschist tendencies date from June 1919, when his emissary, Ernest Bettelheim, organized – or, to follow Radek, "disorganized" – a putsch in Austria. Bettelheim intended to save the Hungarian revolution. This had no official sanction from the Comintern but was abetted by Kun: So concludes Hans Hartmann, *Die verlorene Räterepublik: Am Beispiel der Kommunistischen Partie Deutschösterreichs* (Vienna, 1971), pp. 169 ff. The article by Radek, "The Lessons of an Attempted Putsch: The Crisis in the German-Austrian Party" (1919), and the rejoinder by Bettelheim are reprinted in H. Gruber, ed., *International Communism in the Era of Lenin* (Greenwich, Conn., 1967), pp. 202–217. Apart from the casualties, the consequences of the putsch were deadly for the Austrian Communist party; it "remained an insignificant sect as long as the Austrian republic existed" (Franz Borkenau, *World Communism* [Ann Arbor, Mich., 1962], p. 129). Considering Kun's role in the Austrian putsch and his plans for the Hungarian party, one might imagine that Lukács's criticism of the March Action would be more forceful than it was. See Lukács's comments at the Third Congress: *Protokoll des III Kongresses der Kommunistischen Internationale*, Moscow, June 22–July 12, 1921 (Hamburg, 1921), pp. 591 ff. Elsewhere Lukács was less guarded; see his "Vor dem dritten Kongress" (1921), in *Organisation und Illusion*, pp. 72–86. See Victor Serge's comments on Kun in his *Memoirs of a Revolutionary 1901–1914* (Oxford, 1978), pp. 138–140.

32 Kammler notes the irony that Lukács several months earlier had sharply attacked Levi's similar denunciation of the March Action (*Politische Theorie*, p. 225).

33 Lukács, "The Politics of Illusion – Yet Again?" (1922), *Political Writings*, p. 119.

34 Ibid., p. 121.

35 Lukács, "Organization and Revolutionary Initiative" (1921), *Political Writings*, pp. 115–116. Of course Lukács also criticizes Gorter, in this essay as well as elsewhere; see for instance "Wo stehen wir?" (1920), *Revolution und Gegenrevolution*, pp. 126–128.

36 Lukács, *History and Class Consciousness*, p. 312.

37 Ibid., p. 335.

38 Ibid., pp. 335–336, 337.

39 Lukács referred to the "fate" of Korsch as a political outsider as a reason

to remain within the party ("Preface to the New Edition" [1967], *History and Class Consciousness*, p. xxx).

40 See the survey by Gian Rusconi, "Korsch's Political Development," *Telos*, 27 (1967), pp. 61–78; and Christiano Camporesi, *Il marxismo teorico negli USA 1900–1945* (Milan, 1973), pp. 142–152.

41 K. Korsch, *Karl Marx* (London, 1938). See the Introduction to the German edition by Götz Langkau, "Zum Text dieser Aufgabe," in Korsch, *Karl Marx*, ed. G. Langkau (Frankfurt, 1967), pp. v–xv.

42 Korsch to Mattick (Sept. 20, 1938), "Briefe an Paul Partos, Paul Mattick und Bert Brecht: 1934–1939," *Jahrbuch Arbeiterbewegung*, ed. C. Pozzoli, II (1974), pp. 182–183. The book became *Dialectic of Enlightenment*. Walter Benjamin wrote to T. W. Adorno in 1930, "I read Korsch: *Marxismus und Philosophie*. Really weak steps – it seems to me – in a good direction" (cited in Susan Buck-Morss, *The Origin of Negative Dialectics* [New York, 1977], p. 207). Korsch himself did not highly esteem the Frankfurt School.

43 Wolfdietrich Rasch, "Brechts marxistischer Lehrer," *Alternative*, VIII (1965), pp. 94–99. See the letters in the same issue of *Alternative*, pp. 45–53. Cf. Heinz Brüggemann, "Bert Brecht und Karl Korsch," *Jahrbuch Arbeiterbewegung*, ed. C. Pozzoli, I (1973), pp. 177–188; and Henry Pachter, "Brecht's Personal Politics," *Telos*, 44 (Summer, 1980), pp. 39–48.

44 Sidney Hook, *Towards the Understanding of Karl Marx* (New York, 1933), p. xii. See Cristiano Camporesi, *Il marxismo teorico negli USA 1900–1945* (Milan, 1973), pp. 93–128. Korsch wrote his thoughts on the Hook book to Mattick (May 10, 1935), "Briefe an Paul Partos," pp. 135–136. For a discussion of Hook's Marxism see Richard Pell, *Radical Visions and American Dreams* (New York, 1974), pp. 131–140.

45 Adorno noted that Korsch was "so far left that he practically comes out again on the right" and that compared to him even the situation of a Trotskyist would be "enviable" (Adorno to Krenek [Oct. 20, 1938], in T. W. Adorno and Ernst Krenek, *Briefwechsel* [Frankfurt, 1975], pp. 131–132).

46 K. Korsch, *Marxism and Philosophy* (London, 1970), p. 84.

47 Anna Lesznai, as cited by David Kettler, "Culture and Revolution: Lukács in the Hungarian Revolution of 1918," *Telos*, 10 (1971), p. 69.

48 The most detailed studies of the earlier Korsch are Paul Breines's "Korsch's Road to Marx," *Telos*, 26 (1975–1976), pp. 42–56; and Michael Buckmiller's "Marxismus als Realität: Zur Rekonstruktion der theoretischen und politischen Entwicklung Kark Korschs," in *Jahrbuch Arbeiterbewegung*, ed. C. Pozzoli, I (1973), pp. 15–106; and his *Karl Korsch und*

das Problem der materialistischen Dialektik (Hannover, 1976). Korsch's widow, Hedda Korsch, does not accept Buckmiller's interpretation; she maintains that Korsch entered the KPD with doubts and reservations (private interview, Hedda Korsch, Los Angeles, April 3, 1978).

49 See Breines, "Korsch's 'Road to Marx,'" pp. 49-51; and Buckmiller, "Marxismus als Realität," pp. 26-31.

50 K. Korsch, "Praktischer Sozialismus" (1920), reprinted in Korsch, *Kommentare zur deutschen "Revolution" und ihrer Niederlage* (The Hague, 1972), pp. 24-25.

51 See generally Werner Angress, *Stillborn Revolution: The Communist Bid for Power in Germany 1921-1923* (Princeton, N.J., 1963). Thalheimer's later analysis is valuable; he criticized the identification of Germany of 1923 with Russia of 1917 and explained that Brandler deferred to the Russians because of the success of their revolution (A. Thalheimer, *1923: Eine verpasste Revolution?* [Berlin, 1931]).

52 See for example F. L. Carsten, *The Reichswehr and Politics 1918-1933* (Berkeley, Calif., 1973), p. 194; and Erich Eyck, *A History of the Weimar Republic*, Vol. 1 (New York, 1967), p. 268.

53 K. H. Tjaden, *Struktur und Funktion der "KPD Opposition" (KPO)* (Erlangen, 1970), pp. 30-40.

54 Trotsky's *New Course*, criticizing Soviet leadership, had just appeared as a booklet (January, 1924). Yet even to the participants the relationship between the two factional fights - Soviet and German - was mysterious. For some details on the maneuvers see Otto Wenzel, "Die Kommunistische Partei Deutschlands im Jahr 1923," Ph.D. dissertation, Freien University, Berlin, 1955, pp. 266 ff.; Issac Deutscher, *The Prophet Unarmed: Trotsky 1921-1929*, Vol. 2 (New York, 1965), pp. 144-163; and E. H. Carr, *The Interregnum 1923-1924* (Baltimore, 1969), pp. 238-251. That Trotsky and Brandler drew opposite conclusions from the German October seems not to have mattered in linking them. See L. Trotsky, "On the Road to the European Revolution" (1924) and "Through What Stage Are We Passing?" *The Challenge of the Left Opposition 1923-1925* (New York, 1975), pp. 163-174. See also the memoir of Brandler by I. Deutscher, "Record of a Discussion with Heinrich Brandler," *New Left Review*, 105 (1977), pp. 47-81. Radek served to link Trotsky and Brandler inasmuch as he was associated with each. See Warren Lerner, *Karl Radek* (Stanford, Calif., 1970), pp. 124-125. Cf. Marie-Luise Goldbach, *Karl Radek und die deutsche-sowjetischen Beziehungen 1919-1923* (Bonn, 1973), pp. 132 ff.

55 Zinoviev, "Rede des Genossen Sinowjew über die Lage der KPD" (in der Stitzung der Exekutive der Komintern January 1924), *Die Internationale*,

VII (1924), p. 44. For Zinoviev's position before the shake up see his *Probleme der deutschen Revolution* (Hamburg, 1923).

56 Cf. Theo Becker, *Der politische Erfahrungsgehalt der geschichtsphilosophischen Kritik Karl Korschs am dogmatischen Marxismus (1923–1930)* (Hannover, 1977), pp. 93 ff. Becker criticizes Buckmiller on several points.

57 Hermann Weber, *Die Wandlung des deutschen Kommunismus*, Vol. 1 (Frankfurt, 1969), p. 63. Cf. Ossip Flechtheim, *Die Kommunistische Partei Deutschlands in der Weimarer Republik* (Offenbach, 1948), pp. 100 ff.

58 According to Ruth Fischer in her *Stalin and German Communism* (Cambridge, Mass., 1948), Maslow had met with Shlyapnikov, a leader of the Russian Worker's Opposition, who in 1921 had been sent to Berlin (p. 182). Daniels confirms that Shlyapnikov was in Germany seeking contact with the left of the KPD; see Robert V. Daniels, *The Conscience of the Revolution: Communist Opposition in Soviet Russia* (New York, 1969), p. 162. Schapiro records Shlyapnikov's German trip, his meeting with Maslow, and the affinity between the Worker's Opposition and the KAPD (Leonard Schapiro, *The Origins of the Communist Aristocracy* [New York, n.d.], pp. 330–331). Fischer claims they met at the home of Arthur Rosenberg, a leftist and later a historian. Helmut Schachenmayer repeats the account but gives no further sources; see his *Arthur Rosenberg* (Wiesbaden, 1964), p. 24. In any case Lenin did attack Maslow for "playing at leftism" and alluded to his provocative contacts with the Russian left opposition; see V. Lenin, "A Letter to the German Communist Party" (August 14, 1921), *Collected Works*, Vol. 32 (Moscow, 1965), p. 519.

59 Carr noted in regard to this investigation, "few references to this episode exist in party literature" (*The Interregnum*, p. 217). Cf. Fischer, *Stalin and German Communism*, pp. 361–362. Erich Wollenberg (1892–1973) mentions the incident in his unpublished memoirs (Archives of the Hoover Institution).

60 Cf. Pierre Broué, *Revolution en allemagne 1917–1923* (Paris, 1971), p. 557.

61 Zinoviev, "Artikel des Genossen Sinowjew" (March 26, 1924), in *Bericht über die Verhandlungen des IX Parteitages der Kommunistischen Partei Deutschlands*, held in Frankfurt from April 7 to April 10, 1924, ed. Central Committee of the KPD (Berlin, 1924), pp. 78–79. At least to some of the delegates the letter was a surprise. The alliance between Zinoviev and the left had been struck against the right of Brandler and Thalheimer; now Zinoviev was attacking the left. "What is happening now?" asked one delegate. "The general line [of Zinoviev's letter] now shows: the main

danger exists in the left and one must struggle against left deviations. That is a shift since January" (p. 289).

62 Zinoviev, "Briefe Sinowjews und Bucharins an Thälmann und Schlecht" (March 31, 1924), reprinted in Weber, *Die Wandlung des deutschen Kommunismus*, Vol. 1, pp. 399–400.

63 Zinoviev, "Briefe Sinowjews an Maslow und Fischer" (March 31, 1924), in H. Weber, "Zu den Beziehungen zwischen der KPD und der Kommunistischen Internationale," *VfZ*, XVI (1968), p. 191. The new leadership of Fischer and Maslow sought to parry the attack. Fischer claimed that stray pronouncements defending Rosa Luxemburg "here and there" "misled the Executive of the Comintern" into believing "the formation of an ultra-left wing was a real danger." In fact, the danger was on the right (R. F. [Ruth Fischer], "Der Frankfurter Parteitag," *Die Internationale*, VII [1924], p. 232). The Politburo of the KPD replied to Zinoviev's letter to the Ninth Congress; it declared that intellectuals participated in both wings of the party and that "under the appearance of a struggle against the 'ultra-left,' there is in reality a struggle against the party leadership" (Polbüro, "Einige Ergänzungen zum Artikel des Gen. Sinowjew," *Die Internationale*, VII [1924], pp. 247, 250).

64 Max Levien to Maslow (April 1, 1924), in Weber, "Zu den Beziehungen," p. 195.

65 K. Korsch, "Ein Nachwort statt Vorwort" to "Marxismus und Philosophie," *Grünberg Archiv*, XI (1925), p. 121. Other endorsements of Lukács can be found in Korsch's writings; for example, in 1922 he commended Lukács's review of Dilthey's book on Hegel (K. Korsch, "Eine Antikritik" [1922], *Kommentare zur deutschen "Revolution,"* p. 64).

66 K. Korsch, "Über materialistische Dialektik" (1924), reprinted in Korsch, *Marxismus und Philosophie* (Frankfurt, 1966), p. 173.

67 "One section (Boris and Samosch, both Russians) demanded a breach of all political and organisational ties between the Communists and the Russian state" (Rosa Leviné-Meyer, *Inside German Communism: Memoirs of Party Life in the Weimar Republic* [London, 1977], p. 65).

68 Boris [Roninger], "Zur Programmfrage," *Die Internationale*, VII (1924), pp. 328 ff.

69 G. Sinowjew, "Bericht über die Tätigkeit der Exekutive," *Fünfter Kongress der Kommunistischen Internationale*, Vol. 1, (n.p., n.d.), Feltrinelli Reprint (1967), p. 53.

70 Fischer, *Fünfter Kongress*, p. 202.

71 What is surprising is not the identification of Korsch as an ultra-leftist but the claim that it was based on a misunderstanding, and that at this date

Korsch was not an oppositional figure. According to Douglas Kellner, the notion that Korsch resisted Comintern leadership before September 1925 is a "legend." See his "Korsch's Revolutionary Marxism," in Karl Korsch, *Revolutionary Theory*, ed. D. Kellner (Austin, Tex., 1977). Kellner is attacking the following interpretations: E. H. Carr, *Socialism in One Country III* (Harmondsworth, 1972), pp. 111–115; Paul Breines, "Praxis and Its Theorists," *Telos*, 26 (1972), pp. 67–103; as well as David Bathrick, "Introduction to Korsch," *New German Critique*, I/3 (1974), pp. 3–6, and Fred Halliday, "Karl Korsch: An Introduction," in Korsch, *Marxism and Philosophy*. It is true – to take up one additional point – that "Lenin and the Comintern" did not telegraph Korsch's heresy, but this was not necessary. It was a subtle, almost opaque, defense of Lenin against deviations. Yet it contained a qualified apology for the Luxemburgian and Hegelian dimensions of Marxism, and it criticized the codification of Leninism. Moreover Zinoviev, with no ambiguity, attacked the article at the Fifth World Congress. "The editor of the magazine, Comrade Korsch, 'defends' Comrade Lenin from many deviations from Leninism. I believe that we should give Comrade Korsch the friendly advice to study above all Marxism and Leninism . . . I believe that it is not too much to demand of the German Party, when I ask that the magazine *Internationale* be placed in the hands of Marxists" (Zinoviev, *Fünfter Kongress*, p. 54). If there is still doubt, Korsch later complained of attacks on this article. In a review some months after the Congress he mentioned in passing that his "Lenin and the Comintern" was "unjustly and without foundation attacked at the Fifth Congress as a critique of Leninism . . ." (K. Korsch, "J. Stalin, *Lenin und der Leninismus*," *Der Internationale*, VII [1924], p. 668). See also Henri Rabasseire [Henry Pachter], "Kellner on Korsch," *Telos*, 28 (1976), pp. 195–198. Apart from the political facts, Kellner's argument that the condemnation of Korsch was based on a misunderstanding is based on a misunderstanding. "There was supposed to be some kind of profound connection between 'idealist deviations' and ultra-leftism: Hegel would have smiled" (Kellner in Korsch, *Revolutionary Theory*, p. 46). Whether Hegel would have smiled is difficult to know; however, insofar as the history of Western Marxism is co-terminous with the retrieval of Hegelian thought, there is "some kind of profound connection."

72 A. M., "Einige Bermerkungen zur Programmfrage," *Die Rote Fahne*, June 17, 1924.

73 "Diskussion über den Bericht vom 5. Weltkongress: Zentralausschutzsitzung vom 20. Juli," *Die Rote Fahne*, July 25, 1924. "We have explained that the article of Boris in the *Internationale* was a significant mistake because it sought to use the mood of the working class radicalism to

smuggle in anti-Bolshevik tendencies . . . The editor of the *Internationale* has admitted the error."

74 Ruth Fischer, "Parteitag der Bolschewisierung," *Die Rote Fahne*, June 28, 1925.

75 See for example "Die zweite Reichstagung des marxistisch–leninistischen Zirkels," *Die Internationale*, VIII (1925), p. 78.

76 "The position of the present 'ultra-left' group in the KPD (Scholem, Katz, Rosenberg, Korsch) is in the last analysis based on their absolute incapability of applying Bolshevik tactics to the concrete relations in Germany" (G. Sinowjew, "Brief des Exekutivkomitees der Komintern an den X Parteitag der Kommunistischen Partei Deutschlands," *Die Rote Fahne*, July 9, 1925).

77 "Die erste Rede des Genossen Sinowjew: Aus den Verhandlungen des EKKI über die deutsche Frage," *Die Rote Fahne*, Sept. 26, 1925. This speech was delivered on August 13 but was made public on Sept. 26 and 27. See also speeches of Comrades Bukharin and Zinoviev, *Der neue Kurs*, ed. Central Committee of the KPD (Berlin, 1925). Zinoviev charged that although the party claimed to be Marxist, it tolerated Korsch. "When we said that Korsch is no Marxist, but a petty-bourgeois gone mad, and you should remove him, that was not done" (p. 22).

78 "Briefe der Exekutive der Kommunistischen Internationale an alle Organisationen und die Mitglieder der KPD," *Die Rote Fahne*, Sept. 1, 1925; reprinted in H. Weber, ed., *Der deutsche Kommunismus: Dokumente*, (Cologne, 1964), pp. 218–242.

79 Ibid., pp. 222, 233, 227, 230. Excerpts of the "open letter" are in H. Gruber (ed.), *Soviet Russia Masters the Comintern* (Garden City, N.Y., 1974), pp. 49–55.

80 Leviné-Meyer, *Inside German Communism*, p. 86.

81 Of Korsch's denunciation of the Comintern for "red imperialism" Kellner says: "I have yet to discover any evidence for this story and suspect it is part of the Korsch legend" (*Karl Korsch*, p. 69). The evidence is everywhere; Korsch even tried to explain it away. An anonymous article in *Die Rote Fahne* made the standard distinction between decent proletarians and irresponsible intellectuals on the left. As an example of the latter it cited Korsch's remarks from the Frankfurt District meeting. It quoted him as saying "that through the alliance of the Soviet Union with capitalist states, the revolutionary propositions of the Comintern could be placed in danger. In this connection, Korsch characterized the campaign for international trade union unity, as a 'product of Russian foreign policy, and spoke of 'red imperialism,' and a 'possible 1914 of the Comintern'" ("Neider mit dem kleinbürgerlichen antibolschewistischen Geist," *Die*

Rote Fahne, Sept. 22, 1925). Ernst Meyer in a letter cataloging the responses to the "open letter" also cited Korsch's remarks. Korsch "spoke of a possible '1914' of the Comintern. Comarade Korsch, followed so closely the style of the antibolshevik pressure that he spoke of a 'red imperialism' (of the Soviet Government)" (Meyers to Klinger [Oct. 3, 1925], in Weber, *Die Wandlung*, Vol. 1, pp. 413–414). Heinz Neumann attacked Korsch at length and referred to the same statements (Neumann, "Der neue Kurs der KPD," *Die Internationale*, VIII [1925], pp. 528–529). Cf. the later attack on Korsch, A. S., "Die bürgerliche Konterrevolution und der Renegat Korsch," *Die Internationale*, IX (1926), p. 565. Korsch answered these charges; and although he sought to minimize them, he did not deny uttering these remarks. At the end of September Korsch published a short "explanation" in several party newspapers that tried to refute three legends about *Korschismus*. According to these legends Korsch made an "anti-bolshevik and anti-Soviet speech" at Frankfort; a "group" existed with membership of Korsch, Boris, Rolf, and Dr. Weil; and Korsch was forming a left faction ("Eine Erklärung des Gen. Korsch," *Neue Zeitung*, Sept. 24, 1925). An editorial note following the "explanation" printed in *Die Rote Fahne* observed correctly that the explanation was lame. "The above explanation provides no clarification on the dispute. Comrade Korsch does not give the text of what he has said, nor does he concretely dispute what the Frankfurt party newspaper reported he said" (*Die Rote Fahne*, September 27, 1925).

82 Heinz Neumann, *Maslows Offensive gegen den Leninismus* (Hamburg, 1925), pp. 6–7.

83 For the immediate future see Siegfried Bahne, "Zwischen 'Luxemburgismus' und 'Stalinismus': Die 'ultralinke' Opposition in der KPD," *VfZ*, IX (1961), pp. 370 ff.

84 K. Korsch, *Der Weg der Komintern* (Berlin, 1926), p. 24. Excerpts of the "Platform of the KPD Left" are in Gruber (ed.), *Soviet Russia Masters the Comintern*, pp. 56–60.

85 "Letter to Erich Gerlach" (Dec. 16, 1956), in Korsch, *Revolutionary Theory*, p. 295.

86 A. Deborin, "Lukács und seine Kritik des Marxismus" (1924), reprinted in *Geschichte und Klassenbewusstein heute*, ed. F. Cerutti et al. (Amsterdam, 1971), p. 92.

87 Cited in Iring Fetscher, *Marx and Marxism* (New York, 1971), p. 95. Ladislaus Rudas, a Hungarian and former ally of Lukács, joined in the offensive, and he also alluded to the "left" communist link. See his "Orthodoxer Marxismus?" *Arbeiterliteratur*, 9 (1924), p. 496.

88 Lukács, *History and Class Consciousness*, p. 24.

89 A. Deborin, "Des Revisionismus letzte Weisheit," *Unter dem Banner des Marxismus,* I (1925–1926), p. 85.
90 A. Deborin, "Materialistische Dialektik und Naturwissenschaft" (1925), reprinted in A. Deborin and N. Bucharin, *Kontroversen über dialektischen und mechanistischen Materialismus,* ed. O. Negt (Frankfurt, 1969), p. 97.
91 Rudas, "Orthodoxer Marxismus?" pp. 502–504.
92 Deborin, "Lukács und seine Kritik des Marxismus," in Deborin and Bucharin, *Kontroversen,* pp. 193–194.
93 Deborin, "Materialistische Dialektik und Naturwissenschaft," p. 114. This article tries to demonstrate the continuity of Hegel and Engels in regard to the dialectic of nature. Deborin appeals to Engels's *The Dialectics of Nature* to prove his argument.
94 The best guides through the maze are David Joravsky, *Soviet Marxism and Natural Science* (London, 1961); and René Ahlberg, "*Dialektische Philosophie" und Gesellschaft in der Sowjetunion* (Berlin, 1960). There is a brief survey in Predrag Vranicki, *Storia del Marxismo,* Vol. II (Rome, 1973), pp. 100–106.
95 Cited in Joravsky, *Soviet Marxism,* p. 96. Minin and the mechanists have been characterized as fermenting a renaissance of (Russian) nihilism; see P. Vostokov, "La Philosophie russe durant la période post-révolutionnaire – I," *Le Monde slave,* IV/11 (1932), pp. 288 ff.
96 Deborin, "Materialistische Dialektik und Naturwissenschaft," p. 130.
97 Joravsky, *Soviet Marxism,* pp. 221–222. See the careful account of Soviet attitudes toward technology in Kendall E. Bailes, *Technology and Society under Lenin and Stalin* (Princeton, N.J. 1978). That the height of the attack on the technical specialists coincided with the height of the support for the Deborinites (1928–1931) confirms the implicit authoritarianism of scientific Hegelianism.
98 Cited in Ahlberg, "*Dialektische Philosophie,*" p. 79.
99 Cited in Joravsky, *Soviet Marxism,* p. 122.
100 See René Ahlberg, "The Forgotten Philosopher: Abram Deborin," in *Revisionism,* ed. L. Labedz (New York, 1962), p. 140.
101 M. Mitin, "Über die Ergebnisse der philosophischen Diskussion" (1931), in Deborin and Bucharin, *Kontroversen,* p. 365. Wetter views the condemnation of the Deborinites as a "decisive turning point in the history of Soviet philosophy." It opened the way for an exclusively official doctrine. See Gustav A. Wetter, *Dialectical Materialism* (London, 1958), p. 175. Deborin later "confessed." "We Marxists of the older generation stood under the strong influence of Plekhanov . . . Inasmuch as I concentrated my attention on the common links among Feuerbach, Hegel and Marxism,

I lost to view what Marxism forcefully contradicted" (cited in Ahlberg, "*Dialektische Philosophie*," p. 111).

102 Mitin, "Uber die Ergebnisse," p. 350.

5. The subterranean years

1 See the charting of Gramsci and Bordiga's fortunes in Gwyn A. Williams, "The Making and Unmaking of Antonio Gramsci," *New Edinburgh Review*, No. 27, pp. 5–15. Cf. G. A. Williams, *Proletarian Order: Antonio Gramsci, Factory Councils and the Origins of Communism in Italy, 1911–1921* (London, 1975), pp. 302–308; and the Introduction to A. Peregali (ed.), *Il Communismo di sinistra e Gramsci* (Bari, 1978), pp. 5–31.

2 For Lukács's critique see "N. Bukharin, Historical Materialism," *Political Writings 1919–1929*, (London, 1972), pp. 134–143. For Gramsci see his "Critical Notes on an Attempt at Popular Sociology," in *Selections from the Prison Notebooks*, eds. Q. Hoare and G. N. Smith (New York, 1971), pp. 419–472. Korsch also criticized Bukharin, although more briefly; see his comments in "Über materialistische Dialektik," *Internationale*, VII (1924), pp. 376–379, reprinted in his *Die materialistische Geschichtsauffassung und andere Schriften* (Frankfurt, 1971), pp. 131–136. For a comparison of Gramsci and Lukács's critiques see Aldo Zanardo, "Il 'manuale' di Bukharin visto dai communisti tedeschi e da Gramsci," in *Studi gramsciani*, ed. Istituto Antonio Gramsci (Rome, 1958), pp. 337–368. Cf. Robert Paris, "Gramsci e la crisi teorica del 1923," *Nuova Rivista Storica*, 53 (1969), pp. 167 ff. For a discussion of the Bukharin text see Stephen F. Cohen, *Bukharin and the Bolshevik Revolution* (New York, 1973), pp. 107–122.

3 A. Bordiga, "Abstentionist Communist Fraction of the Italian Socialist Party" (1920), included in A. Gramsci, *Selections from Political Writings 1910–1920*, ed. Q. Hoare (New York, 1977), p. 211.

4 Gramsci's conception of the factory councils was vulnerable to these criticisms; see Franklin Adler, "Factory Councils, Gramsci and the Industrialists," *Telos*, 31 (Spring, 1977), pp. 67–90.

5 For instance, it published A. Pannekoek, "Lo sviluppo della rivoluzione mondiale e la tattica del communismo," *Il Soviet*, III/22 (Sept. 5, 1920), and subsequent issues; E. Sylvia Pankhurst, "La situazione in Inghilterra," *Il Soviet*, II/42 (Oct. 20, 1919). Pannekoek's article is discussed in Chapter 3.

6 A. Bordiga, "La situazione in Germania e il movimento communista," *Il Soviet*, III/18 (July 11, 1920). Cf. A. Bordiga, "Il Partito Communista Tedesco," *Il Soviet*, III/11 (April 11, 1920).

7 Editorial note to G. Lukács, "Sulla questione del parlamentarismo," *Il*

Soviet, III/12 (April 25, 1920). The English translation, "The Question of Parliamentarianism," is in his *Political Writings 1919–1929*.

8 Editorial note to G. Lukács, "Sulla questione del parlamentarismo," *Il Soviet*, III/14 (May 16, 1920).

9 Andreina de Clementi in *Amadeo Bordiga* (Turin, 1971) argues that Bordiga belongs within a Western Marxist tradition. This book has provoked some sharp replies. See Silvano Levrero, "A proposito di Bordiga," *Critica Marxista*, IX (1971), pp. 122–135. For a more balanced discussion see Simonetta Ortaggi, "Il dibattito fra Lenin e gli 'estremisti' europei sull'ideologia borghese," *RSC*, V (1976), pp. 28–71. Cf. Giorio Fiocca, "Il dissenso Gramsci-Bordiga in alcuni studi degli anni '60," *Storia e Politica*, XI (1972), pp. 95–106; and Dino Ferreri, "Note su 'estremismo storico,' e 'Leninismo,'" *Critica Marxista*, IX (1971), pp. 152–177. Franco Livorsi in his anthology of Bordiga, *Scritti scelti* (Milan, 1975), does not accept the argument of de Clementi. He points to Bordiga's rejection of Korsch's proposal of a united opposition as evidence. See "Il tentativo di proseguire la lotta allo stalinismo all'interno dell'Internazionale: La lettera a Karl Korsch del 1926," in *Scritti scelti*, pp. 196–200. Cf. Christian Riechers, "Kommentar zu Bordigas Brief," in *Jahrbuch Arbeiterbewegung*, ed. C. Pozzoli, I (1973), pp. 248–263.

10 A. Bordiga, *Protokoll: Erweiterte Exekutive der Kommunistischen Internationale*, Moscow, Feb. 17 to March 1, 1926 (Hamburg, 1926), p. 126.

11 Ibid., p. 286.

12 Ibid., p. 227. From Tasca's archives comes a record of a meeting and exchange between Bordiga and Stalin not included in the official account. See "Verbale della riunione del 22 febbraio 1926 della delegazione italiana al Comitato esecutivo allargato dell'Internazionale communista con Stalin," *Annali Feltrinelli*, VIII (1966), pp. 258–270.

13 Alastair Davidson argues that Gramsci was equally distant from the Comintern and Bordiga; see his *Antonio Gramsci: Towards an Intellectual Biography* (London, 1977), pp. 204–231. Cf. his "Gramsci and Lenin 1917–1922," in *Socialist Register 1974*, ed. R. Miliband and J. Saville (London, 1974), pp. 138–146; and the review of his book by Franklin Adler in *Telos*, 34 (1977–1978), pp. 182–184.

14 "Minutes of the Political Commission nominated by the Central Committee to Finalize the Lyons Congress Documents" (1926), in A. Gramsci, *Selections from Political Writings, 1921–1926*, ed. Q. Hoare (New York, 1978), pp. 321–322.

15 Bordiga, *Protokoll: Erweiterte Exekutive*, p. 289.

16 Maurice Merleau-Ponty, *Sense and Non-Sense* (Evanston, Ill., 1964).

17 M. Merleau-Ponty, *Adventures of the Dialectic* (Evanston, Ill., 1973).

18 Jean-Paul Sartre, "Materialism and Revolution," *Literary and Philosophical Essays* (New York, 1962), pp. 198–256; and *Being and Nothingness* (New York, 1966). See Pietro Chiodi, *Sartre and Marxism* (London, 1976), pp. 35–38; and Wilfred Desan, *The Marxism of Jean-Paul Sartre* (Garden City, N.Y., 1966), pp. 13–20.

19 For *Socialisme ou Barbarie* and *Arguments* see Mark Poster, *Existential Marxism in Post-War France* (Princeton, N.J., 1975), pp. 201–263. The writings of Cornelius Castoriadis are in process of re-publication; see his Introduction to the first volume of *La Société bureaucratique* (Paris, 1973). There is a discussion of Castoriadis and Lefort in Dick Howard, *The Marxian Legacy* (New York, 1977), pp. 222–301.

20 Maurice Nadeau, *The History of Surrealism* (New York, 1966), pp. 119–120. Lichtheim called the "Philosophies" group a "prefiguration" of the post-1945 writings of Sartre and Merleau-Ponty (G. Lichtheim, *Marxism in Modern France* [New York, 1968], p. 87).

21 N. Guterman and H. Lefebvre, *La Conscience mystifiée* (Paris, 1936).

22 H. Lefebvre, *La Somme et le reste* (Belibaste, 1973), p. 110. Yet Guterman recalls that they were unfamiliar with Lukács at the time they composed *La Conscience mystifiée* (private letter, Oct. 12, 1979).

23 Guterman and Lefebvre, *La Conscience mystifiée*, p. 251. See Henri Lefebvre, *Everyday Life in the Modern World* (New York, 1971). For a restatement of this tradition see Bruce Brown, *Marx, Freud and the Critique of Everyday Life* (New York, 1973).

24 Leo Lowenthal and Norbert Guterman, *Prophets of Deceit*, with an Introduction by Max Horkheimer and a Foreword by Herbert Marcuse (Palo Alto, Calif., 1970). (First edition 1949.)

25 See the discussion of "surplus" in Paul Baran's *The Political Economy of Growth* (New York, 1965), pp. 22–43. Baran cites Horkheimer's *Eclipse of Reason* (New York, 1947), a book that made no impact on American social science; it opened with a discussion of "objective reason" (pp. 3–57).

26 Paul Sweezy, "P. A. Baran: A Personal Memoir," *Monthly Review*, XVI/11 (March, 1965), p. 33. See Martin Jay, *The Dialectical Imagination: A History of the Frankfurt School and the Institute of Social Research 1923–1950* (Boston, 1973), pp. 31, 307.

27 The best account and survey is Martin Jay's *The Dialectical Imagination*. See my review, "Marxism and the Critical School," *Theory and Society*, I (1974), pp. 231–238; and our exchange "Marxism and Critical Theory," *Theory and Society*, II (1975), pp. 257–263. The literature on the Frankfurt School has become immense, and it spans the spectrum from careful monographs, such as Susan Buck-Morss, *The Origin of Negative Dialectics: T. W. Adorno, Walter Benjamin and the Frankfurt Institute*

(New York, 1977), to hatchet jobs, such as Zoltán Tar, *The Frankfurt School* (New York, 1977). See my review in *Sociology and Social Research*, 63 (1978), pp. 168–171. Another book to be avoided is Phil Slater's *Origin and Significance of the Frankfurt School* (London, 1977). See my review in *Telos*, 31 (Spring, 1977), pp. 198–202; and the exchanges by Slater, "The Ideological Significance of a Critique of the Frankfurt School in Britain," and Timothy Plaut, "On Slating Slater," and my comment, all in *Telos*, 33 (Fall, 1977), pp. 152–158. Other studies include Gian E. Rusconi, *La teoria critica della società* (Bologna, 1968), which is excellent and well informed; Pierre V. Zima, *L'Ecole de Francfort* (Paris, 1974), by a student of Lucien Goldmann; and Jean-Marie Vincent, *La Théorie critique de l'école de Francfort* (Paris, 1976). Both Helmut Dubiel, *Wissenschaftsorganisation und politische Erfahrung: Studien zur frühen Kritischen Theorie* (Frankfurt, 1978); and Alfons Söllner, *Geschichte und Herrschaft: Studien zur materialistischen Sozialwissenschaft 1929–1942* (Frankfurt, 1979) reached me too late to use. See also the exchange between Martin Jay, "The Frankfurt School's Critique of Mannheim and the Sociology of Knowledge," *Telos*, 20 (Summer, 1974), pp. 72–89, and James Schmidt, "Critical Theory and the Sociology of Knowledge: A Response to Martin Jay," *Telos*, 21 (Fall, 1974), pp. 168–180; and the rejoinder by Jay, "Crutches vs. Stilts: An Answer to Schmidt on the Frankfurt School," *Telos*, 22 (Winter, 1974–1975), pp. 106–117.

28 Carl Grünberg, the first director, stated that he used Marxism "not in the sense of a political party but purely scientifically" (C. Grünberg, "Festrede gehalten zur Einweihung des Instituts für Sozialforschung an der Universität Frankfurt a. Main 22. Juni 1924," *Frankfurter Universitätstreden*, XX (1924), p. 10.

29 Korsch denied that Weil belonged to the ultra-left ("Eine Erklärung des Gen. Korsch," *Neue Zeitung*, Sept. 24, 1925). See the discussion in Chapter 4. Weil also played a small part in the Rosa Luxemburg legacy. He corrected the edition of "The Russian Revolution" that Levi had published, and he also made available to Paul Frölich, Luxemburg's biographer, some of her letters. See Felix Weil, "Rosa Luxemburg über die russische Revolution," *Grünberg Archiv*, XIII (1928), pp. 285–290. On transmitting the letters to Frölich see Charlotte Beradt, "Einleitung," *Rosa Luxemburg in Gefängnis* (Frankfurt, 1973), pp. 12–13.

30 See Paul Breines, "Praxis and Its Theorists: The Impact of Lukács and Korsch in the 1920s," *Telos*, 11 (Spring, 1972), p. 70; and M. Jay, *The Dialectical Imagination*, p. 5. Hedda Korsch recalls that the manuscript of "Marxism and Philosophy" was read in the study group (private interview, Los Angeles, March 15, 1978). Other participants included Boris Roninger,

who had been charged with Korsch as an ultra-leftist. A list of projected books sponsored in 1929 by the Institute named a book by Roninger on capitalist trusts. See Paul Kluke, *Die Stiftungsuniversität Frankfurt am Main 1914–1932* (Frankfurt, 1972), p. 511.

31 For a close examination of the efforts to found the Institute see Kluke, *Die Stiftungsuniversität Frankfurt am Main*, pp. 486 ff.

32 See Helmut Gumnior and Rudolf Ringguth, *Max Horkheimer* (Reinbek bei Hamburg, 1973), p. 51; Max Horkheimer, *Verwaltete Welt? Ein Gespräch* (Zurich, 1970), pp. 11–12; Jay, *The Dialectical Imagination*, pp. 26 ff; Kluke, *Die Stiftungsuniversität*, pp. 508–509. For some details on Marcuse from this period see Barry M. Katz, "Praxis and Poiesis: Towards an Intellectual Biography of Herbert Marcuse," *New German Critique*, 18 (Fall, 1979), pp. 15–16. According to Jürgen Habermas, a former research assistant of the Frankfurt School, "As a school, it had been alive only during a few years of American exile . . . it did not exist in Frankfurt, neither before nor after the Nazi-period, but during the thirties, in New York" ("Psychic Thermidor and the Rebirth of Rebellious Subjectivity," *Berkeley Journal of Sociology*, XXV [1980], p. 3).

33 See Max Horkheimer, "Vorwort" (September, 1933), *Zeitschrift für Sozialforschung*, II (1933), p. 161. Cf. Alfred Schmidt, "Die 'Zeitschrift für Sozialforschung': Geschichte und gegenwärtige Bedeutung," *Zur Idee der kritischen Theorie* (Munich, 1974), pp. 36–124.

34 Heinrich Regius, *Dämmerung* (Zurich, 1934), p. 7. See the Introduction by Alfred Schmidt to M. Horkheimer, *Notizen 1950 und 1969 und Dämmerung* (Frankfurt, 1974), pp. xix–lxx. A partial translation of *Dämmerung* is in M. Horkheimer, *Dawn and Decline: Notes 1926–1931 and 1950–1960* (New York, 1978).

35 These words are not contained in the *Dawn and Decline* edition.

36 Horkheimer, *Dawn and Decline*, p. 78; Regius, *Dämmerung*, p. 167.

37 Horkheimer, *Dawn and Decline*, pp. 40–41; Regius, *Dämmerung*, pp. 71–75.

38 Horkheimer, *Dawn and Decline*, pp. 62–64; Regius, *Dämmerung*, pp. 122–130.

39 "The Authoritarian State" is dated Spring, 1940. "Vernunft und Selbsterhaltung" is dated Winter 1941–1942. Both first appeared in a mimeographed volume entitled "Walter Benjamin zum Gedächtnis" (1942). A slightly different version of "Vernunft und Selbsterhaltung" appeared as "The End of Reason" in *Studies in Philosophy and Social Science*, IX (1941), pp. 366–388, the continuation of the *Zeitschrift für Sozialforschung*. "Die Juden und Europa" appeared in *Zeitschrift für Sozialforschung*, VIII (1939), pp. 115–137.

40 Paul Breines, "Introduction to Horkheimer's 'Authoritarian State,'" *Telos*, 15 (Spring, 1973), p. 2.

41 M. Horkheimer, "The End of Reason," p. 388. See Rosa Luxemburg, "What Does the Spartakus League Want?" in *Selected Political Writings*, ed. D. Howard (New York, 1971), p. 368.

42 M. Horkheimer, "The Authoritarian State," in *The Essential Frankfurt School Reader*, ed. A. Arato and E. Gebhardt (New York, 1978), p. 104.

43 Ibid., pp. 98–99.

44 W. Benjamin, "Theses on the Philosophy of History," in Benjamin, *Illuminations*, ed. H. Arendt (New York, 1969), pp. 253–264. For a discussion of the relationship of Benjamin and these "Theses" to Adorno see Susan Buck-Morss, *The Origin of Negative Dialectics*, pp. 168–175. Cf. Rolf Tiedemann, *Studien zur Philosophie Walter Benjamins* (Frankfurt, 1973), pp. 128–166. Buck-Morss puts to rest some of the more outrageous charges that the Frankfurt School suppressed Benjamin's Marxism.

45 Horkheimer, "The Authoritarian State," pp. 109, 117, 111.

46 H. Marcuse, *Hegels Ontologie und die Theorie der Geschichtlichkeit* (1933) (Frankfurt, 1968), p. 1.

47 H. Marcuse, "Preface to the Original Edition" (1941), *Reason and Revolution: Hegel and the Rise of Social Theory* (Boston, 1960), p. xv.

48 H. Marcuse, "Supplementary Epilogue" (1954), *Reason and Revolution*, 2nd ed. (New York, 1954), p. 433; "Preface: A Note on Dialectic" (1960), *Reason and Revolution*, p. xiii. Marcuse explained that he dropped the Epilogue because he intended to discuss its themes "more fully in my forthcoming book, a study of advanced industrial society" (p. xiv). This book became *One Dimensional Man: Studies in the Ideology of Advanced Industrial Society* (Boston, 1964).

49 Georg Lukács, "Preface" (1962), *The Theory of the Novel* (Cambridge, Mass., 1973), p. 22. The metaphor originally appeared in Lukács's *The Destruction of Reason*, a book which Adorno quipped demonstrated the destruction of Lukács's own reason (T. W. Adorno, "Erpresste Versöhnung: Zu Georg Lukács: 'Wider den missverstandenen Realismus,'" in Adorno, *Noten zur Literatur II* [Frankfurt, 1961], p. 153).

50 See Robert Conquest, *The Great Terror: Stalin's Purge of the Thirties* (New York, 1969), pp. 428–436. Cf. Margaret Buber-Neumann, *Kriegsschauplätze der Weltrevolution: Ein Bericht aus der Praxis der Komintern* (Stuttgart, 1967), pp. 346 ff.

51 Cited in Conquest, *The Great Terror*, p. 429.

52 See Margaret Buber-Neumann, *Als Gefangene bei Stalin und Hitler* (Stuttgart, 1968). The family was not fortunate in its choice of husbands and lovers. Buber-Neumann's sister, Babette Gross, was the companion to

Willi Münzenberg; his disappearance remains unexplained. See Babette Gross, *Willi Münzenberg: A Political Biography* (Michigan State University Press, 1974).

6. Class unconsciousness

1 H. Marcuse, *One Dimensional Man* (Boston, 1964), p. 238.

2 K. Marx, "On the Jewish Question," in Marx/Engels, *Collected Works*, Vol. 3 (New York, 1975), p. 172. Cf. my "Reversals and Lost Meanings," in *Critical Interruptions*, ed. P. Breines (New York, 1970), pp. 66–70.

3 K. Marx and F. Engels, *The German Ideology*, ed. S. Ryazanskaya (Moscow, 1964), p. 519.

4 K. Marx, "Preface to the First Edition," *Capital*, trans. Ben Fowkes (New York, 1977), p. 92.

5 F. Engels, "Outlines of a Critique of Political Economy," in Marx/Engels, *Collected Works*, Vol. 3, p. 434.

6 H. Marcuse, "Zum Problem der Dialektik," *Die Gesellschaft*, VII (1930), pp. 29–30.

7 T. W. Adorno, "Die Idee der Naturgeschichte" (1932), in Adorno, *Gesammelte Schriften*, Vol. 1 (Frankfurt, 1973), pp. 354–355. The consistency of Adorno is demonstrated by his use of much of this material thirty years later in his *Negative Dialectics* (New York, 1973), pp. 354–360.

8 M. Horkheimer, "Bemerkungen zur philosophischen Anthropologie" (1935), in *Kritische Theorie*, Vol. 1 (Frankfurt, 1968), pp. 220–221. Cf. George A. Kelly, *Idealism, Politics and History* (London, 1969), pp. 290–291.

9 G. Lukács, *The Theory of the Novel* (Cambridge, Mass., 1973), p. 64; *Die Theorie der Roman* (Neuwied, 1963), pp. 62–63.

10 See G. Lukács, "The Question of Educational Work" (1921), in *Political Writings 1919–1929* (London, 1972), p. 92.

11 H. Marcuse, *Reason and Revolution: Hegel and the Rise of Social Theory* (Boston, 1960), pp. 343–344. Cf. Alfred Schmidt, *The Concept of Nature in Marx* (London, 1971), p. 191.

12 Marx, *Capital*, p. 284.

13 T. W. Adorno, *Negative Dialektik* (Frankfurt, 1970), p. 347; *Negative Dialectics*, pp. 355–356. Translation slightly altered.

14 K. Marx, *Grundrisse*, trans. M. Nicolaus (Harmondsworth, 1973), p. 104.

15 I am concerned here with contemporary accounts of revisionism and reformism in the SPD, not with those by modern historians and social scientists. As elsewhere in this book, a premium is placed on theories that accurately anticipated future developments. Out of an immense recent literature on the SPD Hans-Josef Steinberg's *Sozialismus und deutsche*

Sozialdemokratie: Zur Ideologie der Partei vor dem I. Weltkrieg (Hannover, 1967) remains one of the most provocative. Other important studies include Dieter Groh, *Negative Integration und revolutionärer Attentismus: Die deutsche Sozialdemokratie am Vorabend des Ersten Weltkrieges* (Frankfurt, 1973), and see the review by Helga Grebing in *IWK*, X/1 (March, 1974), pp. 105 ff.; Carl E. Schorske, *German Social Democracy* (1955) (New York, 1965); Richard Hunt, *German Social Democracy 1918–1933* (1964) (Chicago, 1970); and the collection edited by Hans Mommsen, *Sozialdemokratie zwischen Klassenbewegung und Volkspartei* (Frankfurt, 1974). References to additional studies can be found in Jacques Droz, "Historiographie d'un siècle de social-démocratie allemande," *Le Mouvement social*, 95 (April–June, 1976), pp. 3–24; and in two bibliographical journals: *Internationale wissenschaftliche Korrespondenz zur Geschichte der deutschen Arbeiterbewegung* and *Bibliographie zur Geschichte der deutschen Arbeiterbewegung* (Friedrich-Ebert-Stiftung).

16 Charles Andler, *Le Socialisme impérialiste dans l'allemagne contemporaine: Dossier d'une polémique avec Jean Jaurès* (Paris, 1918), p. 56. See the discussion in Harvey Goldberg, *The Life of Jean Jaurès* (Madison, Wisc., 1968), pp. 435–438. For a later statement of Andler see his *La Décomposition politique du socialisme allemand 1914–1919* (Paris, 1919). Cf. Jean Bourdeau, *Le Socialisme allemand et le nihilisme russe* (Paris, 1894).

17 F. Domela Nieuwenhuis, *Le Socialisme en danger* (Paris, 1897), pp. 116, 112. Cf. F. D. Nieuwenhuis, "Der staatssozialistische Charakter der Sozialdemokratie," *AfSz*, XXVIII (1909), pp. 101–145.

18 Robert Michels, "Die deutsche Sozialdemokratie im internationalen Verbande," *AfSz*, XXV (1907), pp. 153, 167.

19 F. D. Nieuwenhuis, *Le Socialisme en danger*, p. 32.

20 See the letter of Nieuwenhuis to Michels (December 6, 1906), which notes their spiritual–intellectual kinship; cited in Wilfried Röhrich, *Robert Michels* (Berlin, 1972), p. 64.

21 Cited in Anthony D'Agostino, *Marxism and the Russian Anarchists* (San Francisco, 1977), p. 124. Over the years Max Nomad has been Machajski's exponent and defender; see his *Aspects of Revolt* (New York, 1961), pp. 96–117. See also Paul Avrich, *The Russian Anarchists* (Princeton, N.J., 1971), pp. 102–106; and Richard Gombin, *The Radical Tradition* (London, 1978), pp. 65–70.

22 Cited in D'Agostino, *Marxism and the Russian Anarchists*, pp. 133, 127–128.

23 Hans Müller, *Der Klassenkampf und die Sozialdemokratie* (1892) (Frankfurt, 1969). See the discussion in Dirk H. Müller, *Idealismus und*

Revolution: Zur Opposition der Jungen gegen den Sozialdemokratischen Parteivorstand 1890 bis 1894 (Berlin, 1975).

24 R. Blank, "Die soziale Zusammensetzung der sozialdemokratischen Wählerschaft Deutschlands," *AfSz*, XX (1905), pp. 507 ff. See the comments by Max Weber to this article, "Bermerkungen im Anschluss an den vorstehenden Aufsatz," *AfSz*, XX (1905), pp. 550–553. Michels contested that the electoral figures could be interpreted as a shift in the composition of the party itself. See his "Die deutsche Sozialdemokratie," *AfSz*, XXIII (1906), p. 555. Also see his "Proletariat und Bourgeoisie in der sozialistischen Bewegung Italiens," *AfSz*, XXII (1906), pp. 82–83, for a discussion of the use of electoral figures in evaluating socialist parties.

25 Recently the concept has been reexamined and restudied. See the survey in John Field, "British Historians and the Concept of the Labor Aristocracy," *Radical History Review*, 19 (Winter, 1978–1979), pp. 61–85.

26 V. Lenin, *Imperialism* (New York, 1939), pp. 104–108. The final reason that Sombart adduced for "why there was no socialism in the United States" participated in this logic. High wages and standard of living killed the interest in socialism, or, in his famous words, "All socialist utopias come to nothing on roast beef and apple pie" (*Why Is There No Socialism in the United States?* [White Plains, N.Y., 1976], p. 106).

27 Arghiri Emmanuel, *Unequal Exchange* (New York, 1972), pp. 179–180.

28 See the important discussion in Wolf Wagner, *Verelendungstheorie – die hilflose Kapitalismuskritik* (Frankfurt, 1976). Michels studied the history of the concept; see his *Die Verelendungstheorie: Studien und Untersuchungen zur internationalen Dogmengeschichte der Volkswirtschaft* (Leipzig, 1928).

29 See Wilfried Röhrich, *Robert Michels* (Berlin, 1972); and Arthur Mitzman, *Sociology and Estrangement: Three Sociologists of Imperial Germany* (New York, 1973), pp. 267–338.

30 G. Lukács, "Michels: *Zur Soziologie des Parteiwesens*," *Grünberg Archiv*, XIII (1928), p. 309.

31 R. Michels, *Political Parties* (New York, 1959), pp. 365–376, and 212. This is a re-publication of the 1915 English translation. The more recent edition of *Political Parties* (New York, 1962), with an introduction by Seymour Lipset, is a small scandal. Nowhere does it mention that nearly all of Michels's long and substantial footnotes have been deleted. For a provocative reconsideration of Michels see Frances Fox Piven and Richard A. Cloward, *Poor People's Movements* (New York, 1979). "The intellectual left has dealt with Michels largely by ignoring him" (p. xvi).

32 Claus Mueller's *The Politics of Communication* (New York, 1973) contains

a useful survey of recent literature. See also Jürgen Habermas, *Legitimation Crisis* (Boston, 1975); Stuart Ewen, *Captains of Consciousness: Advertising and the Social Roots of the Consumer Culture* (New York, 1976); and Stanley Aronowitz, *False Promises: The Shaping of American Working Class Consciousness* (New York, 1973).

Index

"abstentionists" (boycottists), 106, 107
Adler, Max, 141 n1
Adorno, T.W., 34–5, 92, 109, 115, 119; "The Idea of Natural History," 118; and Horkheimer, *The Dialectic of Enlightenment*, 120
Althusser, Louis, 15–17, 24–5, 36; *For Marx*, 16, 17; *Reading Capital*, 16
Anderson, Perry: *Considerations on Western Marxism*, 7
Andler, Charles, 50, 54, 55, 121
appearance/essence, 22
Arendt, Hannah, 18
Arguments (journal), 108
aristocracy of labor (theory), 61, 122–4, 166 n89
Aristotle, 118
Austro-Marxism, 141 n1, 169 n21
autonomy, 95, 122
Avenarius, Richard, 60

Bakunin, Michael, 20, 39
Baran, Paul: *Political Economy of Growth*, 110; and P. Sweezy, *Monopoly Capital*, 109–10
being, 56–7
Belinsky, Vissarion G., 39, 40
Benjamin, Walter, 113; "Theses on the Philosophy of History," 114
Berdyaev, Nicolas, 40
Bergson, Henri, 51
Bernstein, Eduard, 47, 52; Luxemburg and, 67, 68, 69
Bettelheim, Bruno, 18
Bettelheim, Charles, 13; *Cultural Revolution and Industrial Organization in China*, 13–14
Bettelheim, Ernest, 171 n31
Bettelheimerei, 61
Blanquism, 68
Bloch, Ernst, 33, 34
Bogdanov, A., 60
bolshevism/Bolsheviks, 4, 12, 59, 62, 67, 72, 77, 96
bolshevization, 67, 70–71, 97, 98, 108
Bordiga, Amadeo, 8, 76, 77, 106–8, 166 n90
bourgeoisie, 5–6, 18, 20, 111–12; critique of, 30–2; Dutch, 72; impact of, on working class, 67, 72, 73–4, 79–80; relation to Marxism, 25–8, 30–1, 61–2; second nature and, 118–19; success/defeat, 12
Brandler, Heinrich, 94–5, 98

Brecht, Bertolt, 92
Breton, André, 33, 34, 50
Brown, N.O., 61
Brzozowski, Stanislaw, 55
Bukharin, Nikolai, 96, 97; *Historical Materialism*, 96, 106
Bulgakov, Serge, 28

capitalism, 4, 9, 11, 14, 19, 41, 56, 62; critique of, 18; evolutionary progress of, 14, 25–8, 30, 95, 113; "natural" laws of, 118; relation to Marxism, 25–33, 112; second nature and, 118–20; secondary characteristics of, 31–2; view of nature, 117, 118
Carnap, Rudolf, 22, 134 n46
Castoriadis, Cornelius, 108
centralism, 69, 70
centralization, 78, 90–1, 95, 170 nn26, 27 (*see also* organization)
Chailland, Gérard: "Guerilla Inflation: The *Foco* Theory as a Theory for Failure," 15
Chernyshevskii, Nikolai, 142 n9
China, 19; Cultural Revolution, 13–14
Chinese Revolution, 3, 11, 12, 14
class consciousness, 62, 78, 120, 121, 123–4; knowledge as, 74; and proletariat, 69, 91; theory of, 124–6
class struggle, 84
class unconsciousness, 117–26
Claudin, Fernando, 5
Cologne working-class movement, 135 n70
colonialism, 26, 28
Comintern, *see* Communist International
communism (*see also* council communism; "left" communism): bolshevization of, 67; critical, 45, 46; methods for attaining, 135 n70
Communist International, 19, 59, 60, 62, 63, 70, 80, 81, 106, 108; Amsterdam Bureau, 76, 88, 89; Berlin Bureau, 76; Fifth World Congress, 96–7; and Italian political parties, 63–4; and KPD, 64–5, 66, 94–9; "left" communism threat to, 72, 76, 77; Vienna Bureau, 76, 88, 89–90
Communist League, 26, 135 n70
Communist parties, 59, 60–1, 62, 103, 124, 169 n22; Dutch, 61, 73; French, 9, 109; Hungarian, 89; Italian, 63–4, 106; Soviet, 11–12
Comte, Auguste, 21
Congress of Livorno, 63, 64
consciousness, 7, 38, 39, 43, 44, 72, 75–6, 90, 92, 100 (*see also* class consciousness); critique of, 46, 57; determined by social existence, 86; and economic reorganization, 85–6; and laws of history, 118; Leninist party as, 88–9; and self-consciousness, 22
conservatives/conservatism, 6, 31–3
council communism, 12, 17, 81, 166 n90 (*see also* factory councils; workers' councils)
Croce, Benedetto, 44, 46–8, 49, 54; correspondence with Sorel, 50–1; *What Is Living and What Is Dead of the Philosophy of Hegel*, 57
Cuban revolution, 14–15
culture, 72, 85, 115

Deborin, Abram, Deborinites, 83, 99–103
Debray, Régis: *Revolution in the Revolution*, 15

Democritus, 118
determinism, 41, 46, 51, 119
development: laws of, 100; universal, 40, 41
dialectical materialism, 38-9, 45, 54, 56-7, 100, 102
dialectics, 7, 19, 24, 38, 57, 75, 115, 141 n1; of history, 19-20, 53, 119; in Italy, 45; laws of, 38; in Marx, 26-7; of nature, 38-9, 53, 100-1, 118, 119; universal validity of, 52-3, 100-1, 102
Dietzgen, Joseph, 62, 75-6; *The Nature of Human Brainwork*, 75
discipline, 70, 88, 89, 90-1, 95, 114, 122
dissidents, opponents, 17, 20, 93; charges against, 34-5, 48, 103, 105
domination/resistance, 19
Douglas, Mary 35
Durkheim, Emile, 21
Dutch Communist party, 61, 73
Dutch Marxists (later "Dutch School"), 8, 62, 72-6, 89
Dutch Socialist party (SDAP), 73

economics, 6-7, 34
Elkins, Stanley, 18
Ellul, Jacques, 31
emancipation (freedom), 67, 75, 84-6, 91; conscious leap into, 91-2; and laws of history, 118
Emmanuel, Arghiri, 123
Engels, Friedrich, 3-4, 24, 26, 42, 45, 47, 52, 67, 100; *Anti-Dühring*, 54; critique of, 7-8, 53-4, 55-8, 88; *Dialectics of Nature*, 101, 118; *Feuerbach and the End of Classical German Philosophy*, 52; labor aristocracy theory, 123; and Marx, *The Holy Family*, 42; Marxism of, 39, 52-8; "natural" laws of capitalism, 118; *The Origin of the Family*, 52; *Socialism: Utopian and Scientific*, 151 n126
England, 26, 30, 37, 76, 144 n28
evolutionism, 26, 30, 54
European Marxism, *see* Western Marxism

Fabian Society, 94
factory, 28-9; as model for revolutionary organizations, 69-70
factory councils, 77, 89, 106, 108 n4
fascism, 6, 60, 105, 109, 117
Feuerbach, Ludwig, 48-9, 75, 179 n101; and Marx, 55, 56
Fichte, Johann, 11, 138 n91
Fischer, Ruth, 94-5, 96, 97, 98
France: development of a Western Marxism in, 108-9; Hegelianism in, 39, 42, 49-51, 150 n106; Marxism in, 8, 9, 29, 37, 62
Franco-China Friendship Association, 13
Frankfurt School, 4, 33, 34, 35, 62, 92, 105, 109-16, 185 n44; concept of second nature, 120; literature on, 182 n27; negative vision of nature, 117, 118
Frankfurt University, 110
freedom, *see* emancipation
French Communist party, 9, 108
Frölich, Paul, 156 n7, 183 n29

Gentile, Giovanni, 46, 47, 48-9, 50, 54, 55, 72; *La filosofia di Marx*, 48
German Communist party (KPD), 5, 63, 66, 78, 93, 94, 107, 158 n27, 165 n88; and Comintern, 64-5; importance of, 63; Ninth Party Congress, 95-6; Tenth Party Congress, 97-8

German Communist Worker's party (KAPD), 8, 77–9, 80–1, 89, 99, 107, 165 n88
German idealism, 45, 58, 62, 115, 141 n1
German October (1923), 60, 94, 98
German proletariat, 71–2
German Revolution, 78–9, 94
German Social Democrats (SPD), 12, 30–1, 41, 63, 87–8; Party School, 73; reformism in, 121–4
German socialism, 42, 68, 71–2, 121–2
Germany, 29, 30, 37, 39, 63; "left" communism in, 77, 80–1, 87; mass strike, 68, 73, 74
Gorter, Hermann, 59, 61, 72, 73, 75, 76, 91, 105, 166 n89; *Der historische Materialismus*, 72; and KAPD, 77; "Open Letter" to Lenin, 77, 80
Gottschalk, Andreas, 26
Gramsci, Antonio, 4, 8, 37, 44, 58, 87, 166 n90, 180 n4; and Bordiga, 105–6, 107, 108; rooted in German idealism, 62
"Grand Hotel Abyss," 115
Gross, Babette, 185 n52
Grünberg, Carl, 110
Guevara, "Che," 14
Guterman, Norbert, 50, 109

Hahn, Hans, 22
Hegel, Georg Wilhelm, 7–8, 15, 23, 44, 55, 72, 92, 114, 179 n101; commentaries, translations, 43, 49, 50, 109; dialectic of nature, 101; Engels's understanding of, 54; French literature of, 108–9; impact on Marxism, 20, 22, 23–5, 37, 57; Marxism of, 37–58; *Phenomenology of Mind*, 38, 43–4, 48, 54, 60; philosophy of nature (concept), 57, 150 n106; *Science of Logic*, 24, 38, 44, 54, 58, 60, 102
Hegelianism, 40, 102, 106, 126, 144 n28; French, 39, 42, 49–51, 150 n106; historical, 38, 39, 40, 43, 46, 49, 50, 51, 53, 57–8, 62, 83, 86, 97, 100; Italian, 39, 42–9, 53–4, 106, 146 n49; of Lukács, 83–4; scientific, 38, 39, 40, 41, 43, 52, 57–8, 83, 100, 102, 179 n97; two traditions of, 37–8, 43, 57, 60, 83, 100, 101; in Western Marxism, 42–51
hegemony, 12; of bourgeois ideology, 62, 79–80
Heine, Heinrich, 57
Herr, Lucien, 50, 55, 87, 150 n106; *La Révolution sociale*, 51
historical materialism, 39, 54, 75–6
historicism, 8, 16, 24, 115
history, 8, 12–13, 16, 18, 43, 44, 57, 100; compromises rigor of science, 24–5; dialectic of, 19–20, 53, 119; "leap" out of, 114; made by man, 45–6, 67, 76, 119, 126; proletariat subject of, 69; relation to nature, 117–20; revisionism in, 13–14, 16–17; story of humanity as actor and victim, 22, 23; subject attaining consciousness through, 38, 39
Hook, Sidney: *Towards the Understanding of Karl Marx*, 92
Horkheimer, Max, 34, 35, 109, 110–14, 118; "The Authoritarian State," 113–14; *Dämmerung*, 111–12; "The End of Reason," 113; "Reason and Self-Preservation," 113
Hotel Lux, 115–16
humanism, 35

Hungarian Communist party, 89
Hungarian Socialist party, 87–8
Hungarian Soviet Republic, 86
Hungary, 90
Hyppolite, Jean, 50; *The Phenomenology*, 49

idealism, 49, 94, 99; German, 45, 58, 62, 115, 141 n1; Hegelian, 102–3
Illich, Ivan, 31, 32
immiseration (theory), 123
imperialism, 11, 67, 123
Independent Social Democrats (USPD, Germany), 78, 93, 157 n20, 158 n27
India, 26
individuality, 40, 41, 42, 57
industrialism (ethos of), 122
industrialization, 26–7, 28–9, 30–1, 33, 69
Institute of Social Research, Frankfurt, *see* Frankfurt School
intellectuals: bourgeois, 111–12; left, 95–6, 98; Marxist, 115
International II, 28, 46, 59, 151 n127
International III, *see* Communist International
Internationale, 96–7
Italian Communist party (PCI), 63–4, 106
Italian Socialist party (PSI), 63–4
Italy: critiques of Engels, 53–4, 55–8; development of a Western Marxism in, 105–8; Hegelianism in, 39, 42–9, 53–4, 106, 146 n49; "left" communism in, 76, 77; Marxists in, 29, 37

Jacobinism, 68
Jacoby, Russell: *Social Amnesia*, 9
JaJa, Donato, 48, 54

KAPD, *see* German Communist Worker's party (KAPD)
KPD, *see* German Communist party
Kant, Immanuel, 23, 46
Kapp, Yvonne, 52
Kapp putsch, 78
Kautsky, Karl, 67, 68, 73, 74–5
Khruschev, Nikita, 11, 17
Kierkegaard, Sören, 23
Kireevsky, Ivan, 40
knowledge, 43, 48, 56–7, 74; as subjective activity, 49
Kojève, Alexandre, 49, 50, 150 n106
Kolakowski, Leszek, 134 n46
Kommunismus, 58, 59–60, 76, 79, 88, 107, 110, 116
Korsch, Hedda, 183 n30
Korsch, Karl, 4, 59, 62, 72, 92–9, 106, 108; expelled from Communist party, 99; *Karl Marx*, 92; and Lukács, 83–4; *Marxism and Philosophy*, 83, 92–3, 97, 103
Koyré, Alexandre, 50, 150 n106
Kun, Béla, 66, 89–90, 96, 115, 170 n31

labor aristocracy, *see* aristocracy of labor
labor process, 28–9
Labriola, Antonio, 42, 44–7, 48, 50, 54, 146 n49, 153 n152, 154 n156; and Croce, 47–8; *In Memory of the Communist Manifesto*, 46; *The Materialist Conception of History*, 46; *On Historical Materialism*, 46; *Socialism and Philosophy*, 46, 47
Labriola, Arturo: *Marx nell' economia e come teorico del socialismo*, 55–6
Lafargue, Paul, 47, 54–5
Lagardelle, Hubert, 87

leadership, 77, 78, 87, 112, 113–14
Lefebvre, Henri, 50, 108–9; and N. Guterman, *La Conscience mystifiée*, 109
Lefort, Claude, 108
left, the, 3, 18; "decisive," 99; Italian, 64; ultra-leftism, 95
"left" communism, 17, 61, 62, 72, 76–81, 83, 87, 88, 91, 93, 97; divergence in, 106–7; German, 95–6; Horkheimer and, 113
Lenin, V. I., 2, 3, 12, 24, 41, 48, 53, 62, 65, 66, 67, 107; defended national liberation movements, 166 n89; *Development of Capitalism in Russia*, 27; evaluation of technology, 29; Hegel notebooks, 50; *Imperialism*, 123; and "left" communism, 72, 88, 106; *Left-Wing Communism, an Infantile Disorder*, 76, 80; and Luxemburg, 62, 64, 66, 67, 68–9, 159 n39; and March Action, 158 n25; *Materialism and Empirio-Criticism*, 60; *One Step Forward, Two Steps Backward*, 69; reproached Maslow, 95; translations, 109; use of parliaments and trade unions, 77; *What Is to Be Done?*, 4, 69
Leninist party, 77, 88–9, 91, 92
Leninism/Leninists, 3, 12, 62, 67, 80–1; Bordiga represented, 106; deviation from, 99; orthodox, 8; repudiated by Western Marxism, 61; success of, 12
Levi, Paul, 8, 61, 63–7, 77, 78, 90, 99, 108, 170 n27; expelled from Communist party, 65, 158 n25; and USPD, 157 n20; *Unser Weg: Wider der Putschismus*, 65–6
Lewis, John, 17
Loria, Achille, 47
Lowenthal, Leo, 110; and N. Guterman, *Prophets of Deceit*, 109
Lukács, Georg, 6, 7, 57, 58, 59–60, 62, 74, 76, 77, 83–92, 95, 106, 107, 110, 126; analysis of capitalism, 85–6, 91; attacked as ultra-left, 97; "Bolshevism as Moral Problem," 84; "The Changing Function of Historical Materialism," 86; denounced intellectuals for pessimism, 115; *History and Class Consciousness*, 34, 35, 53, 76, 83, 86, 88–9, 91, 92, 93, 103, 109, 119–20; on Michels, 124; "The Old Culture and the New Culture," 85–6; on organization, 61; "Organization and Revolutionary Initiative," 90; "Party and Class," 88, 89; philosophical and political critique of, 99–103; polemic against Engels, 118; "Politics of Illusion - Yet Again," 90; "The Question of Parliamentarianism," 88, 89, 107; *Soul and Form*, 84; *Theory of the Novel*, 84; translation of, 108; "What Is Orthodox Marxism?," 11
Luxemburg, Rosa, 61, 73, 76, 87, 96, 99, 113, 166 n89, 183 n29; critique of Lenin, 62, 64, 66, 67, 159 n39; critique of Russian Revolution, 59, 62–3, 66–7, 72, 77; "Mass Strike," 170 n27; murder of, 4, 63
"Luxemburgism," 62, 67, 97

Mach, Ernst, 60
Machajski, Jan W., 122
Mao Tse-tung, 3, 13, 53, 57
Maoism, 4, 12, 13
March Action (1921), 60–1, 65–6, 89, 90, 94, 169 n26, 170 n27

Marcuse, Herbert, 34, 58, 109, 110, 111, 114–15, 117, 118, 119; *Hegels Ontologie und die Theorie der Geschichtlichkeit*, 114; *One Dimensional Man*, 19; *Reason and Revolution*, 114
Martov, Julius, 2
Marx, Karl, 1, 8, 23, 24, 41, 42, 43, 55, 67, 93; advocated incremental social transformation, 26; analysis of modern industry, 26–7; *Capital*, 8, 20, 24, 25, 33, 52, 55; on capitalism, 25–7, 33; *Civil War in France*, 52; *Class Struggles in France, 1848–1850*, 52; colonialism, 26; *Communist Manifesto*, 26, 55; consciousness determined by social existence, 86; "critique of political economy," 6; *Critique of Political Economy*, 45; dialectics in, 26–7; and Dietzgen, 75–6; *The 18th Brumaire*, 67; and Engels, dialectic of nature, 101; and Engels, *The Holy Family*, 42; and German idealism, 45; and Hegel, 15, 25, 45, 86; on history, 22; interpretation of, 38; meaning of science to, 20–1; and methods by which communism is attained, 135 n70; "natural" laws in, 118, 119; reality to, 49; on revolution, 17; substance of, retrieved by unorthodox Marxists, 33–4; surplus value (theory), 47; and technology/industry, 28–9, 30; "Theses on Feuerbach," 49, 55–6; translations, 49, 50, 55, 109
Marxism/Marxists, 6–7, 39, 67, 99; acceptance of the judgment of history as truth, 3; ambivalent relation to bourgeois society, capitalism, 5–6, 25–33, 112; and class unconsciousness, 120–4; classical, 6–7; coherence of, 6, 11; compulsive objectivity of, 9; conflicting approaches to history and society, 21–3; critical, 124; critiques of, 93, 122; Darwinian, 45; defeated by nazism, 5; diversity in, 1–9; of Engels, 52–8; essence of, 69; French, 50–1; German, 94–6; of Hegel, 37–57; industrial ethos of, 122; internal opposition to, 3, 4–5, 11–12, 41, 52 (*see also* dissidents, opponents; Marxism, unorthodox); Italian, 42, 44–9; "legal," 27–8; literature on, 1, 7–8, 46–9; Luxemburg and, 67–8; myth of success, 4 (*see also* success/defeat); national traditions of, 6, 37, 39, 40; philosophy and politics in, 7; positivist, 45, 46; question of organization in, 61 (*see also* organization); responsible for failure, 115; as science, 5–6, 7, 16, 27, 34, 35, 42, 51; scientific, 86, 94, 101; threatened by historicism, 16; two divergent traditions in, 52–8; as unified system, 44, 52, 53; validity of, in Russia, 40–2; victims and victimizers, 117; vulgar, 31, 45, 46, 52, 86, 87–8, 91, 93; *see also* Soviet Marxism; Western Marxism
Marxism/Marxists, orthodox, 11–36, 58; asceticism of, 35; and capitalism, 25–33, 94; critique of, 51; and Frankfurt School, 115; French, 8, 9, 29, 37, 62; Hegel's impact on, 20, 22, 23–5, 37, 57; paralyzed by economic orientation, 34; puritanism of, 35–6; reaffirmed by Deborin, 100–1; reliance on Engels, 39, 53; success/defeat, 1–5,

11–17, 18–20; and technology, 28–9; Western Marxism as alternative to, 105
Marxism, unorthodox, 33–4, 37, 53, 60
Marxisms, 1–2; failure of, 3, 4–5
Masaryk, Thomas, 55
Maslow, Arkadi, 94–5, 96, 97, 98, 99, 116
mass strike, 68, 73, 74
materialism, 4, 49, 57; passive, 56
"mechanists," 101, 102
Merleau-Ponty, Maurice, 8, 37, 49, 58, 105; *Adventures of the Dialectic*, 108; *Sense and Non-Sense*, 108
Michels, Robert, 121, 122; *Political Parties*, 123–4
Mikhailovsky, Nicholas, 40, 41–2; "What Is Progress?", 41
mind, 72, 86
Minin, S.: "Overboard with Philosophy," 101
Mitin, Mark Borisovich, 102–3
Mondolfo, Rodolfo, 55, 56–7; "Feuerbach and Marx," 56; *Il materialismo storico in Federico Engels*, 54
Morris, William, 33, 34
Munich Soviet Republic, 3
Münzenberg, Willi, 186 n52
Münzer, Thomas, 118

national liberation movements, 166 n89
nationalism, 67
natural laws, 118–19
natural sciences, 6, 21–3, 101
nature, 37; dialectic of, 38–9, 53, 100–1, 118, 119; Hegelian philosophy of, 38–9, 44; history and, 117–20; negative vision of, 117–18
nazism, 5, 110–11
Neapolitan Hegelians, 42–4
necessity, 119
neo-Kantianism, 42
Netherlands, 61, 72, 73, 77
Neue Zeit, Die, 41
Neumann, Heinz, 99, 116
Neurath, Otto, 22
Nietzsche, Friedrich Wilhelm, 23, 31, 32
Nieuwenhuis, Ferdinand: *Socialism in Danger*, 121, 122
nihilism, 179 n95
Novalis (Friedrich Hardenberg), 84

"objective reason" (concept), 110
objective relations, 84, 85
"objectivists," 144 n22
objectivity, 7, 9, 40, 41, 54
opportunism, 122, 123
organization, 61, 64, 67, 88, 91–2, 96, 106, 124; and class consciousness, 74–5; corruption in, 90–1; factory as model for, 69–70; party as, 88–9; and reformism, 122–3

PCI, *see* Italian Communist party
PSI, *see* Italian Socialist party
Pankhurst, Sylvia, 76, 107
Pannekoek, Anton, 59, 72–6, 87, 105, 107, 161 n63, 169 n22; "World Revolution and Communist Tactics," 79, 166 n89
parliaments: 77, 78, 79, 87, 88, 106–7, 163 n75
party, the, 90–2, 102, 106, 170 nn26, 27; Horkheimer on, 113–14; as organization, 88–9 (*see also* organization)
"partyness" (concept), 102–3
passivity, 62, 69, 123

pessimism, 34, 126
philosophical traditions: Hegel in, 23–4
"Philosophies," 109
philosophy, 6–7, 16, 45 (*see also* politics/philosophy conflict); in Marxism, 48–9; Soviet, 101–3, 179 n101; of praxis, 49, 54, 56–7
Plekhanov, Georgi, 41, 44, 60, 68, 179 n101; *The Development of the Monist View of History*, 41
Poland, 144 n28
political parties, 64
politics, 6–7; Frankfurt School and, 111–12; in Marxism, 48; transformation in, 84–6; of underclass resistance, 18
politics/philosophy conflict, 58, 59–81, 83–103; denunciation of heresies in, 99–103
Pollock, Friedrich, 110, 111
Popper, Karl, 21, 133 n46; *The Open Society*, 23–4
populism/Populists (Russia), 27, 39–40, 41
populist sociologists, 41, 143 n15
positivism/Positivists, 21–3, 24, 35, 42, 44, 45; term, 133 n46
Poulantzas, Nicos: *Fascism and Dictatorship*, 16
power: cultural, 74; of society, 125
"practical socialism," 94
praxis (concept), 49; revolutionary, 53, 56–7
press, the, 32
process, 62; historical, 53
production, 26–7
progress, 5–6, 27, 114; of capitalism, 30
proletarian organization, 75, 77, 89, 91, 106 (*see also* organization)
proletariat, 6, 11, 15, 59, 101, 121 (*see also* aristocracy of labor); as actor/subject of revolution, 67, 69, 78; of advanced capitalist countries, 61, 123; autonomy and self-regulation of, 77, 87, 89; and capitalism, 25, 33; class consciousness, 69, 91; emancipation of, 67, 75; German, 63; impact of bourgeois culture and values on, 72, 73–4, 79–80; international, 71; and March Action, 65; and organization, 74–5; politics and, 88; revolutionary, 125–6; as subject of history, 66, 68, 91; success/defeat, 17–18, 19; West European, 65–6
Proudhon, Pierre, 20
psychoanalysis, 9, 103, 115
putsch(s), 65–6, 78; Austria, 171 n31

Queneau, Raymond, 50

"radical left tendency," 59, 72 (*see also* "left" communism)
reductionism, 31, 123, 125
reformism, 120–4
Regius, Heinrich (pseud.), *see* Horkheimer, Max
Reich, Wilhelm, 16, 34
reification, 119–120
Reisberg, Arnold, 159 n30
repetition, 119; in history, 117; in nature, 118
resistance/progress, 17–20
revisionism, 2, 69, 73, 97, 103, 122, 123, 124; Marxist, 47, 120–1
revolution(s), 11, 12, 14–15, 27, 29, 30, 67, 99, 114 (*see also* March Action; Russian Revolution); Chinese, 3, 11, 12, 14; and class consciousness, 78; Cuban, 14–15; European,

revolution(s) (*cont.*)
6, 59, 60, 70–1, 103, 117; German, 63; Hegel's philosophy the intellectual arm of, 43; history of, 17; international view of, 166 n89; organization is supreme intellectual question of, 90–1; parliaments and trade unions as vehicles for, 77, 80, 87, 88, 106–7; proletarian, 107; proletariat attaining class consciousness heart and soul of, 69; renunciation of, 122–4; uniqueness of, 86
revolutionary praxis, 56
revolutionary process, 39
right, the, 18
Rolland-Holst, Henriette, 73, 75, 76, 163 n75, 169 n22
romanticism, 28, 33, 34, 35, 139 n97
Roninger, Boris, 96, 97, 110, 183 n30
Rosenberg, Arthur, 174 n58
Rosenkranz, Karl, 42, 43, 44, 49, 146 n49
Roser, Peter, 134 n70
Rote Fahne, Die (newspaper), 98
Rudas, Ladislau, 100
Russell, Bertrand, 23
Russia, 7, 61 (*see also* Soviet Union); Hegelians in, 39–42; unique development of, 39–41
Russian Marxism, *see* Soviet Marxism/Marxists
Russian Revolution, 3, 5, 11, 12, 14, 60; importance of German Communist party to, 63; Luxemburg's criticism of, 59, 62–3, 66–72; as model, 3, 67, 71, 79–80, 107–8, 165 n89; natural scientists in, 102; *1905*, 68

SDAP, *see* Dutch Socialist party
SDP, *see* German Social Democrats
Saint Louis Hegelians, 43
Sartre, Jean-Paul, 6, 8, 49, 50, 58, 105; *Being and Nothingness*, 108; "Materialism and Revolution," 108
Schapper, Karl, 135 n70
Schelling, Friedrich von, 143 n10
Schlegel, Friedrich von, 84
scholasticism, 48
Schopenhauer, Arthur, 23
science, 7, 45, 48, 57, 115 (see also *Wissenschaft*); Marxism and, 20–5; Marxism as, 5–6, 7, 16, 27, 34, 35, 42, 51
scientific socialism, 20–1, 44, 54–5
scientism, 6
second nature (concept), 118–20
self-criticism, 15–17, 92
Serge, Victor, 3
Shlyapnikov, Aleksandr, 174 n58
social Darwinism, 42
socialism, 6, 11, 20, 71, 94, 112, 138 n91; as central point of universal philosophy, 45; demands spiritual transformation of masses, 70; evolutionary, 14, 25–8, 30, 94, 113; French, 51; German, 42, 68, 71–2, 121–2; lack of, in U.S., 188 n26; scientific, 20–1, 44, 54–5; and technology, 28–9; of unorthodox Marxists, 33–4
Socialisme ou barbarie (journal), 108
Socialist Realism, 19
sociology, 21; "subjective," 41
Sombart, Werner, 139 n91, 188 n26
Sorel, Georges, 44, 47, 50, 51, 53, 54, 87, 154 n153; *The Decomposition of Marxism*, 55; "Fragments of a Study on the Decomposition of Marxism," 55
Soviet, Il (journal), 76, 106–7
Soviet communism, 61
Soviet Communist party, 11–12

Soviet Marxism/Marxists, 2, 8, 40–2, 73, 100, 106; arrest of foreign Communists, 115–16; challenged by Italian Marxism, 107; corroded into pronouncements and principles, 103; dialectic of capitalism and socialism, 27; and dialectic of nature, 38–9; emerged out of and against Russian populism, 39–40; Hegelian tradition in, 37–8, 57; as the orthodoxy, 8; political differences with Western, 4–9, 58, 59–61, 62; reliance on Engels, 53; as scientific and unified theory encompassing society and nature, 42; success/failure, 4, 5; threat of "left" communism to, 72; Western Marxism as alternative to, 105
Soviet Union, 5, 29, 99; philosophy in, 101–3, 179 n101
soviets, 77
Spaventa, Bertrando, 42–3, 44, 46, 48, 50, 146 n49; *Studii sopra la filosofia di Hegel*, 42
Spengler, Oswald, 31, 32, 33
"spirit" (*Geist*), 67, 72, 73, 74, 75–6, 80
Stalin, Joseph, 3, 11, 14, 17, 24, 29, 38, 53, 99, 102
Stalinism, 2, 8, 105
Sten, Jan, 99–100
structure, 35
Struve, Peter, 28, 144 n22
subject/object relationship, 22, 53, 56–7, 100
subjectivism, 34, 35, 143 n15
subjectivity, 7, 9, 40, 42, 44, 51, 73, 75–6, 92, 100, 115; and class consciousness, 74; dialectic of, 43, 48; distrust of, by Soviet Marxists, 41; in German Revolution, 78–9; of Hegel, 38, 39, 54; in political transformation, 69, 84–5; proletarian, 62
success/defeat, 2–5, 17–20, 81; identification of class consciousness with, 125; in Orthodox Marxism, 1–5, 11–17, 18–20
"surplus" (concept), 109–10
surplus value (concept), 47, 109
surrealists, 34–5, 50, 109
Sweezy, Paul, 14; Paul Baran and, *Monopoly Capital*, 109–10
syndicalism/syndicalists, 12, 55, 87–8, 89, 107, 170 n26
system (Hegel), 38, 41, 43–4
Szabó, Ervin, 54, 55, 87–8

Taylorism, 29
technology, 5, 28–9 (*see also* industrialization)
Temps modernes, Les (journal), 108
Thalheimer, August, 94–5
"theoretical practice," 15–16
trade unions, 33, 61, 68, 69, 96, 177 n81; as vehicle for revolution, 77, 78, 80
Trotsky, Leon, 4, 60, 66, 94; *"Left-Wing" Communism*, 165 n89; and March Action, 158 n25
"21 Conditions," 60

USPD, *see* Independent Social Democrats (USPD)
ultra-leftism, 26, 95–9, 175 n63, 183 n29
unconscious society (concept), 119–20
United German Communist party (VKPD), 159 n27
United States, 37, 109; Hegelianism in, 144 n28; lack of socialism in, 188 n26
universal, the: development, 40, 41;

universal (*cont.*)
in dialectics, 52–3, 100–1, 102; laws of nature and society, 57
Untermann, Ernst, 162
utopianism, 33, 34, 35
utopian socialism, 20, 21, 27, 28

Vera, Augusto, 43–4, 49–50, 146 n49
Vico, Giambappista, 22
Vienna Circle, 21, 22, 23, 133 n6

wages, 33
Wahl, Jean, 50
Weber, Max, 30
Weil, Felix, 110
Wellmer, Albrecht, 134 n46
"West European deviation," 99
"West European Theoretical School, The," 97
Western Europe: differed from Russia, 61, 64, 65–6, 67, 79–80, 108, 165 n88 (*see also* Russian Revolution, as model)
Western Marxism, 3, 5, 8, 62; boundaries between philosophy and politics in, 83–103; critically reexamined Engels, 39, 53; defeat in, 4–5; and dialectic of nature, 39; and the Frankfurt School, 110–16; French, 49–51; Hegelian tradition in, 37–8, 42–51, 57; inception of, 59–81, 83–108; and "left" communism, 77, 78; major theorists of, 58; predominance of philosophical works in, 6–7; psychoanalytic thought in, 9; revolution of relation of history and nature, 117–201; separation of, from Soviet, 4–9, 58, 59–61; subterranean years, 105–16; term, 59; viable alternative to Soviet, 105
Willich, August, 136 n70
Wissenschaft, 20–1, 22–3, 45
Wittfogel, Karl, 110
Wittgenstein, Ludwig, 23
women, 15, 18, 19
workers' councils, 77, 88–9, 99, 113–14, 170 n26
Worker's Dreadnought, The, 76–7
working class, *see* proletariat
World War II, 105

young Hegelians, 42
youth, 15
Youth International, 170 n26

Zeitschrift für Sozialforschung (series), 110
Zhdanov, Andrei, 19
Zinoviev, Grigori, 94–7, 98, 99, 163 n75, 176 n71